Hackney Empire New Act of The Year award
(NATYS) winner 2019

"Beautifully written." —Clive Anderson, BBC
Radio 4, *Loose Ends*
"Important voice"
— *The Times*
"Deliciously tart lines"
— *The Evening Standard*
"Compelling rarely heard perspective"
— *FESTMAG*
"Cutting edge confident comedian"
— *FRINGEREVIEW*
"A must see"
— *The Scotsman*
"Trailblazing"
— *The Guardian*
"Dark and refreshing"
— *BROADWAYBABY*
"Engaging, stark and vivid"
— *THREEWEEKS*

This edition first published in Great Britain 2020
Jacaranda Books Art Music Ltd
27 Old Gloucester Street,
London WC1N 3AX
www.jacarandabooksartmusic.co.uk

A CIP catalogue record for this book is available from the
British Library

ISBN: 9781913090104
eISBN: 9781913090302

Cover Design: Rodney Dive
Typeset by: Kamillah Brandes

Printed and bound by CPI Group (UK) Ltd,
Croydon, CR0 4YY

I would like to dedicate this book to my beautiful mum, Gakari, who passed away before the publication of this book: Mama may you brighten heaven the way you did earth.

To my delightful daughter Neve so full of love and so much compassion. To my beautiful daughter Inez you validate the joys of motherhood.

To my siblings who weathered the storm. Wairimu, you mothered me when Maitu couldn't, Mungai the soldier amongst us and Wainaina our darling brother, may the strength Maitu instilled in us see us through.

Finally to Dave, my husband, who stood by me.

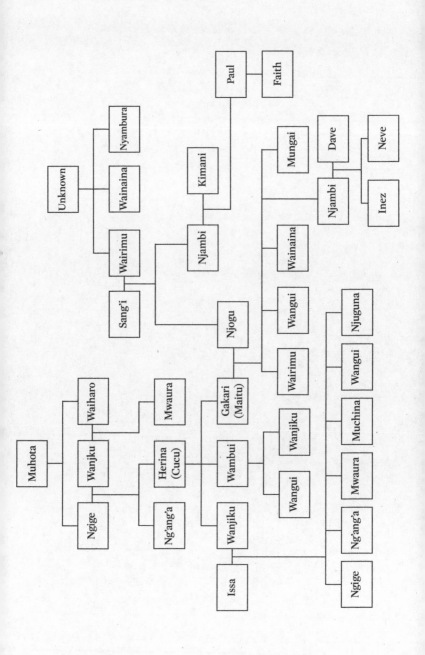

Through the Leopard's Gaze

Njambi McGrath

PART ONE

PART

ONE

Our Family Would Have Been Perfect

Our family would have been perfect if Kui had not been the malignant tumour that lay dormant in the family abdomen—spewing her cancerous pathogens, infecting each one of us in her wake, propelling our demise. She was the tumour whose pronged tentacles wrapped themselves tightly around our throats like a hangman's noose, squeezing the airways until we could hardly breathe. Our family would have been perfect if she had not been the caustic soda that dissolved the marrow from the skeletal bones leaving us hollow and weakened. We would still have been together if she'd kept her mouth shut.

Our family would have been perfect, living in our pink pebble-dashed house on top of the ridge in the Garden of Eden in the Central Province of Kenya. My family would have been perfect if the leopard had not chosen Juli, our pet dog, as her prey and if Maitu had not been superstitious. It was she who found Juli's cold dead body in the thicket, bringing the evil spirit that would trigger a sequence of events that ate into the core of our being. Our family would have been fine if Tanzania had not been hit by 5.7 Richter scale earthquake which shook the foundations of our home.

Our family would have been fine if Baba's brain had not been infected with a parasite taking hold of his body like a zombie snail. His anger—the parasite—metamorphosed him into the robotic monster who couldn't control his temper, attacking us in a frenzied fury as if we were the enemy. It would have been perfect if Baba would have deemed it unreasonable to chase Maitu with an axe, having punched her until he was spent, leaving Wairimu to pick up the pieces at only thirteen. Wairimu was the ray of sunshine, a beacon of hope that brings relief after the devastation of a catastrophic event.

My family would have been perfect if *I* hadn't found the stolen items in the maid's suitcase, and if she hadn't sent a poison letter to Baba. My family would have been perfect if Baba had not punched me and kicked me until I lost consciousness. We would have been fine if I hadn't woken up fearing for my life and taken off walking all night before being picked up by two shabbily dressed farm workers who smelled of stale sweat and pesticides.

Our family would have been perfect if brute history had not been the defective gene embedded into our being, rendering us incapable of normal functionality. We would have been fine if we were not Gikuyu and if the Gikuyu had not been farmers. It would have been fine if the white man had not coveted our land and thrown my tribe into concentration camps. My family would have been perfect if Cucu Herina had picked a side: either support the white man like her brother Guka Robinson or fight the white man like her other brother Guka Mwaura. If she had picked a side Cucu Herina and her three daughters would not have been amongst the women held on open fields that slowly became concentration camps which they built with their bare hands.

Our family would have been perfect if the famine that engulfed the camps had not sent Maitu in search of food and a few pennies to save her mother and sisters. Our family would have been fine if Maitu had not travelled on the late afternoon train, and if Baba had not caught sight of Maitu's flawless face with her big brown eyes that captivated his heart. Our family would have been perfect if Baba had not fallen madly in love with her and if she hadn't looked at him with such disdain. It would have been perfect if Maitu had not been walking on the secluded path by the eucalyptus trees by herself and if Baba hadn't run into her. Our family would have been perfect if Baba had not felt compelled to punish her for rejecting his undying love, by ripping her clothes apart and taking away her innocence.

Our family would have been perfect if Kui had been the dying baby Baba cradled in his arms, instead, she was the cancer that invaded Maitu's adolescent abdomen, gnawing our family, leaving ubiquitous open sores, weeping; destroying every shred of love that might have existed.

Our family would have been perfect if Baba's mother had not died, leaving her baby son suckling furiously, clasping onto the frail life that ebbed slowly from her body. If she hadn't left her infant son on her cold withered breast until passers-by found him barely alive, making him an incomplete human, our family would have been fine.

Of course, I would never have dared look into the dark well of my past; rousing ghosts from within. A journey that would leave me on the verge of a nervous breakdown, threatening to ruin my marriage and everything I ever worked for. The genie would have remained firmly trapped in the bottle, if Wainaina had not disturbed my peace by inviting me to his wedding. Me and everyone else.

Prologue

"Most of what matters in our lives takes place in our absence."
Salman Rushdie

My past ambushed me as if I was unsuspecting prey; threatening to crumble all falsehood. It was a corpse rising to the surface bloated with secrets, decomposing flesh peeling away reluctantly, sinew still clinging in the final attempt to hide the truth. I spent most of my adult life burying those pernicious memories, coping the only way an African knows how, *praying*! And all it took was one little wedding invitation. It was the summer solstice. The deceptively long day had already curtailed my evening, my escape from the daily slog. The clock had struck nine when I gazed up its blazing-sun-shaped face, a wedding present. I was relatively happy, as happy as a damaged soul can be, living in my middle-class London home with my English husband and delightful daughters. That night I did what I usually do most nights. I cracked open a miniature bottle of prosecco. The fizzing bubbles teased my lips for a sip. I was staring at a little spider that had down-sailed to just above my glass as if mesmerised by the fuzzing bubbles rising to the top. I jumped at the vibrating phone on the black stardust granite worktop. 'WAINAINA MOB' flashed on the screen. I picked up, pleased to hear from my older brother. Although he rarely rings me, we have an unspoken bond. A bond of shared experiences; of little lost souls by the wayside, clambering to cling onto the reeds of life's fast flowing river; of having dwelt in the same womb. A bond that makes blood thicker than water.

Wainaina's engagement news was sandwiched between discussions of Kenyans in the diaspora and the strength of the shilling. 'I am getting married in December,' he announced joyfully. 'What? Who to?' I asked, sounding surprised. I didn't even know he was dating. 'Congratulations you cheeky bugger, you kept that quiet,' I teased. 'December is barely six months away!' In true Wainaina style, he gave people little preparation time. It was exciting, he was finally getting married. My mind was already racing ahead. There was so much to organise, the tickets, visas, outfits, accommodation—'Baba will be attending, with his wife!' He interrupted my thoughts. My wandering brain calibrated, tuning back to the bandwidth at Baba's mention.

'What? Sorry, I was daydreaming,' I half laughed, thinking I misheard him.

'I would like Baba to attend with his wife,' he

16

repeated, sounding serious this time. The thought of coming face to face with our father sent a cold shiver down my spine.

For hours after the phone call I stared at the intricate octagonal shape the spider crafted. The web clung to two slats of the plantation shutters, now his abode, to be abandoned once it finished with it or died, whichever came first. I felt anger rising at the spider. Leaving his web behind for others to clear the mess. I swirled the mouthful of freshly opened prosecco, allowing the bubbles to tingle on my tongue. Suddenly I was thirteen again, vulnerable and scared.

Unexpected Visitor

It was nearing morning when the two men whose faces I could not recall dropped me off dishevelled and still bleeding; my pink night-dress clinging to my thin hairy legs. A combination of dust and their overpowering stench of stale sweat and pesticide lingered in my nostrils long after they were gone. The men had understood; things were better left unsaid. The driver spoke only once when we reached the intersection to ask where I wanted to be dropped. A destination was the last thing on my mind. I forced my adolescent brain to think. 'Kiambu,' I replied at last. The driver changed the indicator from left to right, and drove on until we eventually pulled up to the *matatu* terminal.

We arrived as Kiambu awoke. For those arriving from the tranquil countryside, Kiambu town was an assault on the senses. The orchestra of impatient horns; the thud of the barrels unloading from brewery lorries; turn boys touting for passengers, each shouting louder to capture the attention of commuters. Smart city types hopped onto the towers of asphalt whose eroded bases were now filled with dirty rainwater. Shiny films of rainbow coloured grease from the aging vans floated on top of the stagnant water, giving them a magical look. The commuters hurried to the waiting matatus whose engines revved like old timers recapturing their youth. Some hopefuls challenged themselves to open the morning paper to escape the assault of music blaring out of oversized speakers. Market traders were alighting from the country buses, their baskets laden. Impatient drivers hooted at the matatu drivers stopping in the middle of the road to pick up passengers. An already overcrowded matatu stopped for a rather large woman. The turn boy instructed her to climb into the front seat. The four passengers already sat at the front shifted their buttocks so that only one cheek took up the seat space. The driver sat in his place as if folded in two, eating a large juicy pear, the syrup dribbling through his fingers. His elbow was clenched inwards to secure the driver's door. The woman climbed in, squeezing herself, forcing a thin man out of his seat, leaving him suspended above them. The turn boy heaved against the door until it closed, helped by another man. The woman's large flesh smeared on the window as the turn boy slapped the side of the van yelling, '*Twende*—let's go!' The driver tossed the core of the pear into the street and sped off.

The chorus of chaos crashed into my eardrums like

glass crashing on a concrete floor. As we drove into the matatu terminus, the calm that had engulfed me shattered. The bumpy ride with the men had been eerily soothing, like the calm before the storm. When the car stopped, the man on my left jumped out of the truck, rushing to the back to get my suitcase. He hopped over a muddy puddle narrowly missing one and splashing on a scornful woman. He placed my suitcase along the wire hospital fence decorated with dusty purple bougainvillea that struggled to grow, the few dwarf leaves only just clinging on.

I shuffled my bottom along the seat until I got to the edge and swung my legs out. It was the first time I caught sight of my legs. My feet were covered with wellingtons of mud from when I had waded through the muddy patch whilst crossing the river. The moonlight was dim, not enough to see where I was going. I had miscalculated the jump, landing in the edge of the stream, frightening slumbering frogs. I had stood for a minute listening to the waterfall and the pump, convinced I had heard a different noise.

The crippled man was the first sight to people alighting the buses. He usually sat at the junction of Kiambu Road and Hospital Road. He crawled on his abdomen, his bottom sticking out like the abdomen of an insect, two long withered legs sticking out on either side of his hips. When he moved, he resembled a giant spider, hauling himself by his oversized muscly arms. On his hands, he wore flip-flops emblazoned with Samara bed and breakfast, making them look like feet. His flip-flops were meant for the right leg. He slid his hand from the flip-flop to raise his begging bowl in my direction, his eyes weeping with pity.

'*Saidia sista, tafadhali*—help me sister please.' I looked at him. I had no money. He sneered at me and shouted, 'That's why your husband beat you.' I turned away, lifting my oversize suitcase, and began to walk.

'I am only thirteen,' I whispered to myself.

The impervious clouds finally gave way, the sun's rays beaming on my angst. I walked into the grounds of the General Hospital as uniformed workers marched out, their eyes droopy with the night shift. Two policemen hovered around a navy truck waiting for the driver to stop. The two harried officers rushed to the raised back of the truck, covered with beige canvas with plastic panes from which a face peered. They slid the latch noisily and opened the door, which continued to swing back and forth. They jumped in the lorry and emerged carrying the lifeless body of a woman. One held the arms while the other carried her by the legs. Her head was bent unusually far back, her wig nearly sweeping the floor. I stood to stare. They were hurrying towards the mortuary where we collected Uncle Njiru's body on the morning of his funeral. The policeman at the head end walked almost too quickly, stalling in the process and stepping on her wig, pulling it off.

'*Ngoja*—wait, put her down,' he said. He lifted the wig and placed it back on the dead woman's head so that the long hair was at the front, covering her face. He then parted the hair, so her face was visible, before resuming her transportation. The policeman at the leg end used his leg to knock on the door. After a few moments, the doors swung open, letting out the pungent smell of death. I wondered about that woman. What took her life away? Did she start her day worried like the people in the matatu, hurrying to get to work on time for fear of upsetting their boss? What if her boss was angry with her, only to find out the reason for her lateness was because she had died? Would he or she feel ashamed, shocked or relieved?

My suitcase was burning my hand, prompting me to move on. I walked past casualty and approached the maternity ward on the other side of the mortuary. Through the smeary windows, I could see the new mothers holding their wrapped-up bundles of joy. I wondered what life awaited those bundles of joy. At what point do these parents go from loving their babies to being their abusers? When does the love become frustration, impatience and violence? I wondered what expectations those parents had for their children. African parents were laced with insatiable hunger for education, but would their babies have read the manual for high achievers? I shifted my suitcase from my right hand to my left hand. The mortuary was slightly obscured from the maternity ward. The beginning of life and the end of life; the bitter irony of those walking out from hospital with their bundles of joy or those walking out with solemn sorrow to bury their loved ones. I thought of the dead woman carried by the police. What kind of life had she had? Had she fulfilled the aspirations her parents had had when she was their bundle of joy? Why had her life been curtailed so soon?

It was a chilly morning when I walked up the steps to Maitu's two-room house. The row of staff quarters was right up against a wire mesh fence. The thin fence separated the well and the sick. It allowed the well and the sick to peer into each other's world. The well would stare at the sick and wonder what illness they suffered from. The sick looked into the world of the well, wishing their halted lives would resume. Some lives were halted only temporarily and some permanently.

In the daylight, my nightdress seemed very short and see-through, prompting a few strange looks from people. In my haste to leave, I had forgotten to wear shoes and realised just how numb my feet were from wading through the dew and mud, which were now caked, giving the appearance of wearing socks.

Maitu's house was raised and the door sat at the top of the fifth step. I hesitated briefly at the bottom of the stairs, coaxing my weary legs to walk up. Was every step I took, a step to freedom or was it the distance from which I would fall? I had not considered the enormity of my decision until I climbed the steps leading to Maitu's door, fingers curled in, knuckles protruding, about to knock, then it hit me. 'What if Maitu can't take me in?' I thought suddenly, fearful she would send me back to face his wrath. She had only just found a job in the casualty department of the General Hospital and could barely afford to look after herself, let alone me. For the first time since my unconsciousness, I felt panic rising from deep within. Maitu would put me in the matatu and send me straight back to Baba. The prospect of going back to Baba's house was unthinkable. I put the suitcase down, sank on the step, buried my face in my hands and began to weep. I would not let Maitu send me back to Baba. The thought of being back in Baba's house made me cry out louder.

'Njambi!' My torment was interrupted. I raised my head to the direction of the familiar voice. Maitu approached the staff quarters from the maternity block. She was in the light beige uniform worn by the hospital subordinates. Her head was covered in a floral head-scarf. Eyes rounded and full of panic, Maitu broke into a half-run half-walk, forgetting the eggs she carried in her pockets. They were clearly visible from underneath the off-white cardigan she wore. When Maitu worked nights, the Cook always gave her boiled eggs to take home for breakfast.

'What happened?' I had to think very quickly.

I didn't want her to send me back. I couldn't speak. Words simply refused to leave my mouth, tears streaming down my face. By now, Maitu had reached me and was walking round scrutinising me frantically. Maitu's face swelled in fury. She looked like she would explode. Her nostrils widened, puffing air like an angry dragon. She looked like she could pounce any minute, like a lioness that had been cornered. She tried to speak but only jumbled words came out. How, what, which, why?

'Did *he* do this?' her voice breaking off. A siren went past. Her eyes looked at me from head to toe, every eye movement followed by her whole body. Her face scrunched from anger to pain to sorrow in one motion.

'Why? Just why?' There was a thick cluster of dried blood on the side of my head. She placed her hand on my head, prompting me to shout in pain. My hair was caked together with blood, which had streamed down my face, soiling my nightdress and jacket. She tilted my face up carefully to have a better look; my eye was swollen and had turned purple-blue. She opened my jacket, the silhouette of my skeletal frame visible through my nightdress. It was when I moved my arm that I yelled out in pain.

I woke up in hospital the following day. Blinding pain throbbed in my ribs. Maitu had carried me to casualty, where her colleagues rushed to her. They assumed I had been hit by a car.

'Quick, go in there, Dr Okello is alone.' Maitu

ran to the doctor's room crying. He jumped to his feet and helped Maitu carry me to the bed. I was admitted after quick examination with suspected concussion and broken ribs. I was admitted to the women's ward, where Maitu told us of a girl we knew who had been admitted there after she was raped by her father. I wondered if this was the ward for girls abused by their fathers. What would Maitu's colleagues tell their families about me? The doctor had reassured Maitu that my injuries would not be life-threatening but I would need looking after. He had issued Maitu with a note if she needed to take time off work.

It was several days before I could tell Maitu what had happened. One morning, I was woken up by Maitu pouring tea slowly into a pan from a mug, and when there was no more tea in the mug, she poured the tea from the pan back slowly into the cup. I opened my eyes as she was checking the temperature by attempting to sip it.

'Is that mine?' I asked. She looked up from the stones where food preparation took place. It was the first time I had spoken since my unexpected arrival. She rushed to my bedside, a tender smile visible even with the poor lighting of the room.

'You are awake? How are you feeling?' she asked me, holding my hand.

'He said if I go back he will kill me,' I lied, worried Maitu would send me back.

26

'Oh, you will never go back my child, not if I am alive. He is an animal. I'll sooner sell my body than have you go back to that wretched house.' I closed my eyes at Maitu's comforting words, memories of that night still vivid.

'What kind of a man does this to his child?' Maitu shouted angrily. 'He is not a human.' She stopped cursing when I opened my eyes and began to recount the events of the night that would define who I became. The night I lost my childhood!

Kangaroo Court

The court was in full motion. The judge, Baba, wore a sullen expression on his brown face, his thick lips sealed tightly. His soulless brown eyes scrutinised me, giving little away yet causing my heart to thump loudly. I wiped the palms of my hands nervously on my pink nightdress. The flickering light from the emergency lantern reflected on his broad forehead, exaggerating its size. His receding hairline invisible; the bane of Cucu Herina's jokes, who appropriately nick-named him Hitler. The prosecutor, She-whose-name-refuses-to-leave-my-mouth, sat eagerly on the edge of her chair, ready to get the session started. Her long nose, a feature of much speculation as to her origins, sat awkwardly on her face. Some gossiped she might have Indian blood in her, whilst others laughed that her nose extended every time she sniffed a wealthy man whose home she would wreck. Nonetheless her ambiguous look gave little away. Her steely eyes oozed poison as she began to read out my crime. My sleepy eyes played tricks on me. Her yellow headscarf pushed her thick mousy hair to a mould on the back of her head. Suddenly I imagined that they had switched heads and she had Baba's body. The dim light gave them both comical outlines, which nearly made me laugh. The jury, my brothers, had been summoned from their slumber on the sofas where we had fallen asleep whilst watching the small black and white TV. Mungai struggled to stay awake, his adolescent eyelids laden with sleep. As for Wainaina, whose main hobby was sleep, had only managed to sit up, but had quickly fallen asleep and now snored softly with one eyelid slightly open. It must have been after 10:30 pm because the TV fuzzed, black and white dots jumping around the screen as if to remind us transmission was finished.

Although modern and newly built, our combined living and dining room was overcrowded with a mishmash of furniture. In the living area were two rows of sofas, the black set against the wall and opposite, the elegant yellow velvet set. The armchair nearest to the TV and the stone fireplace was Baba's favourite. Next to the TV was a padlocked cream dial telephone. In the dining area was a red rug, complementing the velvet dining chairs nestled under the wooden dining table.

We had spent the evening watching WWF on TV, jumping up and down, my brothers both shirtless, pretending to be Giant Haystacks and Big Daddy, whilst I refereed the match. Exhausted, we had sat down to watch *The Love Boat* and must have fallen asleep because we did not hear the car approaching from the other side of the ridge, nor heard the car door slam when it stopped outside the house. When my two sisters lived with us, we always heard the car from the other side of the ridge, and we knew it took 9 ½ minutes for the car to loop round to the house, so that by the time Baba felt the back of the TV it was barely lukewarm and he never had enough evidence that we had been watching it.

The Famous Five, as we'd called ourselves, were no more; now we were the Pathetic Three. We were no longer masters of deception, making telephone calls from the padlocked handset by tapping the ringer until the call went through. Baba would pace up and down, rubbing his bald head, trying to figure out why the phone bill was always so high before concluding it was corrupt telephone operators.

The Famous Five usually stayed ahead of the judge, but tonight the Pathetic Three had been caught red-handed watching TV. The TV was for grown-ups; we were supposed to spend our evenings studying. The first we knew they had arrived, was when we heard the door slam and we jumped in fright to see them standing there. We groggily made a hasty dash towards our bedrooms, the faint light barely enough to see where we were going. 'Come back here,' Baba growled, pointing to the black sofa, the overhead bulb flickering tiredly as if to symbolise the lateness of the hour. The solar panels had run out of charge and light could disappear at any minute. She-whose-name-refuses-to-leave-my-mouth dashed to the dining table, grabbing a box of matches and hastily striking one before sliding the flame to the wick, brightening up the room.

They had been out and we had played at the back of the house all day, catching grasshoppers and other bugs, storing them in the pink torso, the remnant of the doll Cucu Nyambura brought us from her Indian employers. The blue-eyed pink doll had freaked my brother and me out, he, speculating that the blue in the eyes represented witchcraft. We had torn off the head and limbs but found the torso a useful storage space for the insects we collected.

At dusk, when the fireflies began their dance and mosquitoes were buzzing busily around looking for exposed flesh, we headed indoors in search of food. All there was, was old ugali and sukuma wiki, which we ate cold and then headed to the living room, where I switched on the TV. It was just the three of us now; Maitu and my two older sisters had long left Baba's tyranny, leaving Wainaina, Mungai and myself under the dictatorship of our father, and now her.

'You! Sit there!' Baba barked angrily, indicating that I should move from the comfort of my brothers to the cold black armchair. Something told me that this was serious. I closed my eyes, waiting to feel the rope tying me to the chair, my stomach tight with knots.

'Open your eyes,' he said, forcing my brothers to alertness. To my relief, he did not tie me to the chair. 'Maybe it was not that bad,' I thought. That's what he did to my sister Kui when she was very naughty. He tied her to the dining chair, hoisting her on his shoulders, taking her outside, turning her upside down and threatening to dump her in the pit toilet.

I didn't have to wait long to find out what he'd planned for me because she began to read out my crime. Baba signalled her to pause.

'Turn that off!' He pointed to the TV, still fuzzing, making us all jump in fear. I hurried to the TV, squinting to see the dial, then clicked it to off before sitting back on the black armchair. I sat on the edge of the chair, briefly turning to look at the jury, who could barely hold their heads up. My mind was racing, trying to figure out what crime I had committed. Maybe it was because I was the one that turned the TV on, but how could he have known? It was clear that he seemed only angry with me. As she outlined my crime, it slowly dawned on me that this was a trial; someone had written something about me and sent it to them. It didn't make sense, and I was terrified.

'You liar!' he shouted as I began to protest, his stout figure heading towards me. One left punch on the side of my body landed me on the floor instantly. A

32

kick in my ribs pushed me into the soft padding of the black sofa. The last thing I saw was an object hurtling towards me and then total darkness.

It was still dark when I opened my eyes. I blinked, trying to see where I was. I was engulfed by a heaviness that made it difficult for me to move. I tried to move my leg, but it was pinned down by something. I lay there, trying to make head or tail of what had happened. And then I remembered the axe. Maitu had told me of the axe he had carried on his shoulder whilst he chased her down the hill. I sat bolt upright, fearful he had gone to get the axe. The heavy ball on my leg edged closer to me. It was Stemper, our black, curly-haired dog. I listened, but all was quiet except for the owl hooting from a distance. That was meant to be a bad omen, I remembered Cucu Herina saying; perhaps this was my signal to get away. My trial had ended predictably, and now I needed to leave quickly before he came back.

I walked to the door that led to the corridor where all the bedrooms were located. I crept into the hall on my tiptoes whilst listening for any movement. It was pitch black and all was quiet except for Wainiana's snoring from the room he shared with Mungai at the end of the corridor. I moved into my room, careful not to make a noise. I felt my way to the window, opened the curtains to let in some moonlight, and grabbed a few clothes from a pile on the floor, stuffing them into my blue tin suitcase. I went to my brother's bedroom, leaving my suitcase by the door. The boys were huddled together like puppies; they were very close and seemed to find comfort in one another. I patted them softly, careful not to startle them into making a noise.

'I am leaving,' I whispered. I had to say it several times before they stirred and replied, 'OK.' I walked quietly down the corridor, into the living/dining room and across to the front door. Stemper wanted to come with me but I pushed him back in the house and closed the door.

I knew the path well. I had walked down this way many times when we attended Githatha Primary before Baba transferred us to Musa Gitau Primary. The dim moonlight was enough for me to see where I was going. I went down the hill through our scarcely planted coffee bushes, down the terraces, to the flat riverbed where Maitu *used* to grow vegetables and farmed our fish, now overgrown with weed. I headed towards the little stream humming soothingly as the ice-cold water made its way down the mini waterfall to join the Athi River, which joins up with Galana on its way to the Indian Ocean. I balanced on the plank of wood laid across the stream, careful not to slip, and then I made my jump, ending up in the muddy slosh. I cursed at nearly losing my balance. I got onto the path on the farm that belonged to Githatha Farmers Cooperative. From there I climbed the steep hill through the tea plantation, the lightness of the green distinguishable from the dark green leaves of the thick coffee bushes up ahead.

When I got up the hill, I tried to block off any thoughts of creatures emerging from the thick maze of coffee bushes that lined both sides of the dusty track. I just kept walking. I felt numb. I did not think of the hyenas, or the leopard, but I was aware of the sweat on my forehead dripping down to my eyelids. I sighed with relief when I got to the clearing and only then, did I realise how tightly I had been clenching my tin suitcase, the metal handle biting into my fingers. I stopped briefly to change hands and then carried on walking.

I don't know how long I'd been walking when I suddenly became aware of lights shining on my back, illuminating my pathetic little frame, creating long shadows as a car approached. I carried on walking in the middle of the road. The car stopped behind me. Two men got out of the car, striding to catch up with me. I did not turn round. I just kept on walking. A voice bellowed behind me.

'*Unaenda wapi*—Where are you going?' he asked placing his hand on my shoulder. I froze at his touch. I was worried they would recognise me and take me back to Baba's house so kept my head down. That was the ~~only~~ thing I feared most. I did not care what happened to me. All I knew was that I could not go back to his house.

'Boarding school,' I replied trying to sound as if nothing was amiss, a drop of blood from my forehead landing on my foot. Slight irritation welled up within me for being interrupted. Walking alone in the dim moonlight felt strangely comforting, there was some certainty to it. Certainty that I was escaping and now here they were. I felt their eyes boring into me trying to make out what had happened to me. The old car's headlights were too dim to give much away. If they suspected what had happened to me, they did not let it show. It was obvious from my state I was in trouble. They hesitated, as if trying to figure out what to do.

'Get in the car,' he said finally sounding rather resolute. I turned around, my head still bent down, and walked towards the passenger side of the pickup truck. One of the men followed me, reaching out to take my suitcase. I did not resist; I was too exhausted. I resigned myself to my destiny. He took my suitcase to the boot before climbing into the front of the car, sandwiching me between him and the driver. We sat in uncomfortable silence! My immaturity unable to process my predicament and they, too puzzled to pry. To this day, when I think of that night, all that's etched in my mind is their faceless silhouettes, their shabby clothes and smell of stale sweat and pesticide.

There is something incredible about a child's brain that is able to put up defence barriers to enable them to cope with trauma. When I look back, I can't imagine where I got the carriage to talk to those men and get into the car. My instinct now would be to run and hide but on that night, my brain just refused to engage. I sat still, staring ahead into the abyss, my mind vacant.

Born Again

Maitu's rising anger reached fever pitch as I recounted how She-whose-name-refuses-to-leave-my-mouth had played the prosecutor in my condemnation. Maitu had banged on her chest like a mother gorilla provoked to war. She swore at them, cried out loudly, mucus and saliva dribbling down the side of her mouth. Of all the things Baba had done, this had to be the lowest. He had lost his love for his children: 'He promised to love you for eternity.'

When she was calm and had wiped her tears, she told me a story. Long before I was born, she was heavy with child.

'I had the biting pains two days after your father travelled to Mombasa on the Lunatic Express where he worked as a hawker. It was the end of the month which was the busiest time with customers' pockets bursting with money.' That was the time of the month when Baba undertook longer journeys and made most of his money on the trains. Maitu had been getting ready for the morning with her toddler Wairimu. She got up and a gush of water ran down her legs. She was bent double with pain, unable to move. She sent her toddler to go next door to call the neighbour. Wairimu could see that Maitu was in trouble so did as she was told, bringing the neighbour, who came running in at being called by a small child. She suspected it might be the baby because Maitu was heavily pregnant. The woman arrived to find Maitu squatting on the floor, the head of the baby nearly out. The woman washed her hands quickly and began assisting Maitu with the birth. The baby was born quickly with no complications. The neighbour sent for help to take Maitu to Kikuyu Maternity Hospital in case of anything. After inspection, Maitu and her new baby boy were discharged as fit and healthy with the baby feeding well.

By the end of the second day Maitu's concern grew because the baby had not had any bowel movements and his stomach was beginning to swell. She called the same neighbour, who organised for her transport to Kikuyu Hospital. It was too complex a problem for a small hospital and she was transferred to Kenyatta National Hospital, where they were admitted. The baby's intestinal tract was blocked, with urgent surgery recommended. Maitu had no way of passing the message on to Baba, working on the trains. It was only when he went to Machakos market after alighting the train, that someone told him Maitu had had the baby, and they were in hospital. Baba dropped everything and made his way to Kenyatta National Hospital to find Maitu holding a big baby boy, who bore Baba's big lips and square forehead. He was a miniature version of Baba. Baba held his son and when he opened his eyes, beamed with a broad smile, 'Hello son.' Unbeknownst to Baba was the severity of his son's complications. The baby then closed his eyes again. Forever. Baba was inconsolable. He cried so loudly the nurses came to console him. The baby had waited until he was in the loving arms of his father before he passed to another world. He was only in Baba's life for a day but the baby's image haunted him for years. Baba hugged him tightly, crying and praying. He begged God to allow his safe passage into the next world.

When the nurses took the baby away, Baba and Maitu held on to each other, empty-handed, and that's when Baba made his promise.

'Gakari, every day, I will seek to be a better man for you and Wairimu and the baby angel we have lost. God will bless us with more children and I will love each one of them with every fibre in my body. Forever.'

* * * *

When her friend, the Cook heard of my arrival, she loaded Maitu's pockets with four extra eggs for me.

'That will nurse her back to health,' she told Maitu. Mr Kamau from the pharmacy gave Maitu enough painkillers to last a life-time, as well as other medicines, should I fall ill of other conditions. The nurse who lived on a farm nearby brought a bunch of cooking bananas. Maitu's colleagues were determined to nurse me back to health. I was woken every morning by Maitu's key in the door as she was returning from night shift. She and I would sit on the stools by the cooking stones after her night shift, warming ourselves up with the fire whilst the water boiled to make tea. Once she emptied her pockets of the eggs and placed them in a bowl, I would fetch the salt and cups from the cupboard. One morning she was hitting the shell of an egg with a spoon, causing the shell to crack into many fissures. One by one she started picking fractured shells, purposefully placing them into the bowl as if she was concerned about their welfare. When the egg was clear of shells and was now just a wobbly mass of cooked albumen, she pinched the salt and rubbed the fine dust on to the egg. She extended her hand and handed me the egg, which I sunk my teeth into.

'You know, when you were born, my eyes lit up,' Maitu said, half smiling.

'With joy?' I asked.

'No, there was a power cut and you had big eyes,' she teased me and we burst out laughing. The kind of deep belly laughter that cleanses the soul. It had been years since we laughed. The last few years of living with Baba had been very stressful, his rage and unpredictability engulfed every aspect of my life. Living in Maitu's house was like an oasis of peace. Calm and pleasant. Those days living with Maitu were some of the happiest days of my life.

Maitu's house was basic compared to our house in Riara Ridge. It was two interconnecting rooms with unpainted walls that had turned black with soot. Each room had a medium-sized window with corrugated iron shutters. The kitchen was sparsely furnished with a cupboard which we used to store food and utensils. The cooking took place on three boulders facing each other and firewood on each side. The pan was balanced on the rocks. There were two stools which Maitu had purchased to sit on. The bedroom had a similar layout and had a medium-sized bed in the corner. Maitu had ordered a wardrobe to be built which she would pay the carpenter for on hire purchase. When Maitu came in the morning after her night shift, she would put the water on fire whilst waiting for the boy who delivered our milk. When we heard the footsteps coming up, I would walk to the door to meet him. He always arrived at half past eight without fail; at the steps he would hand me the washed-out squash bottle half-filled with milk. I would pour the milk directly into a pan and place it on the fire. Once the milk had risen to the top, I would blow it into submission before lifting the pan off the stones. It would be left on the side to be used for tea now that it was sterile.

After the initial anger that consumed Maitu, she became contented and happy to have one of her children living with her again. The days after my revelation, Maitu had walked around talking to herself, cursing Baba loudly. All their dreams had come to nothing. When she and Baba waved goodbye to their friends and neighbours in Thogoto village ten years before, they had left full of expectations, leaving poverty and misery behind.

The Promised Land

After driving round the winding, scenic Limuru Road, soaking up the greenery, the old Ford Anglia had come to a stop. Baba had jumped out of the car, run round to the passenger's side, opened the door and let Cucu (grandmother) Herina out. 'Come, Herina,' he had said courteously, helping her out of the car. Next, he helped Maitu out of the back seat. He held both their hands in the late afternoon light, the crickets creating a sense of drama, the sun lazily sliding down to the west. He walked them to a grassy patch, turned them round to face the hills, vast green rolling hills as far as the eye could see. They stood quietly for a moment, Maitu and Cucu Herina curious as to what Baba was up to. He let go of Maitu's hand, turning round to look at Cucu Herina's tired haggard face, her dark skin aged prematurely. The years of forced labour and constant starvation had taken their toll.

'Herina,' he began earnestly. 'I gave you my word

that I would make Gakari an honourable woman. That I would spend the rest of my life atoning for what I *did* to her.' His voice dropped, his head drooping in shame, turning his face away from Cucu Herina's glare, detecting the pain she still bore. Cucu Herina held her hand out to stop him, she had long forgiven him, but he carried on.

'Today, Gakari is a true Gikuyu bride, the land on which you stand on belongs to Gakari,' he proclaimed. He had dreamt of this moment for so long, he took a step back, giving them a chance to digest the news, looking at the delight on Maitu's face, a smile on his face awaiting her reaction.

'What do you mean?' she had asked in joyous disbelief. Maitu's face lit up as she danced around, twirling, her face looking to the sky, laughing like a little girl, her wide-skirted dress making a big circle. Her feet felt light; she could have danced all night. She stopped briefly, turning to look at Cucu Herina, hardly believing her ears as Baba continued.

'Today, Gakari, I paid for this land and you will grow food for your children. On your very own land.' Cucu Herina could not take it all in. Her knees gave way as her body slid into a kneeling position. Maitu rushed to help her to her feet but Baba stopped her.

Let her give thanks,' he said calmly.

On her knees, Cucu Herina brought both her hands to her chest, pulling the top of the neck of her dress

45

outwards, slightly exposing her bony chest, spitting into her chest whilst giving thanks. She raised her hands, turning to face Mount Kirinyaga.

> Ngai, *mwene nyaga*, God of Kirinyaga, you did not forsake the Gikuyu. You knew that one day you would deliver us from the iron fist of the coloniser. You knew they took our goats so we couldn't give you sacrifice, but you still delivered us. On empty stomachs the land and freedom army fought with little else than hope, machetes and reconditioned AK47s. My brother Mwaura, you gave him the courage, seven oaths he took, swore to slay the white man, because you gave him the courage.
> *Thaai thathaya Ngai thaai*
> You delivered us from the iron fist that sucked our blood dry. They took our men and raped our daughters, impregnating them with *chotara*, the bearers of their mothers' shame; the women did not bleed. The white man took their blood, because they survived on black man's blood. They whipped us into the gutters, dug with our own bare hands, determined to wipe the Gikuyu out of their land. They took our innocence but not our spirit; you gave us

resilience. They dehumanized us, made us bury our brothers and sisters like stray dogs in trenches, one on top of the other, their rotting flesh tainting our clothes. Those babies wrapped in bundles of six. With nowhere to rest their souls.

Thaai thathaya Ngai thaai

Today, you have blessed Gakari. She will never have to beg for food like I begged for food, in the clasp of starvation. I had no pride, but stared into the eyes of Kanjii the Indian, pleading to his soul. Every day I stood outside his shop. 'What do you want?' he would shout. 'Just a cup of flour, my children will die if they don't eat.' He was full of contempt, because they told him to hate us. He called me useless, spitting at the sight of me, but I would not relent. What is the purpose of pride if one's children are dead? I knew there had to be humanity in his soul. He finally relented and gave me a cup of flour, not just that day but every day; the day I did not turn up because I had too many bodies to bury, he did not close the shop because somewhere deep in his soul there was a human. Because he was human, Gakari and her sisters did not die. Gakari will have her pride, from this land that is

47

the colour of the blood the Gikuyu spilt,
she will feed her children from this earth
like her ancestors did before the white man.
From this land, she will never beg.
Thaai thathaya Ngai thaai

For many a year, the true sons of this land could only shed a tear from afar. It was bequeathed to those deemed more deserving than a mere African with his incredulous ways. For several generations, Gikuyu men were incomplete. Their rituals suspended. Denied their engagement gifts to their brides. Their laments for the loss of their land to 'Ngai', the God of Mount Kirinyaga, fell on deaf ears. Their sacrifices shunned. A gust of wind had changed direction. A dice tossed in the air. No one could predict the outcome. Like a victor's trophy now coming home. For years, Maitu nagged Baba about it. In fact, it's all she talked about. Every so often, Baba cupped Maitu's face in his hands, looked directly into her big brown eyes and promised that one day he would gift her land. Nothing would delight him more than to see her nourish their little family from her land. This was that day. Joyous tears washing down the sorrow of yesteryears.

On the day Baba collected the deeds, he rushed to Thogoto beaming with pride, scooping Maitu into his arms and showing them to her. He was proud to finally move my mother away from the overcrowded village of

Thogoto. To celebrate, he took Cucu Herina and Maitu to Karumaindo for *nyama choma*—roast meat.

Garden of Eden

When Riara Ridge was created, the fertility gods must
have had a field day, modelling it on paradise. Its
sumptuous earthy red soils bore tenfold whatever was
sown into it. It was a bountiful feast for the eye, the
luscious greenery and a temperature that would sooth
the wrath of any temperamental god, not too hot and
not too cold, not too wet and not too dry. Just perfect.
The life-giving tributaries with the purest ice-cold water
tantalizingly meandered through the undulating hills,
nourishing the lush green pastures along the way. The
gentle waterfalls created a melody complimented by the
humming, buzzing and clicking of the abundant creatures that inhabited this land. Like a peacock exhibits
its plumage for all to marvel, Riara Ridge stood, tall
and proud. An oasis of magnificent beauty, deep in the
highlands of Central Kenya.

It was in this Garden of Eden, on one of these hills,
that Green Gold Farm stood. You name it, it grew,

and Maitu's green fingers transformed it into a gold-mine. The farm was separated in two, and the lower parts were Maitu's domain, where carefully planned planting took place. By the stream, well watered and nourished, Maitu planted rows of arrowroot, white and powdery, delicious when served with cold milk. Their broad venous dark green leaves could be used to make *mukimo*, a Gikuyu staple food consisting of potatoes, maize, beans and various greens, all mashed together. The arrowroot leaves were also used as a funnel with which one would scoop drinking water from the stream. Carrots were interspersed with lettuce, all snacks that Maitu plucked from the ground to silence our rumbling tummies whilst we giggled at the alien-looking tadpoles tickling our feet in the stream. Where the ascent of the hill began were rows of bananas and sugarcane which provided plenty of additional snacks. Above that were the terraces, where the ground was too steep. Baba had asked the workmen to create the terraces to combat soil erosion. This was a technique he had learned as a child, spending hours watching the women and girls dig terraces in a futile attempt to combat land degradation caused by overpopulation in the Gikuyu Native Reserves of Thogoto.

The embattled colonial government, pressured to grant Gikuyu more land, came up with terracing amongst other strategies to make existing land more productive. On the terraces, Maitu planted potatoes, sweet potatoes, maize and hedgerows of passion fruit. It was halfway up the hill where it wasn't too steep that Baba claimed his territory. He would prune lovingly and spray pesticides on the coffee bushes, which he nicknamed green gold. He planned on getting two extra men to help him turn his coffee into his gold, when he could afford it.

The Knock

It was some time in 1982 when we heard the knock. We had just finished the first lesson after the morning break when Miss Maina said, 'Get out your English books children.' I opened my wooden locker and peered inside for my *English, Read with Teacher* book. I placed the book on the desk next to my lined exercise book. Miss Maina was half sat on her desk the way teachers always sat on their desks, wearing a cream chiffon blouse with a bow tied at the neck. Her long pencil skirt reached just below the knee, showing off her beautiful curves. She was just about to begin speaking when there was a knock at the door. She hesitated, got up and strutted to the door. Her hair, which was tonged with an upwards curve from the side all the way round her neck, bounced up and down when she walked, her sweet perfume following her. When she opened the door, she appeared shaken and visibly taken aback. She stepped outside, closing the door behind her. From inside the classroom, we could hear the murmurs of Miss Maina talking to someone else. Their voices were soon drowned out by the class as everybody began chatting.

The door opened moments later, rather abruptly, to an instant silence. Miss Maina walked down the row of desks and stood in front of my desk. 'Come with me outside,' she said with a lowered voice. Puzzled, I pushed my chair back and walked behind her to the door.

Outside the door, Maitu stood, but it did not look like Maitu. She wore a dress that was too long for her and looked similar to Cucu Herina's dress. Her face was swollen like the time she was attacked by a swarm of bees when she accidentally disturbed their nest whilst clearing her section of the farm. She had tried to fight back the frenzied attack to no avail. She had tried to run home; they followed her. She ran in the opposite direction and dived in the river to escape the attack. By the time she made her way up the hill to the house, she was so swollen, she could barely see. Our workman Munyau had run to the neighbours who lived half a mile away to ask for a lift to Nazareth Hospital.

Now Maitu stood outside the door with a big puffy face, black circles surrounding her eyes. I made as if to run to her but hesitated because she appeared too fragile and injured and I did not want to hurt her. I had instead put my small hand inside of her hand, which she squeezed tightly. I tugged and led her away from the sympathetic gaze of my teacher, who looked like she wanted to say something but could not think of what to say. Children were now peeping from behind Miss Maina. When Miss Maina turned round they could be heard scrambling back to their desks.

Maitu and I walked slowly to the playing field past the slide and found a shady spot under the *mugumo* tree facing the hedge. There, we would be out of sight. We both sat down. I, carefully still holding Maitu's hand, waiting until she was seated. We sat in silence. We did not know what to say to one another. I knew he had done this to her. Maitu always said I was perceptive and older than my years. 'Maitu, please do not go back,' I said, crying.

'He came to get me after I ran away. When I refused, he beat me again, in front of Ngwiri,' her lips quavered as she spoke. Ngwiri was a family friend whom Baba had employed as my sisters' tutor when we lived in Thogoto. I felt a pang of pained sympathy in my heart for Maitu. Her spirit appeared to have been shattered. She was a broken woman. I held her hand tightly. I wanted to make her feel better. I wracked my brain looking for something to say, then I remembered.

'*There was once a man who travelled a long distance in the blazing hot sun,*' I began to speak. '*By midday of his third day on the road, he was very thirsty and could not walk any further to find a stream.*' Maitu listened intently. '*He sat by the side of the road trying to catch his breath when he noticed drops of water coming from above. The traveller could hardly believe his luck at finding water. He quickly reached for his gourd and held it out to trap the water. Drop by drop it began to fill up. With every drop, he got thirstier. When he had collected enough, he raised the gourd to his lips, about to take a sip. Just then a big crow swooped down, knocking the gourd from his hand, which fell on to hard rocks, breaking into small pieces. The traveller wailed as the liquid quickly evaporated in the hot sun. "Noooo, you damn bird," he cursed, "what am I to do now?" When he looked up he had an idea. He would climb up the rock face to the source of the water and there he would quench his thirst. He got up and began to climb the rock face using every ounce of his strength until he was at the top. When he got there, he saw a huge serpent spread across the rock, its mouth wide open, venomous saliva dripping out of the mouth. He stopped, realising that the bird had saved his life. Whilst he was up there, he saw down below on the other side an oasis with plenty of water and beautiful plants.'*

Miss Maina had read us that parable during that morning's parade. Maitu seemed heartened by the story. She held me tightly when she walked out of the gate.

'Maitu, God will look after you,' I told her.

'He will,' she said, closing the gate behind her.

Baba was incapable of coping with rejection. Maitu had humiliated him by leaving; he was going to make her pay in every conceivable way. He would deny her everything they had worked for. And now, all these years later, Wainaina's wedding ran the risk of suffering collateral damage, with Maitu's bitterness surpassing Baba's. Her years in the wilderness had created bitterness beyond reprieve. She was a scorned woman. And I would be by her side!

The Den

Maitu had returned to Thogoto empty handed, alone and humiliated. She had moved back into her mother Cucu Herina's one room hut. Many people in the village had been pleased, others envious when she drove off with Baba, my sisters, brothers and I, in our Ford Anglia, to our new life in Riara Ridge. They knew we were moving to the area formally known as the White Highlands because only white people could live there in the colonial days.

Now they mocked her. 'How will she squat to use the outside toilets?' they laughed. In her heyday of prosperity, Maitu never forgot Thogoto, where she came from. After every harvest she'd fill the pickup truck with all manner of produce: sugarcane, passion fruit, arrowroot, sweet potato, carrots, courgettes, aubergines and anything in season. She collected all our old clothes and anything we didn't need to be distributed in Thogoto. She would go door to door, giving to those she felt were in need of food and clothes. Now she had fallen from grace and the very people she had helped now laughed and mocked her. Maitu was tough. She avoided people, staying in the hut or going to till Cucu Herina's shamba.

* * * *

When Maitu fled from the axe-wielding Baba, he excommunicated her. He had instructed the head teacher of our boarding school that Maitu should never be permitted into our school. He threatened to beat us if we ever spoke to her again. Her grief was incomprehensible. Our boarding school was a short distance from Thogoto, where she lived with Cucu Herina before finding the job at the General Hospital. Unable to stay away, she had walked the length of the fence; when she heard children on the other side of the fence playing, she called to them.

'Please can you call my daughter Njambi or sons Wainiana and Mungai?' she requested. The children stopped to listen to the voice on the other side of the hedge. They came running to where I had been playing close by. When I got to the hedge, I heard Maitu cry, 'Njambi, Mungai, Wainaina!' She began sobbing on the other side of the hedge. By now, my brothers had arrived. Mungai, being the smallest, crept under the fence and replied, 'Maitu.' Maitu was ecstatic to see her last born. I followed, then Wainaina. She talked to us, hugging us. 'I thought I would never see you again.' When the bell rang, she said, 'Please come here on Friday after school and I will be here.'

I was the first to run out of my class on Friday after the last period. I headed towards Lay Training, the room that was my brothers' classroom. Wainiana had repeated several times, due to his dyslexia, undiagnosed at the time, until I caught up with him and now, he was in Mungai's class. There were no systems in place to deal with children of different learning abilities. Kenya adopted the British education system which was a one size fits all. Everything was exam driven and those children whose exam results were poor had to repeat the year, sometimes multiple times. This was not only damaging to the children's self esteem but also a waste of school fees as the root cause of the problems were never addressed. Theirs was the same room that seventy years earlier Cucu Herina had sat in, listening to the teachings of missionary Dr John W. Arthur, and years earlier Jomo Kenyatta, the first president of Kenya.

My brothers' teacher, Mr Job, walked out of the classroom with his accordion flung over his shoulder. He gave me a stern look and said, 'Don't come to my choir.' I growled at his comment. I loved singing and had joined the school choir. Mr Job had asked me to sing in different keys but everyone I tried was no good.

'Singing is not for you,' he had said, irritated at my persistence. I was undeterred and turned up several times. 'Your voice sounds like a rusty engine,' he had said the last time. He had cut short my dream of becoming a singer. I didn't like him. I stood aside to let him out and waited for my brothers. 'Come, we are going to the hedge remember?' I reminded them. We rushed to the hedge and found the spot. We could hear movements in the thicket so Mungai crept under, followed by Wainaina and I was the last.

Maitu had created a den in the hedge where she'd spread her *rithu* on the floor. She had laid out the serving dish with chicken casserole, chapatis sliced into triangles and cubed sweet potatoes. 'Come sit down my children,' Maitu greeted us, full of delight. Beaming with accomplishment. Her scars had faded and she looked much stronger. She served us the food, which we ate hungrily. We dunked our chapatis into the gravy whilst digging our teeth into the meaty chicken thighs. 'Maitu, a boy called Sammy and I were playing...' Wainaina began. We each took turns to tell Maitu about our friends. She listened intently, glad to have her litter again.

Maitu lived for that Friday meal. During the week, she offered her services to others in the village, digging, cooking, cleaning, anything to earn enough money to buy us food for that meal. Our meal in the den, in that hedge, became how we saw Maitu. For a few hours, she

61

could escape her misery in that den, like a fox with her cubs hidden from the outside world. When the school term ended Maitu cried because our school holidays were spent at the farm, in Baba's house. Maitu had no chance to see us.

Ray of Sun

Amongst a jeering crowd, there is always the one that identifies with the victim. An old acquaintance remembered Maitu's good deeds and when she ran into her one day at the shops, she called her to wait.

'*Weka wega niwe weika, weka uru niwe weika*— when you do good, you do yourself good, when you do bad, you do yourself bad,' she said. 'I heard about all your kindness when times were good for you. You never forgot the people of Thogoto.' The woman was most sympathetic to Maitu, informing her that The General Hospital in Kiambu was recruiting and that she would put in a good word.

In the meantime, the acquaintance employed Maitu to work on her land. Maitu was not proud and took on the job with zeal. Every morning she rose early to work for the Good Samaritan. She dug, planted, harvested and ploughed. One day the woman came to Maitu carrying a brown envelop. It was a letter with an application form inviting her to attend the employment day at the hospital. The recruitment manager was the woman's brother and she had spoken kindly about her. The woman helped Maitu fill out the form. She signed it the way most people signed the forms, by placing her thumb on a blob of ink then transferring it to the form.

On the staff recruitment day at the General Hospital, Maitu sat patiently on the benches provided, wearing her best clothes. She had been the first at the bus stop, with Cucu Herina wishing her luck. She recognised the recruitment manager, who bore a striking resemblance to his sister. When all the formalities were done, he called her to the side, reassuring her that his sister had provided an excellent reference recommending Maitu as a diligent hard worker. Not only would she be getting a job, but she also qualified for a house at the staff quarters. Maitu could never have wished for anything better than a job and a home.

She was lucky to find employment not only to support herself but also get away from Thogoto village. She was pleased to get the job and a little house where she could begin again. Without us, Maitu's life felt meaningless. When she was off duty, her nights were lonely by the fire, crying, moaning her loss. The little kitten who sat by her feet would comfort her with a faint meow as if to share the empathy. They had both suffered loss of family. The man who worked at the mortuary had given Maitu the pussycat because she 'walked with the world on her shoulders,' he had said. 'Life does get better.' Maitu had lost everything. Her children, her home—the house she lovingly built through sweat and tears—her farm which she tended with such dedication, all gone. It was ironic that she should be given a kitten to keep her company because her children had been ripped away from her, yet that's what humans do so readily with animals.

When I turned up at Maitu's door, she could not believe her prayers had been answered. One of her children needed her now more than ever. She could be a mother again and look after me. I needed her because I was broken, just like she had been. She could see me every day, just like it was meant to be, mother and daughter, wounded but still standing. Maitu's life had been given meaning again. The evenings were transformed from tears to sitting by the fire roasting maize, plucking kernels one by one and throwing them in our mouths. 'Riddle me this,' she would begin. We told stories and laughed. It's like I was born twice, my mother said to me one evening. Let's sing *kanyoni kaja*, I suggested to Maitu. It was my favourite song.

> *Kanyoni kanja, kanyoni kanja*
> Little bird, little bird

Gekugwa nja na mitheko
Fell outside with laughter

Ndakoria atiri, ndakoria atiri
I ask it, I ask it

Wamichore watinda Ku?
Striped one where have you been

Ndatinda koiri, ndatinda koiri
I have stayed in koiri, I have stayed in
koiri

Ngiaragania mbirigiti
Spreading mbirigiti [seeds from the mikin-
duri tree]

Na mbirigiti, na mbirigiti
And mbirigiti, and mbirigiti

Na ndinainukia magoto
And I have not brought home any banana
fibre

Magwa iriaini, magwa iriaini
They fell into the lake, they fell into the
lake

Gwa cucu wa kamerukia.....meru!
At grandma who swallows.....meru!

Like the striped bird, I would fall about laughing. We told stories late into the night and went to sleep in Maitu's bed because she didn't have a spare bed for me. Maitu's small home was calm. There was no fear. I could wake whenever I wanted, and sleep whenever I chose or was tired. I did not spend my evenings pretending to read, fretting about whether I was in trouble or not. It was just peaceful.

Our lives revolved around Maitu's night shifts. She was based in the casualty department. At night, when all the patients had been admitted or discharged, Maitu and other new casualty subordinates slid into their gum boots. They had been recruited following a damning inspection which condemned the cleanliness of the rat-infested hospital. The new general manager was well aware of the staff's attitude problems and hoped that new blood would shake things up. The new recruits were to do the night shift. Someone would start by sprinkling the sanitising white soap powder on the floor, which very quickly turned a mucky brown. Someone else splashed the floors with buckets of water. Maitu followed with a squeegee, pushing the water to the doors and then the drains. Others cleaned the walls, one graffitied 'help' with blood. When all the waiting rooms were clean, they cleaned the toilets and consulting rooms, some of which contained bodies waiting for the mortuary collection. By the first rays Maitu would be parking her squeegee before making her way to the kitchen for her eggs from the Cook.

Although I loved living with Maitu in her house, I began to notice how my discomfort grew when I was outside the house. I was aware that there were people who came to the town of Kiambu to buy provisions who also attended Kiambu High School. I was embarrassed to think my friends from school might see where I was living with Maitu after living in our posh house in Riara Ridge. When walking out of our house I always looked around to see if there was anyone walking on the other side of the wire fence that separated the hospital from the main road. Part of my embarrassment was the questions it would raise amongst my friends, and the thought that I would have to explain why I was living in shabby hospital housing instead of our beautiful house on top of the ridge. These moments were only temporary, but they were there. I wished that our school was not so near and I did not know anyone in the area. As a result, I began to feel guilty for feeling embarrassed about Maitu's abode.

When she had rested enough, we would leave the hospital grounds and go for long walks, exploring our new territory. We loved the convenience of living in the close proximity of shops and public transport. We would stroll leisurely to the outdoor market on the upper side of Kiambu where Maitu gave me lessons on bargaining. We haggled for our vegetables. I, watching Maitu's techniques. 'How much are the sukuma wiki?' she would ask. '5 shillings,' the seller would respond. 'It's too much, why is it that expensive and you have had heavy rains? It's too much,' Maitu would say and begin to walk off. 'I will throw in another bunch, take both for 5 shillings,' the seller would call us back. If there were 5 tomatoes on a pile, we would ask the seller to add a couple more. Maitu would smile, thank her and we had our supper. Slowly, she and I began rebuilding our shattered lives.

Baba's Shame

It was nearing the end of the school holidays after I arrived at Maitu's house. I woke up one morning to see Maitu pacing up and down full of thought. I wondered what was on her mind. For a few days after my arrival we had been wonderfully happy, but now she looked fraught with worry.

'What is wrong Maitu?' I asked her, sitting up in bed.

'Your education!' she growled biting her nails. The new term was about to begin. So much had happened that school was the last thing on my mind. I had just finished the first year of high school and was getting ready to go to Form 2 at Kiambu High School. Maitu could not believe her good fortune when she got the job at The General Hospital. It was walking distance and she could visit me at school with ease. It was a government school for gifted children with high entrance grades and low school fees. I had been amongst the top students in my primary school. The day I received my Certificate of Primary Education (CPE) results, Baba had beamed with delight. He had rung the school as I stood behind the door in the hallway listening to the conversation. I made the top seven, the head teacher had confirmed, and the highest any member of our family had ever achieved. I was on the way to becoming a lawyer. Baba's daughter would be a lawyer, possibly working in the high-rise buildings in Nairobi.

Although I had brought my blue tin suitcase and everything I needed for school, I had not thought about the practicalities of life after leaving Baba's house. I had not considered that Maitu might not have enough money to pay for my school fees. Now Maitu was staring out of the window.

'What will we do?' I asked, wondering if Maitu was considering sending me back. I was now standing close to her feet, my heart beating loudly.

'I am going to go across the road to Ithe Wa Karanja's shop to send a *kiama*—message to Njogu.' My heart missed a beat. The morning breeze slammed shut the window's tin shutters adding darkness to the mood.

'To tell him what?' I asked worriedly.

'I will ask him to send us money for your school fees,' she said, walking out of the door. 'You stay here,' and with that, she hurried down the stairs. I walked to the back of our house and clung to the fence to see Maitu on the other side. I looked at the busy road, matatus speeding past whilst other people walked idly on either side of the road. I wanted to go back to school; I loved studying and playing hockey for the school. I enjoyed being in the drama club, especially playing the little girl in our last performance. What if there was no money to send me to school? I shuddered at the thought. I would never become a lawyer working in the high-rise buildings in Nairobi. Without school, I would probably get married. That thought made me very sad.

I looked down the road to see Maitu cross to the row of shops opposite the fence. She walked up to the shop with a big sign, *Kiambu Hardware Merchants*. The shop was owned by Baba's relative Chief Mwangi.

Chief Mwangi was a tall lean man, always sharply dressed in pinstripeed suits with black shiny shoes dutifully polished by any of his numerous servants. His walk was purposeful and important. Every stride accompanied by a swerve of the alternate shoulder affirming his alpha male status to the residents of Kiambu County. His face was always clean-shaven, and not even his receding line would diminish his good looks. His smile revealed a set of strong beautiful white teeth brightening up his dark complexion, accentuating his handsome chiselled look. This conveniently masked the despicable callousness with which he dealt with people. Chief Mwangi was feared and revered by those under him. Anyone unfortunate enough to cross his path bore permanent testament to his ruthlessness.

His dashing looks did not go amiss with the ladies. He was a Christian and went to church with his family every Sunday. It was rumoured that at the end of the church service, when all the Christians were hugging each other and wishing 'peace be with you', he would be whispering sweet nothings into the ears of women and arranging evening meet-ups with them. Unlike other chiefs, Mwangi only had one wife, but many women in the neighbouring villages enjoyed his visits and he was rumoured to have fathered many children in the area. His wife was a rather tall, fat, strong, scary-looking woman with a very dark complexion. Unlike her husband, there was very little she could do to disguise her mean spirit.

Chief Mwangi was a wealthy man indeed, with a huge farm, a grand stone house, nice car and servants at his feet. He had been elevated to this position during the colonial period by the British district commissioner, for his willingness to chastise villagers who defied colonial rule. In return, he enjoyed all the trimmings of a chief who held status and authority. In colonial Kenya, chiefs were official law enforcers, hand-picked by British officials and their loyalty to the British monarch was handsomely rewarded with money, animals and land confiscated from the poor villagers. Chiefs had to be ruthless and able to command authority amongst their people. As enforcers of the British law they had power to use any means necessary to make their subjects obey the harsh laws, ensuring that taxes were paid and the women in the village were engaged in forced labour digging terraces or clearing forests. Since the introduction of the hut tax, which required the family to hand over a goat or similar, it was always going to be difficult to get compliance. If the tax was not paid, the chiefs were to employ any methods necessary to persuade people to pay. The patriarch received a warning, and if that warning was not heeded, he would be slaughtered in the night, leaving his wives and children distraught and frightened, handing over whatever wealth they had.

Maitu despised the chief and his wife more than the bile that rose to the back of her throat every time she uttered their names. He never knew this of course because Baba would have been very angry had she expressed any negative feelings towards him. Every Christmas, we would wear our Sunday best and line up in front of the car for Baba to inspect us. Once he was satisfied, we excitedly jumped into the back of his pickup truck. The ride through the winding dusty roads to Ruthimitu to spend Christmas with chief Mwangi's family was great fun as we bobbed up and down in the back laughing. Driving through the gate, we would be met by the aroma of roasting meat, smoke rising from the back where numerous animals had been slaughtered.

When Baba was in front of Chief Mwangi, his demeanour changed to that of an eager schoolboy.

He did everything to appease him. Maitu could never hide her irritation at Baba's willingness to humiliate himself. One day it was the chief's wife's fiftieth birthday. Baba, in his eagerness to please, had called all the chief's sons, whom he called brothers although they never saw or treated him like a brother. He instructed them all to stand up in a line and sing a birthday song for their mother. Holding the white iced birthday cake he bought her, he began to sing, like a chorister leading a church choir. '*Maitu witu ii, na hunyu wake ii*—Our mother, with all her dirt.' It was an endearing song sang by young children to their mother as she returned from a hard day's work in the fields. They were neither young nor had she ever known a day's toil. His call was ignored leaving him to sing the song by himself, holding a cake carrying out the actions in front of a very bemused woman. Maitu spat in disdain.

Now I stood on the fence staring into the shop. I could just about see Maitu talking animatedly, throwing her arms around. When she finally came out, she cursed loudly: '*Ndi girimiti, na mwana wakwa nieguthoma*—I am a peasant, I will find a way to educate my child. Njogu is not a real man otherwise he would educate his daughter.'

Chief Mwangi had telephoned Baba to ask for my school fees. Baba had sent a message saying the only way he would pay for my education was if I went back to live in his house. Maitu reasoned with the chief about how Baba had beaten me, only for Chief Mwangi to reply that children and wives needed occasional discipline to keep them in check. Maitu had stormed out, telling them I would never go back to Baba's house.

When my brother Wainaina decided to get married and invite all his relatives, there was no malice, just plain joy. It was never his intention to reignite bad blood. He just wanted his family to celebrate his union with his girl. A celebration of love and not hate! Yet, every time his invitation card caught my eye, the knife in my heart twisted even deeper. But no matter how anguished I felt, it never occurred to me to throw it away. It sat awkwardly but defiantly on the mantelpiece where I had tossed it. I contemplated my next move as I sat lost in the thoughts of through my childhood.

The Good Samaritans

The patients arriving at the General Hospital used the one and only entrance to the hospital site. To the left was the car park. To the right, under the blanket of dark shade from the tall eucalyptus trees—a reflection, some might argue, of the shady dealings that went on in the concrete building that was the mortuary. Everyone was fully aware it was the mortuary, and that they had trouble with their refrigeration because of the odious pungent smell of death that greeted them at the entrance. The frequent power cuts kept the bodies lingering between purgatory and hell; one minute they were hot, next they were cold.

The hospital staff treated their patients with contempt. Patients who were injured in car accidents were brought to the hospital in the back of a pickup truck; that way those needing to jump out before reaching the hospital could do so. The driver usually ran inside to warn the staff of the casualties in the back of the truck, and the staff usually took their time in coming out. Diagnosis was made in the back of the pickup truck by the staff. Those who were thought to have the best chance of survival were dragged out of the trucks screaming and yelling and taken to casualty. Those deemed hopeless were loaded on to trolleys to be taken straight to the mortuary, to save the staff from transporting them twice. Patients on their way to the mortuary could be heard yelling, 'I'm not dead yet, I only have a broken leg.' That was how the mortuary became known as the home of the living dead.

Those unfortunate enough to require treatment had a poor prognosis, with most patients dying, even the ones that arrived with common ailments. I highly doubted the survival rate was even as high as this, that it was probably an exaggeration by the staff. One thing was guaranteed: those patients of the hospital knew it could go either way, not only for the sick but for the well.

All ailments were treated with piriton and paracetamol, whilst any wounds were treated with iodine. People often left with big blotches of purple smeared all over their wounds, and remnants on their clothes. Dispensing of medicine was generally correct in the morning but by the end of the day, after the pharmacist had taken a few swigs of his 'chai', orders got mixed up. Those needing liquid medicine were sometimes given iodine to swallow, whilst others received piriton to apply to their wounds several times a day. Those swallowing iodine were obviously worse off, although their stomach ulcers might have improved.

Patients admitted to the recovery ward fared the worst. All windows faced the mortuary, so they watched bodies being brought in and funeral processions leaving all day. Breakfast in the wards was a slice of white bread smeared with Blue Band margarine, which was flung to the eager patients. Those that were too ill to catch their slice of bread were marked like in a game of netball by the rats that had moved their entire families in under the beds. The tea served was indistinguishable from urine.

Patients arriving on foot usually made a stop at the kiosk to buy pens with which the doctors would write their prescription, and sheets of paper on which to write them. Anything else—for example, readily filled out death certificates covering different causes of death—could be purchased from under the counter, a reflection of the functionality of public services. Kenya—like most of Africa—having been pushed by the World Bank and IMF upon independence to borrow eye-watering loans for ill-thought-out projects, spent a significant amount of its GDP on debt management. This was compounded by the authoritarian president Daniel Arap Moi, whose reign lasted 24 painful years depleting all public funds.

Deprived of funds, the state of the General Hospital perfectly captured the essence of public services. The daytime cleaning staff were no better. They usually cleaned the casualty department when it was full. They would fill a bucket with soapy water in which they soaked the mop. Once all the excess water had been wrung out, the mop was passed to the patients to mop under the benches they sat on. When one finished, they passed the mop to the next person. Many hands make work lighter and it did for the cleaning staff, whose only job then was to wheel the bucket to the toilet door, leaving it there to block the entrance. The first person to use the toilets would have to empty the bucket first. Then the cleaning staff signed the completed rota sheet.

The mortuary was under the watch of a jovial man who had a thin face covered by dark skin with a few blobs of hair on his chin that made up his goatee. Even those who knew nothing of Mr Mbugua suspected that his sense of smell was severely compromised or indeed non-existent because the smell in the mortuary never bothered him. At the end of every month, Mr Mbugua closed the mortuary doors at twelve noon. He would walk out of the hospital gates and make his way past the matatu terminal and over the road to Amani hotel. Hotel is what people in Kenya call restaurants. He would walk into Amani hotel, walk to the counter and collect his order. Once he had paid, he would stride back past the matatu terminal, past the cripple who knew and expected a small gift, then would head into the mortuary. Once in the mortuary, he would lay his rack of meat on the table and began his feast, sipping on his warm Fanta because the people of Kiambu did not drink cold drinks. They feared cold drinks would give them a cold, since in Kiambu a temperature of 23 degrees was considered cold. On hot days, Mr Mbugua would leave the mortuary doors open tossing bits of bones to the hospital cats who seemed well aware of this monthly ritual. If there were new arrivals at the mortuary during his lunch, Mr Mbugua would ask them to be parked on the side whilst his teeth peeled sinew from the bones. All users and staff of the General Hospital also knew that Mr Mbugua was a man of incredible kindness and possessed a heart of gold.

One day, as dusk was turning to night, Mr Mbugua marched to the door and opened it. 'Come in,' he said to the Cook, who was concerned about being summoned to the mortuary. 'We will wait for the others,' said Mr. Mbugua. The Cook, whose kitchen smelled exactly the same as the mortuary, walked straight in through the partially opened door. 'You look more beautiful than ever Esther,' he said beaming. He had a soft spot for the Cook and if he were not a married man, and she was not a married woman, maybe something might have happened between them. The flattery was interrupted by the ever-serious Mr Kamau, the pharmacist, who believed that he was nearer to God because he was able to heal people, the ones that survived anyway. 'You shouldn't need to come back after that medicine,' he always said to the patients on collection of the medication. Most didn't, especially if they had drunk iodine. He was happy to dispense medicine to his friends and family too, without prescription, and Maitu had a large supply. People in Kenya believe that friends and family should be able to benefit from the perks of a job. Some of the medicines Mr Kamau dispensed were for unrelated diseases but anything provided for free was always gladly welcomed.

The nurse who lived on a farm nearby arrived next. She wore her brilliant white Florence Nightingale starched tunic with a watch clipped to the curve of her enormous breast. Around their waists, nurses usually wore elastic belts, mainly to accentuate their voluptuous figures but also to enable smuggling gauze inside their dresses. She too had welcomed Maitu when she began working at the hospital with a large consignment of gauze. Maitu stored it in a big container which she and I used during menstruation as sanitary towels.

Dr Okello from casualty arrived last. 'Moi is going to finish this country, my friends,' he complained as he walked in. 'The patients now have to buy their own syringes if they want injectable medicine. What's wrong with sharing syringes?' he said laughing, shrugging his shoulders. 'I wonder if Ochuka would have done a better job of the presidency. They are going to hang him you know,' continued Dr Okello.

'He deserves it for trying to overthrow the

government. He would have been terrible. He couldn't overthrow a school, *ni bure sana*,' replied Mr Mbugua.

Dr Okello had grown up in the same fishing village near Kisumu as the ill-fated Hezekiel Ochuka, who attempted to overthrow president Moi's government. The two were rivals, with Dr Okello declared the cleverest person in the Western Province. He had done extremely well with his medical degree and had been granted a place at a top UK university. Dr Okello was not a Gikuyu man; he was Luo. Many nurses and women loved to greet him in Gikuyu language so that he could respond in Gikuyu, which made them laugh because of the way he pronounced Gikuyu words.

'Thank you all for coming, and sorry about the smell, we have had trouble with refrigeration,' to which everyone replied in unison, 'We know.'

'So, I will make it quick,' continued Mr Mbugua. 'Our sister Gakari needs our help. Her daughter survived a beating by her father,' they all nodded, 'who now refuses to educate her unless she goes back to live with him. We cannot let that young lady go back to the hands of that monster. She is a clever girl attending Kiambu High, and it's our duty as citizens to assist our sister in her time of need,' he continued. 'Could you arrange a collection in your departments so that we can ease the burden of this family?' Everyone nodded in agreement.

It was the night before school began. Maitu was sat by the cooking stones, turning the roasting maize, a look of defeat on her face whilst I peeled off the maize leaves. The loud knocking made us jump. '*Hudi*,' went the voice. Maitu rushed to the door, responding to the call '*ii*.' Maitu was surprised to see Mr Mbugua the undertaker standing there, holding an envelope.

'Excuse my intrusion Gakari,' he began. 'A few of us got together and got you this,' he said, handing Maitu the envelope. 'It is a small collection for your daughter's fees, it's not much but it will help.' Maitu stood there staring at the envelope, trying to process what he was saying. She could not conceal her delight.

'*Ngai mwathani*—God the almighty, thank you for sending me this angel,' she thanked him, asking him to come in.

'It is great to see the young lady doing so well, she will look after us when we are old,' he replied turning away. 'I must go now, but God bless you.' Maitu hugged me tightly as we jumped up and down. '*Ciakorire Wacu mugunda*.' In that envelope was enough money to send me to school for a year and a half.

Despite the relief and gratitude to her friends without whom I would never have completed my education, Maitu was overcome by great sadness. She thought of her beautiful home on top of the ridge and her well tended farm. Now she was relying on others for charity. For the second time since my arrival, Maitu broke down. The thought of her beautiful home in Riara Ridge was too much to bear.

New Beginnings

I vaguely remember the day we moved into our farm in Riara Ridge. It was the mud-plastered temporary house that we found standing when our parents drove us from Thogoto in the back of our Ford Anglia. Wainaina, Mungai and I had fallen asleep during the journey. Our parents had just transferred us to the beds that Maitu had prepared the day before. Baba's friend had loaned my parents his lorry to carry our furniture ahead of our move. They had brought our brown leather sofas, beds, Mungai's and my cots, the dining table and sideboard. When we woke up in the morning, we were astounded by the stillness of life in the countryside. It was refreshingly quiet yet full of noises of nature. The loud chatter of crickets, the clicking of grasshoppers and the humming of frogs was quite a contrast from Thogoto. We could hear birds singing sweetly, welcoming us to our new surroundings. We ran around carefree, bathing in the beautiful surroundings. The vast nothingness of the ridge was a striking contrast to the chaotic noisy village of Thogoto where the huts were right up against each other.

On the day after we arrived, we sat outside, Baba and Maitu on stools and us on the ground. In the middle was our transistor radio, which blared out music by Kamaru. '*Ni nyuuuuo, ni nyuo ni nyuo ni ya mwana ni nyuo ni nyuo.*' Baba jumped to his feet and held his hand out for Maitu inviting her to dance. She held his hand and jumped to her feet, beaming with a smile. 'Tsee tseee tseee,' she hissed in tune with the music, moving her right leg to do a back step and then to the front whilst wiggling her bottom. Baba stamped his feet on the ground in the style of *mugoyo*, a traditional Gikuyu dance for married men. They danced, losing themselves in music, to the shrills of our laughter at seeing our parents dance for the first time. It was like the world had stopped to listen to our joy. Thogoto seemed a million light years away and nothing could take away the joy and happiness of the days when we lived in our mud-plastered temporary house with corrugated iron sheets, so shiny, as if to dazzle the world.

Our temporary house was functional, with a living room, our parents' bedroom, a bedroom for us five children and a kitchen. My parents had done a lot of preparation before our move. They had installed a tap that delivered ice-cold water fresh from the stream at the bottom of our farm, one of the many tributaries in the Central Province. There was a shiny water tank beside the house to capture rainwater. The first few months of our new lives felt like being on holiday; a beautiful exploration of plants and wildlife. After we settled down, Maitu built an external kitchen, which freed up the old kitchen space which then became my brothers' bedroom. Although it was cramped and dark inside, with only one window in each room, looking back, it was in our temporary mud house that we were happiest. We had moved up a class; we had staff! We were landowners and now fell into the category of farmers, even taking part in agriculture shows.

Maitu, the Builder

It had all the hallmarks of a perfect little home for a family of seven, on a perfect little farm, in the perfect countryside. Our pink pebble-dashed house was designed adhoc-ly by my parents, with Maitu overseeing all the building work. Not only was Maitu the expert in DIY, but Baba spent the majority of his time in Kampala, building a business selling essentials after the collapse of the Ugandan economy driven by Idi Amin's expulsion of the Asians. When the British arrived in East Africa at the turn of the nineteenth century, they brought Asians with them. Their role was to build the railway and be artisans, because the British deemed Africans only useful as servants. Rumours were rife that Idi Amin was negotiating with Britain over whose responsibility it was to take Uganda's Asians, since the British had brought them to East Africa. Eventually Amin was to expel all Asians, whose arrogance he detested. He felt that Africans had not benefited from independence because they were still in shackles, oppressed by the now self-proclaimed Asian supremacists filling in the void left by the British. The British introduced the colour bar in East Africa and declared themselves first-class citizens, whilst Asians were awarded second-class status and Africans third class. Asians became the oppressors of Kenyans and Ugandans. As a child, I remember being puzzled and could never understand how or why an Asian man would whip a grown African man in front of his wife and children.

Within a week, all the Asians were expelled from Uganda, taking with them their trading structures. To Baba, this was a great opportunity to become a major player in Uganda's trade. Baba quickly learnt Hindi because there were still plenty of Asians in Kenya from whom he purchased his merchandise. He also learnt to speak Buganda, to converse with his customers in Kampala. Whilst the Asians were losing their homes, we were just about to gain one.

Every day we ran down the track to meet the lorries that drove up our freshly dug road, delivering breeze-blocks, as our house began to take shape. Maitu had spent hours scrutinising the building plans despite the fact that she was illiterate. Maitu had barely been to school, only managing to learn the alphabet and how to write her name before Cucu Herina extracted her. The decision to keep Maitu out of school did not come easily to my grandmother Cucu Herina, who was fairly

well-educated having spent her teenage years learning to
read and write in the Mission Church of Scotland under
Dr John W. Arthur. Cucu Herina made the decision to
keep her off school one evening in 1951, just before
the declaration of the State of Emergency. Everyone
had gathered around Cucu Herina's hut in Iganjo, for
kunyihia huai—shortening the evening, a favourite
Gikuyu pastime. It was the time when families, friends
and neighbours sat around the fire, clutching on to their
calabashes of *mukimo*, telling stories, sharing riddles,
parents imparting knowledge to their children. Cucu
Herina's friends Bero and Doro were there, very much
looking forward to Cucu Herina's stories, dramatised
with sound effects and hilarious anecdotes. The grown-
ups sat on *giturua*—the traditional four-legged stools,
each leg representing the sacred mountains surrounding Gikuyu land; Mount Kirinyaga, Aberdares, Ng'ong
Hills and El Donyo Sabuk. The children sat cross-legged on sisal sacks, absorbing the grown-up's tales.
Everyone took turns in telling a story, and when it was
my seven-year-old mother's turn, she said nonchalantly,
'Today I saw Muru Wa Itina,' at which everyone's eyes
widened, Cucu Herina nearly dropping her calabash.
Everyone stared at Maitu, full of fear at what she was
going to say.

'What did he do, Gakari?' asked Cucu Herina, full
of concern.

The mention of Muru Wa Itina got pretty much

the same reaction from the Gikuyu people, who would freeze rigid with fear. It was a nickname given to the white district officer. Jim Crow laws adopted by colonialists in Kenya dictated that whites did not introduce themselves to inferior black people so people did not know white people's names. Instead they created names for them based on their character. The Gikuyu had decided that a fitting name for the District Officer would be Muru Wa Itina, Son of the Arsehole. He was the son of an original settler who the people nicknamed *Itina*, Arsehole, after he build a reputation of thuggery and general nuisance. Blacking themselves up, he and his men would creep up on unsuspecting Gikuyu girls, who would be subjected to rapes and beatings. He particularly hated the ones wearing traditional costumes, with ear lobes full of jewellery. He had perfected the knack of using his whip to slice off cleanly the ears of those Gikuyu girls and women wearing *hang'i*, the traditional earrings. Father and son organised rape orgies, and the women he deemed ugly he would insert his pistol into their vaginas and shoot. Now everyone gaped at Maitu full of fear.

'What did he do, Gakari?' cried Cucu Herina.

It was the end of Maitu's first week at Thogoto primary school. The children were all in the classroom, waiting for the teacher to begin the lesson, when they were interrupted by one of the children shouting, 'Muru Wa Itina,' at which all the children ran to the window. The teacher hurried to the window too, to see the ginger-haired district officer walking up the path in his crisp khaki uniform, his shorts flapping around his scrawny legs. Realising he was coming towards his class, the teacher walked out hurriedly to meet the District Officer, bowing at his feet. 'Good morning sir, it is a great day!' Muru Wa Itina's instructions were concise before turning round and walking out of the school.

'Children, close your books, we are going on a school trip,' announced the teacher worriedly. The children jumped up and down excitedly, hardly believing their ears. 'Are we going to see the train?' some asked. Others speculated that it might be a wedding, whilst some thought they would be given bread by the *Bibi wa Kambi*—the white mother, who came to the villages to educate Gikuyu women on how to be 'good mothers.' She was part of a program where volunteers in Britain were encouraged to come and give lessons to African women on how to be good mothers.

'Be quiet,' the teacher shouted irritably as he nervously herded the children out of the school and past Kihunguro underpass to Dagoretti market, where a crowd was already gathered. Maitu and her friend Njeri held hands giggling as they edged towards the crowd. Muru Wa Itina had already arrived, his Land Rover parked on the side, and now he stood in the middle of the crowd.

On the ground they could see crisp white sheets all spread out. 'Bring the children forward,' commanded the District Officer, as the teacher pushed the children to the front of the crowd. 'Take off the sheets!' came the order. The teacher leaned forward, peeling back the crisp white linen. Underneath the sheets were charred, mutilated bodies, with decapitated heads and limbs lying around. Some body parts belonged to women but most were men. Maitu and Njeri just stood there, unable to comprehend what they saw.

'Look at this, children. If your mothers and families want to end up like this, tell them to join the Mau Mau.' That was the day Cucu Herina decided that Maitu would never return to school.

What Maitu lacked in education, she made up for with blind determination. The architect had spent several hours explaining to her what was what and had taught her the language of builders. She glared at the broad sheets of paper that were the plans for her brand-new home full of confidence, simultaneously giving instructions to the builders whilst climbing on top of the seven-ton lorries to count the breezeblocks, making sure the quarry did not deceive her. We ran around Maitu's feet as the strings were being laid out to mark the area where trenches would be dug that would become the foundations of our home.

When my parents bought the farm, Maitu had been

very keen to finally leave Thogoto for a new start. They had decided to build a temporary house to live in whilst waiting for the new house. It was Maitu who possessed all the skills from having watched Cucu Herina build their house. Maitu also built all the other outdoor structures, such as the cattle shed and all enclosures for my brother's pet rabbits, because Baba did not possess the know-how to nail a piece of wood to anything. It was Maitu who walked around with nails between her tightly sealed lips, hammering the wood in place. Maitu was the one on the roof, nailing the corrugated iron sheets in place. When they built the temporary house, Baba had busied himself digging a big hole in which he mixed the loose red mud with water. With his trousers rolled up, he squelched with his feet until smooth, then began plastering the walls with red mud.

Maitu always had solutions to problems. The neighbour's workmen were excavating the ground for a pit latrine. It was already very deep. When the night fell, they did not secure the deep hole, leaving it open. Our cows, that had been out grazing, were now returning to their paddock. Our excited dog barked loudly frightening the herd which bolted. One of the cows ran in the direction of the neighbour's pit. In their haste to leave, the workmen forgot to put the temporary fence back. The cow did not see the hole in the dim light, ploughing in head-first. Realising the problem, Maitu sent her young workman to run to the neighbours to mobilise a few men to help remove the cow from the toilet. She asked that they bring torches and ropes. It was several hours before they could heave the cow out of the hole. Maitu knew it was very badly injured so she made the decision that it should be slaughtered in haste. By morning Maitu was faced with a huge pile of meat and, without refrigeration, there was no way of keeping it.

Maitu sent the workman to go to the shop and borrow a weighing scale. Next she sent messages to the farm workers in neighbouring villages announcing that she was selling cheap meat. Meat was something that the Gikuyu rarely ate, being mostly vegan (It was with the coming of the white man that eating meat became more habitual than sacrificial and only for ceremonies). The farm workers came in their tens, each buying a little meat for their families. That was how we first met the people of Riara Ridge.

* * * *

Like a pregnancy, Maitu nurtured the building project for nine months, and finally her brand-new stone house was complete. She stood back and smiled contentedly. We moved into our new palace—the pink pebble-dashed palace. As the old house was demolished, life took on new meaning. Maitu and Baba were now no longer regarded as peasants and became gentry. Now that we owned a stone house, my parents began to seek social acceptance. We had found a PCEA church in which we became active members, attending regularly. Maitu could now hold women's meetings at home because our house was presentable. The congregants were all farm owners living in their nice stone houses, some newly built, others inherited from the white farmers who fled in haste after independence fearing reprisals for their cruelty.

Baba spent some time at the farm whilst still maintaining his business affairs in Kampala. When he was around, he would drive to Nairobi to look for new merchandise to sell in Kampala, returning home at the end of the day. When it rained, Baba's car often got stuck because all the roads were mud and gravel. If the car was firmly stuck in the mud, he would walk home and call us to help push it. Pushing the car was highly entertaining for us children. Baba would open the driver's door and put one leg on the foot pedal, his other leg firmly on the ground. He would start to heave the car yelling '*hia hi.*' '*Hii,*' we'd respond, signalling we were ready to push. We would heave and push until the tyres span, spewing mud on to our clothes. When there was a slight give, someone would slide rocks underneath the tyre to stop the car from going back into the hole. Eventually the car would become unstuck and Baba would drive off whilst we walked back, with Maitu laughing at us comically covered in mud.

Pink Torso

Sat on the top of the ridge, was our little pink pebble-dashed house with red bricks and a chimney to the side. It stood in the tranquil countryside, contrasting with the thick lush carpet of varying shades of green. Our home was small, but not too small; it had five modest bedrooms, four of which were connected by a corridor that led straight to the garage. There was a small white tiled kitchen at the back and two bathrooms one en-suite in my parent's bedroom and another which was ours and remained unfinished for all the years I lived in Riara Ridge.

When one entered our pink pebble-dashed house through the living room door, one was met by an amalgamation of furniture in the combined living-dining room. To the left was a light green door which was almost always shut. That room belonged to Cucu Nyambura although she never slept in it even once, but we still called it Cucu Nyambura's bedroom. Cucu

Nyambura was Baba's aunt. As children, we never understood why we had a room for her in our home. Hers was the room where, we swept the dust from the living room floor into, when we were too lazy to collect it with a dustpan. We simply pushed the dust and particles underneath the door. It was the room where we discarded unwanted things. No one ever went in there and on the rare occasion when the door was tried, one struggled to push it open because of the dust and other clutter accumulated behind it.

As a matter of fact, Cucu Nyambura never had any intention of ever living with us. She worked as a maid for a wealthy Indian family in the sprawling suburbs of Muthaiga and did not have a family of her own. Once, she asked Maitu if I could go and visit her for a couple of days in the servant quarters at the back of the big mansion. When she came to collect me, I could not conceal my excitement. She always had a soft spot for me and, whenever she could, she always carried me on her back. She angered Maitu when she did this because she never put her arms back to cradle me; instead I hung on to her back like a primate, but it never bothered me. I was excited to be staying with her, skipping as we alighted the bus opposite Muthaiga police station and walked the short distance to her tiny house at the back of the main house. When her employers were out during the day, and Cucu Nyambura was busy doing chores in the main house, I ran around the pristine compound kicking a ball that was lying around. When it was dusk, I stood on the tarmacked drive, staring at the house. It was hauntingly big to a small child. I wondered whether Cucu Nyambura ever got scared when she was alone in the big house. It was then that I got the urge to empty my bladder. At the farm, we could urinate wherever the urge came. I used to enjoy seeing the projection of my urine burrow a hole in the red soil. If it was sunny, I would sit and watch the vapours evaporate, wriggling my nose at the smell. To dry myself I would raise my bottom up high and then down, up and down until the last drop had fallen. At the big house there was no exposed soil, just the tarmac and flowerbeds. I pulled down my pants and closed my eyes with relief as my bladder ejected the urine. I opened my eyes, pants still at my ankles, and followed the stream of urine to the flowerbed. When I finished, I shook my bottom up and down to force the remaining drops of urine to fall. It was then that I was covered with a burst of light, making me jump and stare at the headlights at the gate like a frightened rabbit. I pulled my pants up and ran to the servant quarters, closing the door behind me. I had never seen the Indian but Cucu Nyambura said he was terrifying. I could hear the clanking of the sliding gates as they parted to let the car in. I stood behind the door, my heart pounding.

The car door slammed, and I could hear an angry voice with an Indian accent calling to Cucu Nyambura.

'*Hiyo mtoto yako amekojoa hapa?*—that child of yours urinated in here?' he told her angrily. '*Chukua maji uoshe drive yote*—get water and wash the drive,' he yelled at Cucu Nyambura. '*Kesho asubuhi arudi nyumbani kwao*—tomorrow morning you must return her home. *Nyinyi WaAfrica in wachafu sana*—you Africans are very dirty.' I peeped from behind the door to see the silhouette of a big fat man who looked like the Buddha in the fading light. Later, when we sat down to eat ugali and sukuma wiki, siphoned from the main house, Cucu Nyambura told me I was going back home in the morning. I felt a little sad but also a sense of relief to be going back home to Riara Ridge because the Indian man scared me. In the morning, the Indian man's wife called Cucu Nyambura, to which she ran answering, '*yes memsabu.*'

'*Patia hi mtoto yako*—give this to that child.' Cucu Nyambura put it in the bag and I did not see it properly until we got home. The gift was a strange old imitation of a baby—a doll, as I later found out it was called. It had matted blonde hair, sun-bleached pink skin and blue eyes with blonde eye lashes, some of which were missing. It had one white shoe and a sock on the other foot.

Mungai and I took the imitation baby and ran to the back of the house where we always played. We put the doll down for inspection.

'What is it for?' Mungai asked curiously.

'It is what the Indians keep,' I replied. 'The Indian woman gave it to us.' We scrutinized it from every angle, unsure of its purpose. When it lay flat on its back, one eye closed, leaving the other open. The eyelid of the closed eye would open and close of its own accord. Mungai and I looked at it, full of fearful suspicion. We did not know what to do with it. It had a menacing look. Mungai scrunched his face and made a growling sound at the doll. I scrunched my face and made a growling noise at the doll too.

'I know, the eyes are blue because it's witchcraft.' A lizard darted across, giving us a terrible fright, causing us to run away in the opposite direction. Mungai came back, picked the doll up and threw it into the coffee bushes, away from his play area.

Every time Maitu fried sausages, Mungai always left a tiny bit which he buried in the ground with a bit of fertilizer. Every morning, he ran to the back to see whether a sausage tree had sprouted in the back yard. Kui saw us from the window of her bedroom and ran out to see what we were running away from.

'What's the matter?' she asked.

'That imitation baby has witchcraft,' said Mungai pointing to the doll. Kui was looking at the doll that lay head down in the coffee bushes with great curiosity. She knelt and carefully reached underneath the branches, pulling the doll out by the leg. She stared at it for a moment and then turned its head round on its axis so that it faced backwards, and the rest of its body faced the opposite direction. 'Aaargh,' she said, running with the doll in her hands towards us. We ran away screaming.

'Stop that!' yelled Maitu at Kui. She threw the doll down and headed back to the house. We could hear Maitu scolding her for not doing what she was told. She was meant to sit outside keeping an eye on the hen whose chicks had hatched. An eagle had been spotted and now was circling the house menacingly, waiting for an opportunity to snatch a chick.

Mungai and I returned to the doll. Mungai started dismantling its body and pulling its limbs off. I helped him. I tugged on to the matted hair whilst Mungai pulled the body. When the head came off, we threw it as far as we could, leaving a headless and limbless torso. Mungai was now staring at the torso with renewed interest. His face lit up and he ran towards a train of safari ants. He blocked their way with the torso, forcing them to climb through the hole where the leg joint used to be, snaking their way to the opposite side where the arm used to be. Mungai sat down to watch his creation. We had found a new use for the pink torso. It would be a tunnel for our prisoners, a collection of various insects to go through. The prisoners in the squash bottles would be allowed out by putting the neck of the bottle into the torso and we would watch them escape from the other side.

* * * *

From the back of our pink pebble-dashed house, one was met with the stunning beauty of rolling hills, with no other buildings in sight, just miles of tea and coffee plantations. Tea was introduced to Kenya in 1903 by two British settler brothers on a farm in Limuru, a few kilometres away from our home in Riara Ridge. Coffee had been introduced ten years earlier by a French religious order and together with tea, became Kenya's top export. The light green tea bushes, all neatly trimmed, were separated by dusty red tracks wide enough for the tractors to pass through, dividing them from the dark broad-leafed coffee bushes.

I hated walking through the imposing coffee plantations, choked by their claustrophobic thickness, always imagining wild animals and scary men emerging from the thick maze. One day after school, Kui and I were walking home slowly, chatting about the people at our school. Grasshoppers ticked and jumped across our path, as if to make way for us as we walked down the dusty track surrounded by tall coffee bushes on all sides.

'Which teacher do you fear the most?' asked Kui.

'*Mwarimu Ngonyo*—teacher Ngonyo,' I replied.

'*Wee mwana wa gitonga*—you daughter of the rich,' Kui imitated teacher Ngonyo. I laughed, diving into the grass. When we got to the end of the path, we turned left, which was another dusty track that was even shorter and led to the clearing before the tea plantation. Just then we heard rustling in the bushes and a movement edging closer to us.

'Mujarewa—aaaah run!' yelled Kui. We ran at top speed at the mention of Mujarewa. She was a mad woman who had mythical reverence. No one actually ever saw her, but we all knew about her. A woman emerged from the coffee bushes, heading in our direction and carrying a machete. We must have frightened her as well because she ran, and we ran even faster down the hill, crossing the river and uphill home. That evening we told everyone how we were nearly caught by Mujarewa. Every time we passed near that spot she had emerged from, we always walked very slowly on our tiptoes so as not to disturb her. She probably didn't live anywhere nearby but we believed she might be close.

Walking through the tea plantations was always intriguing. I liked to imagine what it would be like to run on top of the neat carpet of tea bushes, so fast until I could fly and see the world like a bird. I wondered how far the tea plantation stretched. Maybe if I could fly, I would be able to see the end of the world. Every so often, the carpet of tea plantation was interrupted by hundreds of tea-pickers carrying oversized wicker baskets on their backs as they waded through the thick bushes. With two fingers sticking out, they intricately plucked the youngest two leaves and a bud. I was always fascinated by how teapickers methodically flung the delicate leaves over their shoulders straight into the basket with such incredible accuracy.

Baba the Visionary

Whilst it is fair to say that Maitu was the DIY expert, it was Baba who was the innovator and visionary. One day he was standing behind us, marvelling at a big splurge of freshly dropped cow dung, biting his lip in deep contemplation. He seemed to be working out complex calculations in his head. 'Aha,' he said, finally emerging from his reverie. Over the next few weeks he began to bring home miscellaneous items. A large plastic barrel, some tubes, copper pipes and other seemingly irreverent objects. He asked Munyau the workman to dig a deep wide hole in the back of the cowshed. Next the tubes were coming out of the plastic container and the copper pipes welded together, stretching all the way to the kitchen. When Baba called us to each find a spade and scoop the cow dung into the plastic container buried in the ground, we thought he had lost his mind. He had that concentrated look of determination on his face. He even hummed a tune as he scooped the dung, flinging it into the plastic hole. It was a few days later, when Baba was certain everything was ready, that he led us to the kitchen, turned on a tap and then one of the two dials on a small cooker sitting on a table. We looked on with great curiosity. He pulled out a box of matches, adding to the drama by looking at our faces like a magician about to perform a trick. He struck a match, extending his arm to the hissing sound coming from the cooker. He had created bio gas using the cow dung. We stood back marvelling at his creation. Baba was a genius! He was better than the magician that visited our school. When he performed his magic, he asked us to close our eyes and made a magic noise, '*arisirue, arisirue,*' which we presumed to be magic words. Although we had marvelled at the magicians disappearing cards when our eyes were closed, Baba's trick brought fire. Baba's brain was always looking outwards for new inventions, new foods and new ways of doing things.

Baba always bought the groceries because he had the car and went past shops. He preferred to shop in Uchumi supermarket in Nairobi. He bought us unfamiliar foods to try, like apples. Since they were very expensive, he insisted that apples be halved so that everyone got to taste the interesting fruit. Instead of porridge, Baba introduced us to cornflakes, which Maitu always served with hot milk. Spaghetti was the most puzzling of all the food because Maitu did not know how to cook it or what to cook it with. My brothers and I gave it a nickname, *minyoo*—like the worms that children and their parents sifted for after de-worming medicine. Maitu usually cooked a curry-type sauce with potatoes, peas and carrots as an accompaniment to the pasta. There were packets of Knorr chicken and mushroom soup which we added to boiling water for a starter. Most of our eating ideas came from Baba's dining experiences in posh restaurants in Nairobi. Baba had an eye for identifying innovative solutions. Ours was the first house in Kiambu district if not the country to be powered by solar panels providing electricity and hot water.

As brilliantly minded as he was, Baba also did some carelessly stupid things. One day we were just about to wave him goodbye when we noticed smoke rising from the hut our neighbour's workman lived in. He was out and his goat was making strange noises from inside the hut. The smoke got thicker until it became apparent that the hut was on fire. Baba ran to the garage to collect a ladder and ran back to the burning hut. He put the ladder against the hut and began to climb, reaching for the burning dry reeds that thatched the roof. He began pulling the reeds from the house, throwing them to the ground where they started little fires. The flames were becoming more ferocious, and even as young children we could spot the flaw in his plan. Maitu had run to the other side of the garage, dragging the hose-pipe to put the fire out and fearing the worst.

'Get down,' shouted Maitu. The whole roof was now consumed by flames and caved inwards. Baba saw it in the nick of time, jumping off the ladder and dusting himself where his shirt had caught fire.

'I could not save the goat,' he said, burying his face in his hands. Baba managed to escape with only minor burns to his hands.

The Omen

The pace of life had a comfortable normalness as we settled into our new environment. Directly opposite our house, the acacia tree stood towering over the tea bushes, strategically placed, as if to provide its sole inhabitant a platform from which to observe the goings-on of our little pink house. We never saw the leopard, but we all knew it was there. It made its presence known by leaving blood-drained carcasses with puncture wounds in their throats dangling on the tree brunches, as if to assert it's dominance. Baba said he saw the leopard's dazzling shy eyes dancing around the thickets as it walked around its kingdom, when he drove home in the pitch darkness that enveloped the countryside. There were hyenas too. I never actually saw one but Maitu warned us to walk together as a group and never to swing our arms when walking home from the dusty little school over the ridge opposite, in case the hyena thought we were carrying meat.

It was soon after breakfast, when the sun was still kind to one's back, that Maitu set off to the farm like she did every morning. She would walk around carrying her sharpened machete in case anything needed cutting. She busied herself with many jobs such as tending to seedlings, and if she saw barren patches, she would pierce the ground with the machete, lift the soil and throw a seed from her pocket into the hole. There were times when she'd spot the notorious ferns whose roots shot to the bottom at incredible speed, making it difficult to pull them out. If one was not careful the whole place would be overrun by them. Sometimes Maitu would come across a banana plant weighed down by a huge bunch of bananas which needed harvesting. Her machete was also her protection. There was the time when she was clearing a pile of leaves and when she lifted them something heavy moved, prompting her to throw it to the ground. Before the snake could attack her, she moved promptly, one swift move of her arm sliced the head of the snake off. Breathless, she sighed with relief because she recognized it as a poisonous kind. Her machete was her best tool.

That day, Maitu had walked all the way down to the stream feeling quite thirsty. She cut a broad arrowroot leaf, folded it into a funnel, bent down and scooped the refreshing ice-cold water. Once she quenched her thirst, she discarded the leaf by the riverbed, making crabs scram to their holes. She walked up the hill, inspecting side to side, when she noticed some passion fruit creepers drooping low to the ground. That would make the fruit rot, she thought, wandering over to tie them back. It was when she lifted them up that she was met with a waft of nauseating smell and a flurry of flies. Covering her nose, she looked closely to find our dog Juli. She moved away, yelling for Munyau the workman, who came running. '*Ni chau Nyina Wa Mary*—what's wrong, Mary's mum?' I hated it when people called me by my English name. It was boring like Mary and Joseph, and holy, and I wasn't boring or holy.

Maitu pointed to the carcass, which looked like Juli, our dog. Munyau approached with trepidation. He always had the face of a coward despite being almost twice Maitu's and Baba's height. He inspected it, pointing to the neck, which had a familiar wound on it.

'*Ni chui*—it's the leopard,' he said to Maitu, who agreed. Maitu walked to the edge of the terracing and began to cry. She had only just got Juli the dog but she was quite attached to him. Munyau, who was always perceptive, ran for his hoe and began digging a hole to bury Juli. Having buried the dog, Munyau offered Maitu passion flowers to put on Juli's grave, which she did. Munyau was a very kind and beautiful human being. He was a mild-mannered tower of a man, tall, lean and stooped forward as if embarrassed of being tall. His youthful face was pleasant and friendly, always smiling, never taking anything too seriously. He was jovial, obedient and worked diligently, answering to Maitu's beck and call. When we asked him to play with us, he raised us high in the air and ran down the hill whilst we pretended to be aeroplanes. We fell in love with him.

Although people loved dogs and kept them around the home, there were circumstances that were thought to bring a bad omen to the family. If a dog crossed one's path, especially if one was driving, that was thought to bring bad lack to that person. That was exactly what happened to Maitu and Baba's friend Njoroge Wa Njoki. He was driving one day when a dog crossed the road in front of him. When he told his family, they were full of concern, urging him to refrain from using the car until the bad luck passed. He had many errands, it being the end of the month, so he ignored the warning. It was one Saturday morning when Baba woke up having arrived late the previous night, to announce Njoroge's passing in a car accident. Many people would argue that consuming a large amount of alcohol before driving would bring on accidents, but they believed the dog was responsible.

Maitu had been very upset at finding Juli, our beloved dog, in the thicket. Juli was a very unusual dog with a limp and greying colour. He held such importance to us because we had begun our new life with him. Finding a dead body on your land is a bad omen,

114

but finding Juli's was very bad. Maitu tried not to let it bother her, going about her business in different parts of the farm. No matter how much she tried, it is difficult to ignore belief.

One day not long after she found Juli's dead body, Maitu was deep in thought, inspecting the seedlings which were just sprouting out of the ground. This was a reason to feel happy. The rain had been ample, and all her hard work was beginning to show promise. She bent down pulling a few weeds when she became aware of a strange woman approaching, followed by a man carrying the woman's handbag. She could tell straight away that the pair had been drinking from the way they walked, zigzagging everywhere. The intoxicated pair walked carelessly, trampling on Maitu's sprouting seedlings.

'You are trespassing on my property, and damaging my crops,' Maitu rebuked rather angrily. The man's red eyes glared at Maitu menacingly and he stepped forward, grabbing her by the arm and shoving her violently out of the way. The man was tall, young-looking but prematurely aged with overconsumption of *chang'aa*, the illicit brew. His lips had turned a reddish colour on the inside and had an alcoholic tremor.

Despite her size, Maitu was fearless, always ready to stand her ground. The provocation by the pair got to Maitu. She puffed up like a cat about to engage in a fight. She stepped back in front of the man.

'*Kubafu hii*—stupid man,' said Maitu speaking in Swahili. She could tell from their very dark skin and facial features that they were from another tribe, hence speaking in Swahili. The man stopped and stared at Maitu as if trying to focus his eyes on her. He reached out and shoved her one more time. Baba arrived just in time to see it all.

'How dare you touch my wife?' he barked. The man swung a fist at Baba, who ducked. Next, Baba flew into the air with one martial art move, completely missing the man and instead kicking the woman's rather enormous bottom, causing her to squeal and tumble down the terracing. Baba was always painfully aware of his small stature, which he saw as a vulnerability, so he took measures to defend himself. He had bought a gun and made sure everyone was aware he had a gun, which was a deterrent. He also knew that having a rifle on him all the time was impractical, so he took up martial arts, becoming a black belt in Taekwondo.

Baba accidentally kicking the woman down the terraces enraged the man, who came at Baba. Baba, being five-foot-tall, jumped at the man, his arms flung tightly around his neck, his legs encircling his waist. Baba weighed a ton. The intoxicated man lost his balance and together they tumbled, rolling several times down the hill, whilst still clinging together. Fearing for Baba's life, we chased them down the hill. We feared the big man would kill him. At the foot of the hill, both were slightly concussed and held on to each other, trying to figure out the next move. Mungai took a stick and with all his might, began whipping the man. I went for pinching, whilst Maitu tried to separate them. 'Stop that!' We all turned round to see Cucu Herina and the preacher who she had brought to bless our farm. The two scrambled to their feet, the hooligan making a hasty exit towards the river before disappearing into the coffee bushes wiping his bleeding nose. Shaken and embarrassed, Baba stood up and apologized to Cucu Herina and the preacher, exclaiming that young people lacked respect for others' property, before returning to tend his green gold.

The Peasant School

Out of sight over the ridge, nestled amongst the neat rows of coffee and tea, was Githatha. If Riara Ridge was an oasis of splendour, Githatha was an eyesore of squalor. Helmed in by a thorny hedge, it was quarter acre of tightly packed rows of claustrophobic houses, built of concrete and thatched with reeds. When it rained, the roofs leaked, but the unlike the earth floors, which soaked up their misery, the cold grey concrete had no give. It revelled in the wretchedness of the rainy season. Githatha was a manufactured slum, home to several hundred families, all of whom worked at the farm inherited from white owners. The houses were absurdly small, overcrowded and bleak. The purlieu was served by a block of communal ablutions, bare concrete walls decorated with pungent human faeces in varying shades of brown. Lack of night-lights meant the cubicles got less use than the entrance, whilst most preferred to dig holes by the hedge to relieve themselves. A tap dribbled urine-coloured water to the endlessly long queue. A shop scarcely stocked with overpriced basics of sugar, flour and salt but disproportionally large quantities of cigarettes served the slum. Vegetables could be foraged from a designated section of the farm specifically for farm workers. At the centre was the social hall, which was used for barazas and other announcements during the colonial days. Despite the name, no social activities took place in the leisure hall. During the mornings, it was a nursery school. It was in this dark hall that my education began.

In the colonial days, *Bibi wa Kambi* white mother would be driven in her immaculate Land Rover, her wide-brimmed hat covering her milk-white skin. When she walked into the hall, her perfume wafted over the women and girls dressed in rugged clothes still dirty from working at the farm. Although exhausted and impatient about going back home to cook supper for their families, they listened silently to the broken Swahili as the white woman droned on about the importance of cleanliness and good diet. It was her duty to educate the natives on home management.

Firiso was the name given to the white woman's husband. They lived opposite Githatha in a sprawling mansion set in an acre of beautifully manicured gardens only visible if the tall palatial gates opened. It was securely protected by armed guards behind a concrete wall decorated on either side by a rainbow of neatly trimmed bougainvillea. The Englishman and his wife owned the farm before independence. Instead of fleeing like others, he negotiated a deal with the new owners, Githatha farmers' cooperative that he would oversee the day-to-day running of the farm in exchange for a salary and the guarantee of his family's safety. Little did he know that revenge was the last thing on anyone's mind. The floodgates of capitalism had been opened and profiteering was at the forefront of the newfound freedom. The pair became reclusive, never to be seen, but we all knew they were there. No one bothered them.

* * * *

Githatha Full Primary School was built in the colonial era. It was the school that served the slum, educating Africans to read and write basic English and perform simple arithmetic, enough to be useful servants. All the farm workers were required to send their children to the school. During school holidays, the children accompanied their parents on the farms, picking tea and coffee to help boost the daily earnings of the meagre wages they were paid. By the time we attended the school, little had changed. Baba enrolled us there due to lack of options. All the decent schools were in Nairobi, the capital. When Baba was away on business, we would have no means of getting to school without a car and non-existent public transport. I was enrolled at the nursery in the community hall, but my older siblings were enrolled at the big school. School enrolment was not by age—a child was required to stand straight, stretch their arm over their head and touch the ear on the opposite side. Those who could touch their ear could start Standard 1 and those who couldn't went to nursery. There were several people who remained in nursery for several years.

We, of course were not labourers' children. We stood out. We were the generation of sacrilege. The ones who would shame their parents in later years, leaving our ancestors spinning in their graves. We were the generation of pampered spoilt brats who lost the lustre of determination. The generation that forgot of the struggle for freedom. Our parents had borne the full brunt of colonial might. Not only were they defiant to the oppressors, they were savvy, shrewd and determined to rise against the poverty inflicted on them. Baba and other burgeoning entrepreneurs clubbed together to buy out the hedonistic settlers. He and his friends aspired to great things for their children. They were thirsty for everything denied to them: education, freedom, the delightful taste of churned butter. Our enrolment at the school was only temporary. On our first day, we caused a spectacle. We arrived wearing brand new uniforms, shiny black polished shoes and pristine white socks, in contrast with the threadbare hand-me-down uniforms and dirty shoeless feet, toes spread wide for lack of containment by shoes. Each one of us clutched lunch boxes filled with butter and jam sandwiches, farmers' choice pork sausages only previously preserved for whites. The teachers ogled scornfully at what rich people ate.

When Baba was home from Kampala, he'd drive us to school in the back of our brand-new Toyota Hilux. We sat in the back, bouncing up and down as he manoeuvred around potholes. Our arrival at school always created mayhem, attracting attention of the children who chased the car yelling *watoto wa tajiri*—children of the rich.

Baba's Dreams

Although he never said it to me, or anyone, my father would have been very disappointed at how things turned out when I left home on that fateful night. He always said that lack of education was worse than a curse. He believed that the measure of a man's success was how well he managed to educate his children. By his own standards, his success began failing when he refused to pay for my education despite Maitu's plea. Education had been his mantra.

I was the most promising of his children when it came to academia. Every end of term, he always looked at my school report with a big smile on his face. 'If you are going to be a top lawyer working in the high-rise buildings in Nairobi, you need to be no. 1,' he would say. 'I will try,' I would promise. Githatha primary was no good for me, he had said once, shaking his head sadly. He prayed that God would touch Mrs Wambugu, the headmistress of Thogoto Junior—now renamed Musa

Gitau primary after Kenya got its independence. He prayed that Mrs Wambugu would grant us places at her prestigious school. Baba paid her many visits bearing gifts of all shapes and sizes. Egyptian cotton bedding, woollen scarves from his trip to Scotland, silk blouses from the merchants in Kampala, handbags, shoes, and anything else he could lay his hands on.

One day during his visits, she yielded with great news: 'Two places have come up and we can offer your youngest sons places in class three.' Wainiana and Mungai were in the same class despite their age difference. Baba was pleased, but disappointed there was no place for me. I felt upset and envious that my brothers would be leaving me behind as they went to boarding school. Making the journey down the hill and up the hill to my school on the other side of the ridge seemed longer, lonelier and scary. My sisters too had moved to high school leaving me behind.

Githatha primary had been gruelling for my brothers, particularly Wainiana. We were all happy that he was finally leaving. Our affluence was our curse. We were served on a platter to bullies at Githatha primary, who viewed us as legitimate targets. We received threats from several people who promised to close the school with us. Throughout the term, we prayed they would forget by the end of term. Wainaina, the eldest brother, was fodder to the bullies; his weak frail character fell foul of them.

Wainaina— The Delicate Soul

Wainaina sat under the thin shadow of the telegraph pole, his legs pulled in so that his heels touched his bottom. He was sheltering from the sweltering mid-January sun watching a group of boys play football. The scorched brown grass was interspersed with sandy perches, the fine soil whirling around with the boys' movement. It was difficult to tell when Wainaina was tired or sad, his lazy eye made it look so. He watched the boys intently, their threadbare shorts flapping around their thin legs, their feet looking like they wore beige socks from the morning dew and red soil that caked them. Some children sat on the grass giggling and singing whilst others skipped using the plaited bark ropes everyone made at their leisure.

From his position Wainaina watched the game haplessly, the boys tackling, tagging one another as they kicked their homemade football, wishing he could join in. We had learnt by now that we were not welcome to play with any children. The boys stopped playing, grouped together and chatted away in low voices. Suddenly they approached Wainaina, stopping just by his feet. He looked up at them, covering his lazy eye from the blazing sun.

'Would you like to join us?' asked the ringleader. Wainaina jumped to his feet excitedly.

'Yes! May I?'

'The rule of the game is you have to kick the ball as far as possible,' explained the leader, 'and you can go first.' Wainaina could not believe his luck. Finally, some people sought his company. He placed his book bag by the telegraph pole, taking off his jumper to reveal a crisp white shirt in contrast with the dirty browny torn shirts the boys wore. He placed his jumper on his book bag and followed the boys.

'You stand here,' the leader instructed, 'and when I say on your marks, get set, go, you will kick the ball.' That was easy enough, thought Wainaina, standing readily awaiting instructions.

'On your marks,' he cowered in preparation.

'Get set,' he arched his back.

'Wait,' interrupted someone.

'What's wrong?' enquired the leader.

'He's got his shoes on, it's not fair, he must take his shoes off,' said the speaker wryly. Wainaina saw the disadvantage, hastily bent down and began to peel off his shoes and socks, his toes curling upwards at the feel of the hot dusty soil. He set his shoes down by the tele-graph pole, placing his book bag and folded jumper on top. Now he was ready, without unfair advantage over the other boys.

'On your marks,' he cowered, the boys forming a semi-circle behind him.

'Get set,' his back arched again in readiness to spring into action.

'Go!' Wainaina leapt into action, sprinting to the ball; stopping momentarily to swing his right leg back, full of momentum, he kicked the ball with all his might. Upon impact Wainaina squealed like an animal caught in the fangs of a trap. The shriek of his anguished cry was perfectly timed with the ringing of the bell. Wainaina hopped around clutching his toes with his fingers, blood beginning to seep through them. Some of the boys fell to the ground with laughter; others mocked him mimicking his hopping holding their toes. Mungai's tiny frame ran to his brother's aid, looking at Wainaina's bleeding toes. The ball had not shifted from its position. Mungai felt it. It was a rock wrapped loosely with newspaper and string to make it look like a homemade ball. The boys' laughter came in great waves. Mungai's scrunched up face stared at them fiercely and yelled 'you dogs!' The tallest boy went over and pointed at Mungai's head tapping it with his finger. 'Don't mess with me, little boy.' Mungai, almost half his size, pointed and tapped the boy on his knee, replying, 'You don't mess with me little boy.'

Wainaina was feeble, quiet and gave the impression that he was never sure of himself. Sometimes when he told a story, it seemed accidental, as if you had tuned in between transmissions. His stories rarely had a beginning or an ending. His lack of appetite meant he was always very small, which made his angular head appear bigger than it was. Whenever he ate bread with butter or drank tea with milk he vomited. This intolerance to milk and butter meant that his eating habits came to define him more than they needed to. In later years, when we attended boarding school, the cook used to shout through the hatch at breakfast '*turungi*', for Wainaina to collect his black tea, which earned him the nickname *Turungi* boy. He would walk awkwardly across the hall and sit with Mungai, pour half of his *turungi* into his cornflakes and drink the rest. At the start of term, my parents bought him a big tin of Cadbury's cocoa, which the cook kept on a shelf in the kitchen and was visible from the dining hall. Everyone knew it was his, earning him the second nickname of Cadbury. People during lunch would drum the table and sing *Cadbury cocoa, Cadbury cocoa.*

Wainaina struggled with formal education. Every end of term, Baba would sit on his yellow velvet armchair, clear his throat and call, 'Bring your report cards.' Our hearts jumped at the mention of report cards. I would be the first to hand in my card because

I was always amongst the top seven. 'Baba, if I achieve number one to three next term, please can you buy me a watch?' I once asked him. 'Yes, I will buy you a watch if you are one to three,' he promised. I marched off with a smile on my face.

Mungai's report card always earned him a beating because the class teacher's section would read: 'He is very playful in school.' Wainaina was always the last to present his card, only doing so after being prompted again. He would drag his feet as he walked the long way round the table, his head drooping unusually low like it was too heavy for his body. He'd stop a bit too far from Baba and with all his might he would appear to force his arm to stretch so as to hand in his report card. 'Forward!' Baba would shout, making him edge closer.

'Number 30 out of 30,' he would bark without surprise. 'You have the biggest head, and the least in it. When you will ever become a man? At least your sisters can go sell themselves, you would have to chop off your penis to sell yourself,' Wainaina's head sank lower in shame. 'Go get a stick. Both of you.' They would walk out together, whimpering and grumbling, before returning for their beating. That always marked the end of the school term and the beginning of the school holidays.

* * * *

It was Wainaina's meek demeanour, especially his inability to fight for himself, that made us very protective of him. Every time a boy challenged him to a fight, he would request that the boy give him a grace period so he could take off his jumper in readiness for the fight. The boys knew this, and they always granted him the grace period. As soon as his head was covered as he pulled off his jumper, the boy would punch him before running off, and by the time Wainaina's head was free, the boy had hurt him and left. People simply took advantage of him.

Each one of us felt responsible for his wellbeing and that was why his wedding invitation caused me such anguish. The prospect of letting him down was as unthinkable as coming face to face with Baba. Too much water had passed under that bridge. No one felt more responsible for Wainaina than Mungai. Mungai was never far away, keeping a watchful eye over his brother. I was to find out later after the invitation, that it was Mungai who nudged Wainaina to find a bride: noticing he was getting on a bit, with no sign that he would marry. Mungai asked old friends in the vicinity of Riara Ridge for prospective girls to be introduced to him, and when the girl was found, it became his duty to lead the elders in negotiating the dowry, planning and organizing the wedding. The young lady introduced to Wainaina happened to be related to her-whose-name-refuses-to-leave-my-mouth, and by default she would be expected to attend the wedding with Baba. Also attending was the ringleader of the stone football incident, because he had become a prominent police chief. I guess it was no different than any other wedding.

Mungai—His Brother's Keeper

As a small boy, Mungai was very small. His walk was grounded, self-assured, with the alpha stride of a lion's cub. He believed he was bigger and stronger than he was, which in certain situations made him comical. He saw himself as the protector of his older, more vulnerable brother. Unlike Wainaina, but like Maitu, Mungai was fearless; not even Baba made him scared. He was born with a satirical sense of everything around him. He bore from an early age, a good sense of justice. He made a point of holding people accountable for their actions and inadequacies irrespective of their status or age. His moral compass granted him the status of an elder long before his time. He became the person the family turned to if there was a dispute. They say that leaders are born and not made. He certainly was born a leader.

Mungai could never understand why Baba ordered everyone around him to do chores whilst he sat down doing nothing. Once, when he was punished for not polishing Baba's shoes properly, he was so aggrieved that he decided to leave home. He stood by the door separating the hall and the living room, drawing in phlegmy breaths from crying, grumbling at Baba's unfairness.'Everything it's Mungai, cleaning the car, it's Mungai, going to the shops it's always Mungai, what do they think Mungai is?' he grumbled to himself. Our ginger cat was sat high on the wall unit and realized Mungai was the perfect step to the floor. Baba, Maitu and all of us peered at him from the kitchen hatch. Mungai's head was always shaven clean because his hair grew like tiny bubbles of fluff. His head looked like sparsely planted tea plantation. Children at the school had nicknamed him *gachweri*—hair. He was just about to do some more phlegmy grumbles when the cat flew into the air, landing on his freshly shaved head. Without breaking his sentence, he continued, 'Even the cat hates me. I am leaving.' The cat's timing could not have been more comical. Everyone burst out laughing, fuelling his anger.

He moved quickly to the bedroom he shared with Wainaina and packed a small suitcase, came to the living room to say his goodbye. I felt quite sad to be losing Mungai. He was the closest to me in age and we spent a lot of time playing together. Now he was leaving home, Baba and Maitu did not take it seriously. In fact, Baba gave him a few pennies to start a small business. I held on to my little brother, crying. I did not want him to leave. 'He doesn't know how to cook,' I begged my parents, who didn't seem bothered that four-year-old Mungai was leaving home. Baba said we should allow him to go. He walked out of the door, out to the darkness, pulling the door behind him. Two minutes later he walked back in. I was delighted.

Although Mungai was closer to me in age, Wainaina was always *his* brother, he was after all the other man in the family. They would share a lot more in life than Mungai and I. One overcast morning, they sat in sombre silences each staring out of the car window, sweat beads dripping down their temples. The day had come. They were to become men! Baba had woken them up earlier than usual. There was no ritual. The trials and tribulations of the twentieth century had eroded our culture with incredible speed. Within one generation, the British obliterated Gikuyu customs, like the aftermath of a hurricane, leaving debris strewn over our cultural landscape.

Before Baba's time, all the boy's transitioning from boyhood to manhood spent months with their age-sets, grouped together at birth as life long brothers, in jovial camaraderie, touring different places and singing warrior songs, letting the world know they were about to become men. Circumcision was an extremely important occasion for a Gikuyu boy or girl. Classes were held by matriarchs and patriarchs who imparted manly or womanly knowledge to those on the cusp of manhood or womanhood. It was when a young boy became a warrior, an adult like his father—which qualified him to take a seat on the elder's council—or a girl became a woman. Women too were permitted on the council. The dawn of adulthood required ample preparation. The initiates spent months of intense education of social etiquette and the consequences of sexual perversion, which was ostracisation and the moral code for marriage and society in general. Agesets were each other's moral counsellors, brothers or sisters to lean on through out life. When the British arrived, Gikuyu social cohesion was the first casualty. Like a shark frightens a school of herring into disarray, the British disrupted the structure of the tribe by deporting people out of their land and villages to live in native reserves.

Before the arrival of the British, circumcision ceremonies were grand and elaborate affairs. Many ceremonies and dances were held after the 'Njahi' (a type of pulse) harvest season between January and March. This was an ideal time because the granaries were stocked with grain and the planting season was not until April, giving the Gikuyu villagers a break from work. The boys and girls were presented in age sets between fifteen and eighteen years old. Mass initiation of groups of 30–50 boys or girls was the norm. That age set was given a name depending on events on the day. The variation in age was due to several reasons; affordability, famine or natural disasters as it was considered divine displeasure. Presenting a child for initiation was expensive. The cost of the classes was one goat. In addition the father's entitlement of a seat on the ruling council was two goats for a boy.

The day before the initiation ceremony, boys were clean-shaven except for a small tuft of hair on the crown of the head. They would be painted in different patterns from head to toe. The pattern was determined by the divine commands given to the first man on earth called Gikuyu upon his creation by Ngai—God on the holy mountain of brightness (Mount Kenya) named so due to it's snowcaps. Ngai had taken Gikuyu to the peak of the mountain and pointed out below to the hill, ravines, wildlife all of which he granted Gikuyu. It was this time that he granted Gikuyu a set of commandments.

These commandments were incorporated into every aspect of Gikuyu existence, including circumcision. The boys wore colobus monkey capes with leopard skin tails at the back from the waist down. Monkey tails were strapped on knees and anklets were worn, with dancing rattles on the thighs. Cowrie shell belts were worn across the chest and waist. Wooden shields were carried on the shoulder along with dancing sticks. On the day, the boys woke at sunrise and bathed in the ice-cold waters of a river to anaesthetise them before the initiation. Tribal binding rituals were performed, and feasts enjoyed by the entire village.

These traditions had been broken with the travel ban imposed on the Gikuyu people and their incarceration during the State of Emergency. Baba's was the generation that received none of the manly guidance that his forefathers had passed down for generations. Sadly, he had none to impart to his boys.

When I woke up that morning, my brothers were just returning. There had been no rituals, no visit to the river at the crack of dawn for an ice-cold bath to anaesthetise the body, no camaraderie, no ceremony, no feast. Baba had simply taken them to our family doctor in Nairobi who performed the procedure.

Circumcision required stoicism. The procedure was performed with no anaesthetic because real men didn't cry. That was the first trial of a man's resilience and crying was frowned upon, but such matters were never discussed in the presence of women. Undergoing the ritual together cemented Mungai and Wainaina's bond. They always slept in the same bed, huddled together as if to console each other, especially when Baba emasculated them.

Never to Become Real Women

For most of our days in the peasant school, our pain had been relentless. We did everything to fit in. We gave up wearing school shoes after the first week. The ice-cold dew that numbed our soft feet was preferable to standing in assembly with shiny shoes amongst the plethora of dirty, cracked feet. Our efforts were futile. The teachers hated us too. One afternoon during school sports, the girls were all asked to form a circle. We were going to sing songs. Mrs Kimani looked across and asked Wairimu to lead a song. She knew Wairimu had come from a Swahili-speaking school and did not know Gikuyu songs.

'I said lead the song,' she repeated sarcastically. 'Are you circumcised?' she asked. Wairimu bowed her head in embarrassment, before shaking her head from side to side. The girls gasped in horror that a girl of about thirteen was not circumcised. '*Kirigu*,' they hissed. 'Shush,' hushed the teacher, calming the murmur of 'uncircumcised girl.'

'Lead the song,' insisted the teacher, satisfied that Wairimu's humiliation was complete.

'*Jugu karanga in moja kwa peni*—the peanut is one for a penny,' she started the Swahili song, but nobody joined in. She ploughed, on singing the whole song by herself reminiscent of Baba's song at chief Mwangi's wife's birthday.

My sisters and I were questioned about our plans for circumcision. Teachers and children alike were curious as to why we were not circumcised. We had no plans. Modern parents did not circumcise their girls. That's what Cucu Herina was told by the Glaswegian missionary Dr John William Arthur of Mission Church of Scotland as a young woman.

'It is morally repugnant,' he said to the women.

'No man will marry uncircumcised women!' they pleaded.

'Your customs are repugnant. It's not the will of God. You have to become God's children and be born again in the name of God and shun your customs,' he had taught them.

As a child, I was well aware of the division between traditionalists and westernised people. The fact that Mrs Kimani had raised the issue of circumcision was not my main grievance. My friends, social circles and people whose acquaintance I would make in later life all had western attitudes and the general consensus was that girl circumcision was uncivilized and old fashioned. My problem with Mrs Kimani was her intent: her intention was to humiliate Wairimu by asking her intimate personal questions about a taboo. Her motives were born out of malice. I despised her for highlighting this issue to all the bullies and adding it to the list of the things we could be bullied for, unnecessarily adding to our misery.

And so we were branded the derogatory *'kirigu'*— uncircumcised. We would never be real women! Mrs Kimani would be attending the wedding too because she was Wainaina's teacher and had become best friends with her-whose-name-refuses-to-leave my mouth. Wedding invitations in Kenya are a western formality but everyone knows they are not exclusive. Anyone can attend a wedding without direct invitation from the bride, groom or family. A wedding invitation is generally open and a person can bring a guest or indeed several guests. The etiquette is to cook for an infinite number of people, ensuring every guest may eat to their heart's content. Mrs Kimani's presence at the wedding would reignite such raw hatred within me. I have never been able to forget her spite.

* * * *

As weeks rolled into terms, we kept a low profile. We rarely got lifts from Baba, preferring to walk so as not to draw attention to ourselves. We would walk to the top of the hill opposite our house. As if by magic, children would emerge from coffee bushes from a web of interconnecting paths that led to neighbouring farms. We'd converge on the broad path, waving to the tractors that rumbled past. Slowly we began to fit in. We were beginning to enjoy school and made a few friends. Occasionally things flared up but nothing like our first days. Our lives were nearing perfect.

During the last few weeks of the term, there was a buzz amongst the school children. There was a rumour that there would be a screening of a film on the last Saturday of term. 'It will be Bruce Lee,' they speculated. We were sure our father would not permit us to go; we didn't even bother to ask.

When the school day was over, we'd walk home on the broad path before everyone disappeared into the coffee bushes again. When it rained, we were instructed to stand by the acacia tree, calling to our mother, who'd help us cross the swollen stream. It was one such day when we called out to our mother and Munyau, our new workman, came running down the hill answering our calls in his native language of Kamba: 'ndi baa'— I'm here. He strode across the tree trunk that served as a bridge and one by one, he helped us cross the river.

When we got home that day, Maitu was busy packing. Baba had come home early with Cucu Herina in tow. He had bought two plane tickets; he was taking

Maitu on holiday to Mombasa.

'It would cheer her up,' he'd said to Cucu Herina. Maitu still felt worried about finding Juli, our dead dog. It was a bad omen. Maitu packed excitedly, complaining that she did not know what to take to Mombasa. We watched as the two got into our Toyota and disappeared down the dusty track. We spent the evening outside, lying on the wet grass with Munyau, facing the sky and waving to aeroplanes, just in case Baba and Maitu were waving at us.

142

Dinner without Hitler

As soon as darkness fell, our parents became a distant memory. We were engulfed by a carefree joy, delighted to be spending a couple of days with Cucu Herina in the absence of our parents. We scrambled into the outside kitchen to keep Cucu Herina company, where she sat on a low stool swirling the pot of *mukimo* with a flat wooden stick, passing it round to each one of us to taste for salt, teasing our taste buds. On the charcoal burner, the lamb stew bubbled away as if to join the party. Her *mukimo* was so smooth, the balance of pumpkin leaves with potatoes and peas seamlessly blended. Blowing lungfuls of air through the metal pipe, Cucu Herina fanned the flames, filling the place with a sense of mischief.

'Hitler is gone, today you will eat in the outdoor kitchen like peasants,' said Cucu Herina to a roar of laughter. She nicknamed Baba Hitler because he had too many rules. My brother Wainaina laughed so much he fell off his stool.

'Don't crack the wall with your big Njogu's head,' we laughed some more. We sat cross-legged on stools watching her face full of delight. We ate supper sat around the fire listening to stories of the State of Emergency. Cucu Herina was a born entertainer.

'Tell us of when the District Officer gave orders again,' we coaxed.

'Comu herrrre ngoo therrrrre,' she commanded with a nasal sound of the English accent, her back arched backwards, the metal pipe on her shoulder imitating a gun.

'Boooy! Come herrrrre!' she continued; we laughed so much, our bellies hurt. Her eyes reddened. Suddenly all humour was gone. The stare into nothingness. She was distant. Eyes enlarged; the mood turned sombre.

> *Slosh! Slosh! The squelching mud.*
> *Red mud with murderous blood.*
> *Slosh slosh the cracked feet slosh, the*
> *galleys weep.*
> *The crack of the whip.*
> *The birds flee.*
> *Faster the women work.*
> *The puppeteers of evil glare.*
> *When the white man's gone, they'll have*
> *nowhere to stare.*
> *Till their mortal coil.*

The biting pain across her back.
The pangs of hunger.
A baby wails.
Guttural and feeble, quivers in the final
throes.
The mind hastens.
The heart sobs.
My milk's dry.
Impenetrable gloom.
She will never smile again.
The biting morning chill numbs one's soul.
The growl of the German shepherd.
The heart quickens. Tempers fray.
'That's my mud. You are squelching my
mud.'
Someone hums. A mournful hum.
Her baby is dead.
Rigid. Still strapped to her back, not time
to bury.
No time to weep.
Like a vampire's fangs, the white man
craves my blood.
Like an addict, he searches my veins.
Till every ounce, my veins agape.
My breath wanes. Squelch.
'More mud, the walls are gaping,' yells a
resolute mother.
The clefts in her rough feet now widen.

Her galleys too are weeping.
The tears of a people.
But she feels no pain.
'Faster!' yells the humourless guard,
watches like a hawk from the watchtower.
He feels like a god.
An elderly femme sneers.
The world is spinning; she cannot go faster.
The stabbing pain in the crevices of her
chest, that hosted big round busting femi-
nine breasts, now empty. Just wasted strips
of dried banana skin.
Slosh. Slosh, the cracked feet beg. 'How
much more can we take, it's been weeks!'
The chorus is rising. Energizing and defiant.
'Wako wapi wabeberu hawaoni haya.'
Where is the colonizer, he has no shame?
'Niwao walisema hatuna hakili, na huku
watunyonya hafadhali kupe.' They said we
had no brains, now they suck our blood,
we would rather have ticks.
Shut up! The growl of a Johnny.
A pistol cracks.
Wail in a distance. Silence.
Slosh slosh. Tonight's the night.
There will be a roof over our heads.
The children will not shiver.
Slosh. Faster the women work.

146

The first house done.
A hundred women crammed in one hut.
Defies laws of physics.
'I cannot breathe,' the wail of a child. Hush
till the morning.
From a bare field, rises a camp.
The angels of death smile with glee.
'Tis their finest hour.
A woman bent double. A hundred booted
men took her last night.
Hunger bites. Effective weapons of war.
Slosh. Slosh no more.
These hands are spent. But I'm still
standing.
Slosh slosh.

'You built the house all by yourself?' Mungai's eyes full of tearful concern. 'If I was there, I would have built the house in a day for you, Cucu,' offered Mungai. 'Look at my muscles.' He flexed his muscles to show the bony bulge. 'Your mother scolded the guard when she was your age, she was very brave,' added Cucu Herina. Maitu at eight had watched a cruel guard bully auntie Wanjiku, holding up his whip in readiness to beat her. Maitu had matched up to him, warning, 'If you dare touch our Wanjiku I will box you.' Maitu had her fists all clenched in readiness to fight the guard. 'Don't you dare look at me,' she had shamed him, to walk away.

Dancing with Bruce Lee

It was a beautiful Saturday morning and our parents were still away. The sun shone brightly, waking us up. We had a lie-in, a rare treat because Cucu Herina did not want to disturb us. Baba never allowed anyone to have a lie in. He did not believe in idleness. Every member of the household had to contribute to the functionality of the whole, he would say. Every morning he banged on our doors, loudly insisting we all get up by seven whether it was the holidays or not. After breakfast, each of us would be given a job. Some days it would be carrying the *debes* (tin containers), walking round the coffee bushes to harvest coffee.

During the harvest season, Baba drove his pickup truck to villages calling for coffee pickers. People would run and jump into the back ready to be driven to the farm. Upon arrival, they picked up their *debes* and, each taking a bush, plucked the reddest berries. The aim was to fill the large *debes* with berries, after which one would carry it to the foreman, who would log it and empty it into sacks to be taken for processing. After several truck loads of villagers, the whole farm would be transformed into a hive of action. After a couple of days, the farm looked like the aftermath of a swarm of locusts, but the job would be done. At the end of the day people lined up to see the foreman, who would count all the *debes* each person had picked, paying them per *debe*. Parents often brought their children to boost their earnings.

When we worked on the processing, we would pour the coffee berries into a machine which scraped off the skin, exposing the coffee beans. The coffee beans would then be passed through water to remove the sugary coating before being spread out on drying racks. The drying took several days, until all moisture had evaporated. Once dry, the beans would be bagged, to be delivered to the coffee board in Nairobi. The coffee was then freighted to European middlemen, who took all the stock, promising to send payments once the coffee had been graded. Sometimes the farmers waited for a whole year and when the payments came, they were a pittance; other times payments never materialized. Every year that went by, the promise to the Kenyan coffee farmers of finally reaping the rewards of their hard work would die slowly as they fell behind with payments of loans, unable to pay for their children's education. With every passing year, they made a loss, spending money on production but never getting paid for the coffee. Europe was ahead of the game, always finding new ways of getting something for nothing from Africans.

When Baba got his share of the farm, he had been full of hope that the coffee that brought so much reward for the white settlers would now do the same for him. He tended his 'green gold' with pride, hiring workers to prune it and spraying it with pesticide and harvesting. It was never going to be the level playing field awarded to the white farmers. It was only years later that Baba came to the bitter realization that the rules of the game were rigged. He was never meant to be a beneficiary of the cash crops that placed Kenya on the map as a producer of tea and coffee. He drove home one day after collecting payments for two years' worth of coffee, with only a measly two thousand shillings instead of his estimated eight hundred thousand shillings. He would have benefited more selling sweet potatoes in the market. That was the day he came home enraged, took a machete and began slashing the coffee bushes. It was never going to be gold. It was a hole in his wallet losing him thousands of shillings in labour and production for no return. Fortunately for Baba, his other sideline selling goods to Ugandans was way more profitable and they paid on him on time. They had no bias and above all they valued him and his products.

Once the harvesting was over, Baba found us other jobs such as digging and cutting grass for the cows. He would measure with footsteps a piece of ground marked with rocks and that would be your area to cultivate. He would tell us the amount he would pay upon completion after a thorough inspection.

Doing nothing was never an option when Baba was around. Our relaxation time came when he was gone. We became carefree and the farm became our castle. We walked around the four rectangular pools in which Baba now farmed tilapia after the disappointment of coffee farming. We would walk around the pools, looking for the biggest fish and scoop them with our nets, into the buckets. When we had enough, we would rest, taking aim with our catapults at the kingfishers above the trees waiting for their turn to fish. When we felt the hunger pangs, we carried the bucket, one holding each side, to the house, where we would pan fry the tilapia and enjoy eating whilst sat on the steps facing the rolling hills of the ridge opposite. Wainiana, fed up of *turungi*, took the dry coffee beans and roasted them on the pan, filling the house with the aroma of fresh coffee. He would put them in the grinder and make himself a sugary cup of coffee. Wairimu and Kui took the opportunity to walk the mile to the bus stop to catch a matatu to Banana Hill, where they would spend the afternoon chatting with their friends.

* * * *

The gods of happiness colluded to grant us our one wish. That night, it was the full moon; a magical light enveloped the hills. The light green tea leaves fluttered coyly in the gentle breeze, glistening in the moonlight. The stars twinkled gleefully, joining in the mischief, as we climbed up the path ascending from the river.

'We should dress like men,' Wairimu told Kui and me. She wore Baba's shirt and old oversized trousers, fastening them with a tie because none of the belts fitted. Kui was taller than Wainaina, which meant his trousers were extremely tight, her rounded bottom looking as if it would escape any minute. I squeezed into Mungai's clothes. Despite my narrow boyish frame, they still seemed tight.

'We should also speak in low voices, like men,' Wairimu instructed. She thought we should all pretend to be boys to avoid being harassed by unruly young men; as if we weren't drawing enough attention to ourselves by looking like an ill-thought-out drama group.

As soon as we'd eaten the leftovers from the night before, we disappeared through the coffee plantation, accompanied by Mulu, our milkman, who was delighted to be asked. We walked excitedly, unable to contain our delight. Our legs couldn't carry us fast enough. Earlier that day, Mungai and I had had the chance to tell Cucu Herina about the film being screened at Githatha.

Mungai and I had wandered to the river, looking for tadpoles, carrying our fishing nets flung over our shirt-less shoulders. Cucu Herina had come with us, walking round Maitu's territory tending to her plants. It was then we asked.

'Can we go, Cucu, please?' we begged. Cucu Herina was fun, caring and kind, and besides loved defying Baba's rules. She saw no reason why we couldn't go to the outdoor cinema, so she granted us her blessing. It was the day after Baba and Maitu went to Mombasa, leaving Cucu Herina in charge, and coincidentally, also the night of the screening of Bruce Lee.

As we got to the top of the hill, we were full of excitement at the booming sound of the commercials bellowing through several ridges. Our footsteps quick-ened. By the time we got to the gates to the playground next to where the projectionist was stationed, the ground was already full. It was a sea of white eyes and shiny teeth glistening from the light of the massive screen erected on scaffolding. All our classmates had arrived early, many already in prime positions, necks bent back to absorb the full glare of the screen. We spoke in low, men-like voices as we manoeuvred through the legs to find a spare patch of grass. Mothers with babies on their backs, fathers with children on their knees, even teachers came. Many of our classmates recognized us straight away, greeting us joyfully and wondering why we were dressed like scarecrows, much to Wairimu's

153

disappointment. The Doom commercial was on and Ojuang, the nation's favourite comedian, was on the table hiding from a cockroach. He was cowering on the table, calling Mama Kayai to come help him. Everyone was rolling around with laughter at Ojuang's cowardice. Mama Kayai walked into the room carrying the bottle of Doom and killed the cockroach, to Ojuang's relief. By the time the theme song to the film began, excitement was reaching fever pitch. Bruce Lee's appearance provoked nothing short of hysteria. The exhilarating fight scenes were received jubilantly by a chorus of excitement, every fling of the arm or high kick greeted with, '*Yeega, hwa, hwa.*' The crowd swayed with every move, like long grass in strong wind. The dialogue was irrelevant. We didn't understand the language. We did not care. It was about the moves. The film did not disappoint.

Long after it ended, people still chatted excitedly about the prowess of the unbeatable Bruce Lee. We didn't even notice our journey home, despite walking the long way round on the tarmacked road. It was only when we reached the bridge of death that we realized. It was called the bridge of death because drunk drivers speeding down the smooth road were unaware of the unexpected bend, which caused the cars to overturn with the drivers drowning in the river only to be found the following day. That night I dreamt I was dancing on the sunny dunes into the horizon with Bruce Lee.

The Tremor

Baba did not come home for the move into our new home; he was away in Kampala. Far away from Riara Ridge, at the end of the Lunatic Express, was the city of Kampala, the capital of Uganda. Being a frequent visitor gave Baba a vantage point. He knew it well. It was at that time that whole economy in Uganda ground to a halt. People could not buy soap, sugar, salt or even flour. To them Baba became a saviour, bringing all the basics to an insatiable clientele. Business was booming. With all the Asians gone from Kampala, there was no one to trade. Baba was like a kid in a candy shop.

Maitu moved everything, helped by my sisters and our five boy cousins, sent by aunty Wanjiku from Thogoto village to assist with the move from our temporary house. 'Be careful,' Maitu called as they rushed to take everything into our brand-new house. There wasn't much to move. The beds and other big items were moved by Maitu, Munyau the workman and

Ngige, our eldest cousin. We carried little items like our clothes and shoes. Moving into our brand-new stone house was truly fantastic. The house had big windows and loads of light. The rooms were spacious and clean with black and white tiled floors. It was smoke free because we would use gas instead of charcoal. Open fires and cooking with charcoal always had its challenges: not only were the fumes dangerous for health but babies and children constantly fell into open fires. One day, soon after moving to Riara Ridge, we were expecting visitors from Thogoto who were seeing our new farm for the first time. Maitu had lit two charcoal stoves because she needed to cook many dishes. She placed them outside and was gone for only one minute when Mungai came running from the back of the house. When he got close to the stoves, he tripped, falling between them. He was lucky that Maitu was close by, grabbing him up before he got severe burns. He sustained second-degree burns on either side of his ribcage.

* * * *

Maitu had just cooked supper; the new wooden dining table was set with the gorgeous new plates. There were placemats protecting the white crotchet tablecloth that she had bought from Limuru market. The delicious aroma from the freshly fried chapattis, piled high and sandwiched between two plates to keep them warm, and the meat stew steaming from floral china-ware filled our nostrils, making us very hungry. We now sat on deep padded velvet dining chairs, having given away our old-fashioned stools to Munyau, our dutiful workman. My cousin, Cina, stroked the velvet seat as if trying to figure out what the fabric was. Ngige, my eldest cousin, was asked to pray for the food and that's when we heard it. It came from deep beneath our feet, growling like a hungry monster aroused prematurely from sleep. At first it was an ominous rumble that filled us with fear. We looked around the room; there was nothing visible. The rumble grew stronger, like the stomping of a million soldiers going into battle, but much stronger. It was coming for us. Our hearts pumped blood into our ears. Maitu put the serving spoon down and held on to cousin Ngige with one hand and Wairimu with the other. We looked round in dismayed terror.

'We are going to die,' cried Mungai. I held his hand.

'I don't want to die,' I said and began to cry. Cina stood up, holding the small bible he always carried in his pocket, and said, 'It's the end of the world as described in Peter 3:10: "But the day of the Lord will come like a thief, and then the heavens will pass away with a roar, and the heavenly bodies will be burned up and dissolve, and the earth and the works that are done will be exposed", they said it in church only this Sunday gone, "But you who suffer tribulation will be given relief along with us at the revelation of the Lord Jesus from heaven with his powerful angels in a flaming fire, as he brings vengeance on those who do not know God and those who do not obey the good news about our Lord Jesus. These very ones will undergo the judicial punishment of everlasting destruction from before the Lord and from the glory of his strength...' even he couldn't carry on! His eyes open wide. Frightened.

The ground began to vibrate faster, causing our bodies to shake like rag dolls. The table shook. Plates slid from side to side, crashing into one another; the cutlery bumped up and down on the table as if by magic, the beef stew splashing all over Maitu's new tablecloth.

'Stop shaking the table, Wangui!' Maitu shouted at my sister.

'It's not me,' she replied as Maitu's focus changed, looking around at the walls that seemed to tremble, as we held onto each other, stiff with fear. At the peak of the tremor, the whole house shook. Cousin Ngige ran towards the door and opened it before being thrown outside. To us, it seemed like an eternity, but it was gone as quickly as it came, leaving us still shaking, our frightened eyes almost gawking out of their sockets in the deafening silence that followed. Maitu walked outside and called to Munyau, who hurried over to the house, just as frightened.

Puzzled by the tremor, Maitu, cousin Ngige and Munyau decided to walk to the nearest neighbour, who lived a kilometre away, to ask if they had felt it, whatever it was. That night we ate supper without them and fell asleep before they returned, and it was only the following day we found out there had been a 5.7 magnitude earthquake, originating from Tanzania. The radio called it *mtetemeko wa arthi*—shaking of the earth. It ominously shook the foundations of our lovely pink pebble-dashed home.

The structural damage to our home was repairable but no amount of patchwork could hide the damage that it inflicted. The tremor had shaken more than the core of our foundation. It was as if the curse that Juli, our dead dog, left was beginning to manifest itself. Her spirit was out to get us. The euphoria we felt at being in Riara Ridge began to diminish. We began to notice things we had never noticed before. Our farm now felt isolated, with our nearest neighbour being a kilometre away. The silence we once enjoyed now, began to feel unnerving. There were no convenience shops close by, which meant we were completely reliant on Baba for all purchasing of goods. When our cousins left, the place felt eerily lonely. We wondered if they had felt the tremor in Thogoto village. Could it be that this beautiful ridge had a curse? This was something at the back of Maitu's mind. Her discovery of Juli's body still bothered her. She hoped *this* was the omen of finding Juli's body and prayed there would be no more. Maitu began to pray more, she joined the women's guild and every Sunday she wore the blue headscarf with 'guild' etched on it. When Baba returned, he said he had felt the tremor in Kampala. That made Maitu feel better because the curse was not only in Riara Ridge.

'Everything will be fine,' he had promised Maitu.

The Tumor

None of us remember exactly when Kui's narcissism began, but we all know it was the catalyst that propelled our family's demise. She was the second born, which did not hold the significance of the first born or the last born. She was neither pretty nor ugly. She was just there. Lacking in personality or anything outstanding until she found something that commanded all our attention. Like a cancer, she lay dormant, then quietly gained momentum, eating at the flesh that bound our family together. Kui's cancerous mutation began around the age of ten. She woke up one morning having vomited in her bed with a raging temperature. Baba was the first person to see her. 'What is the matter *Muthoniwa*?' he asked in the hallway, leaning over to take a look at her. *Muthoniwa* means my in-law, because Kui was short for Wangui, Cucu Herina's Gikuyu name. She took Cucu Herina's name because Wairimu was named after Baba's mother. The Gikuyu customs dictates that the first child is always named after the father's mother or father and the second one after the mother's mother or father if the genders alternate. The Gikuyu believe that when a child is born, they only become human around the age of two when the spirits of the ancestor colonise them. Before then, a baby is just flesh and bones but not human. The Gikuyu also believe that people who were bad on earth would ultimately become sinister and evil spirits bringing torment and misery to people. The evil spirit must have had a vendetta against Cucu Herina, by choosing Kui, her namesake as a host that would destroy the core of our being. After all the Waswahili have a saying 'kikulacho ki nguoni mwako' meaning that what eats you or destroys you is in your garment. It's ironic that Kui should be the one, because Cucu Herina was the very essence of decency, morality and pillar that held our clan together and that her name sake should be the one to bring it down.

'I don't feel well,' Kui replied with a hoarse voice. Baba picked her up and felt her head.

'Gakari, get her dressed, I will take her to the doctor,' Baba called to Maitu who came rushing out of their bedroom. Maitu walked over to them, felt Kui's head and said, 'I think I will come with you too.'

Maitu got Kui ready and dressed hurriedly carrying her to the car. When Baba drove them back home early that afternoon, Kui was lying on Maitu's lap. The doctor had said she had a viral infection and recommended she be given her antibiotics with lots of fluids.

'Give her Ribena,' he had said, 'it's got a lot of Vitamin C.'

At dinner Kui sat between Maitu and Baba, who cut up her food into small chunks and helped her eat whilst constantly feeling her forehead for the temperature. When she finished eating, Maitu mixed some Ribena, diluting it in a glass of water which Kui gulped down, watched by all of us.

'Can I have some?' asked Mungai looking rather enviously.

'No, it's Kui's medicine, she needs to get better,' replied Maitu, wiping Kui's mouth. 'Drink your water,' Maitu said, topping up Mungai's glass with water.

Over the next few days, Maitu and Baba fussed over Kui as she slowly got better. The first thing Baba did when he came in was to feel her forehead. He would crouch down to her level and say, 'I am glad you are getting better.' 'Eat a little bit more food,' my parents coaxed her during supper.

Her antibiotics worked and slowly she was on the mend, with colour returning to her face. When she was back to her normal self, she still got some attention, which soon ebbed away into insignificance. At dinner, Kui took up the place between Maitu and Baba which belonged to Mungai, being the youngest. Now he wanted to sit in his usual place. He was the last born and needed a lot more help with his supper than Kui did. Kui refused to get off the chair, making Mungai cry.

'Wangui, let your brother sit in his chair,' Maitu scolded. Kui looked at Baba to see if he would intervene to defend her but Baba was too busy reading his newspaper. Kui walked back to her chair with a look of dejection. But everything had changed for Kui; she had now experienced what it would be like to have her parents dote on her. For a brief moment, she had been the centre of attention. Now Maitu only spoke to Baba about the bumper harvest she was expecting, noting that the coffee berries seemed to have multiplied tenfold. Maitu and Baba did not mention Kui once. Every night during her illness, Baba always asked how Kui was doing, getting a full update from Maitu, but now that she was better, she faded into obscurity.

It was a few days after Kui's illness that her mystifying condition emerged. We had all walked up the hill on the other side of the ridge and were just about to join a group of children walking to Githatha primary. It was at the clearing where all the tractors went by that Kui suddenly stopped. We stopped too to see what she was doing. It was then that *it* happened. Her fists began to clench like she was getting ready to punch someone. The muscles in her neck pulled so tightly that the veins began to appear as her jaw stuck out like the front of a ship. Her head and neck appeared to stiffen and began to jerk sideways. Her lips pulled apart into a grimace, occasionally sticking her tongue out like a lizard. This went on for a couple of minutes. The children began to gather as we all watched her with intense curiosity. Her eyes were now fluttering and she was beginning to say something incomprehensible. It sounded like *'akua akua*—I'm dying, I'm dying'. She appeared to have been possessed. She had the same demeanour as the people who were filled by the Holy Spirit and spoke in tongues during the church service. Her body began to tilt backwards and crashed to the ground. Children ran towards the school shouting, whilst others tried to alert the villagers, 'She is dying, she is dying.' My brothers, sister and I just stood there full of confused panic, unable to comprehend what to do or how to help her.

Once on the ground, she began kicking her legs, her heels digging into the gravel, throwing dust in the air. Her arms jerked as if charged by electricity. She was now having a full-blown convulsion. Saliva was dribbling from the side of her mouth; her eyes were closing and opening as if she was trying to get rid of an eyelash. Faint, incomprehensible words came out of her mouth that made no sense. We were frightened for her. Kui had been ill and now we thought she was dying. Someone shouted, 'Put a stick in her mouth to stop her biting her tongue, that's what you do with epilepsy.' We had heard about people with epilepsy; observing her, it seemed logical to think that Kui was having an epileptic fit. A big boy dived into the grass looking for a stick. Unable to find one, he ran to the nearest coffee bush and broke a branch, which he began stripping the leaves off. After a few minutes, before the boy could force the stick into her mouth, Kui stopped fitting. Her arms and legs relaxed, and she opened her eyes fully. She then sat upright and began looking around in confusion. She started smiling sweetly.

'Where am I?' she asked.

'Kui,' we got down on the grass to see whether she recognized us. 'Kui, it's us, your sisters and brothers.' She furrowed her eyebrows as if trying to figure out what we had said. She reached for a small stick and started breaking it into small pieces. This added to our confusion and no one spoke. Eventually Wairimu knelt down and said, 'Kui, what happened?'

'I don't...' she replied. 'I don't remember.'

'How do you feel?' Wairimu continued.

'I don't know,' she replied.

'Come, I will take you home,' Wairimu offered, helping her to her feet.

By now a couple of teachers were running up the road to assist Kui. They arrived to find her sitting down smiling sweetly. She got up and began walking to school. The teachers insisted that she go home but she said she had no recollection of what happened, and that she felt fine. During break, we all went to her classroom and she was still smiling but we were full of concern.

When we got home that evening, we recounted the incident to our perplexed parents. What happened to Kui was alarming to all that heard about it. She was the talk of the town for days. Maitu began to cry, praying to God. That night, Kui sat between Maitu and Baba, who watched her closely, Baba assisting with cutting her food. She seemed fine and wanted to chat. We all tried to be extra kind and to let her know we cared deeply for her. She smiled, seeming to enjoy the attention we all gave her.

The following morning, despite insisting she was fine and wanted to go to school, Baba and Maitu felt Kui needed to see a doctor. They left us to eat our breakfast and get ready by ourselves whilst they hurried to the car with her. The incident sounded like a very serious condition which required the attention of specialist doctors at Kenyatta National Hospital, so a referral was made by our family doctor. Upon consultation, Kui was admitted whilst the doctors carried out tests on her. Maitu would be staying by her bedside while Baba came home in the evening to be with us. Wairimu, although thirteen years old, was to take care of us. She was to get us ready for school and after school, she was to light the fire and prepare supper. It was a long week as everyone waited anxiously for Kui's news. News had even reached my grandmother Herina in Thogoto village, who asked her church to pray for Kui.

When we heard the familiar hum of the car from a

167

distance, we ran to the road to meet Baba and Maitu. The car drove slowly up the drive, with Kui sat between our parents. Even Munyau and Kariuki, the new workman, came running to hear the news about Kui.

'What did the doctors say?' they asked as Maitu got out of the car. Maitu looked exhausted, with bags underneath her eyes from lack of sleep. The hospital did not provide beds for carers and Maitu had slept on the hospital chair.

'They could not find the disease,' she said, looking disappointed.

'Don't worry, Mama Wairimu,' said Munyau, comforting Maitu. 'God will cure her,' he continued.

'Yes, God is great, he will hear my prayers,' replied Maitu. We had the supper Wairimu cooked in silence, our parents full of worry.

Kui had more episodes over the following week. Maitu and Baba returned to Kenyatta National Hospital on numerous occasions, insisting on seeing different doctors for different opinions. They all said the same thing. They could not offer her treatment as they did not know what she was suffering from and were perplexed by her disease. Our parents told us in no uncertain terms that we should not cause Kui any stress whatsoever, for fear of exacerbating her condition. Maitu stocked up on Ribena, which she kept on the top shelf of her white tiled kitchen. Slowly the weeks turned into months but Kui's symptoms did not subside.

It was always there. High on that top shelf, above the stand-alone gas cooker. The bottle of Ribena which Mungai and I craved so much, yet the refreshing taste that beckoned our taste buds was reserved for Kui. She was the one needing to get better. Everyday Maitu measured the capfuls of purple liquid, diluted it in a glass and passed it over our heads to Kui, like a trophy only she was entitled to. Our eyes followed the glass as it made contact with her lips. We would watch the liquid disappear into her mouth and watched it go down her throat. When she placed the glass down, Mungai and I scrambled to grab it. Whoever got it would place it on their lips with the hope that one little drop of Ribena would land on their tongue. When we went anywhere, Maitu used to carry Mungai on her back, him being the youngest; now it was Kui needing to be carried if she got tired. Maitu was of a small frame but was used to carrying heavy loads, so she often struggled with Kui strapped on her back.

At leisure, I used to sit close to Maitu and follow her knitting pattern, using small sticks she had sharpened for me to use as knitting needles. But those days with Maitu were gone, absorbed by Kui's illness. Without her, my knitting stopped. Mungai and I used to get washed by Maitu in the big blue plastic basin, now we had to clean ourselves since Maitu was gone with Kui in search of treatments. Kui became a law unto herself. Immune from all the house rules. She did not need to take her plate to the kitchen after eating nor partake in household cleaning or even going to the farm. When she went to the farm, she would just sit watching us work whilst chewing on her sugar cane. We had to do everything for her and anything she wanted we had to get. If she was mean or unkind, our parents excused her behaviour, blaming it on her illness. If any one of us upset her, she called Maitu and we got a smack or a clip on our ears. We walked on eggshells. In the evenings, she sat on the sofa watching TV whilst we had to sit at the table doing our reading.

Kui's episodes continued in the same dramatic fashion. At school, people now called her Wangui *Kibaba*—the epileptic. No one dared come close to her; even the teachers began to fear her. If a teacher scolded her, she had an episode, leaving them fearing for their jobs. If she didn't do her homework, nothing was done about it. Her condition controlled everything around her. My parents' concern for Kui grew as they sought after a cure. Maitu would be gone for weeks on end with Kui admitted in different hospitals. She was determined to try every doctor in the country.

One day, in the weeks when Maitu was gone, I was stood outside the house watching a frog hopping around. Mungai was at the back of the house, looking after his prisoners with Wainaina. Wairimu had gone to the shops to get something when Kariuki, the new workman, walked up to me and sat on the ground by my feet.

'You are very beautiful,' he said. I looked down. He reached out, held me by my hand and pulled me to him. He began to stroke my cheek. He then moved his hand down to my crotch and began to squeeze me. I stood there saying nothing. Doing nothing. He shifted his bottom closer to me, his legs encircling me until I was towering over him. He loosened his trouser belt with one hand whilst still squeezing my crotch with the other hand. He unbuttoned his trousers and put his hand inside his trousers, all the while still squeezing my crouch. He squeezed too hard so that I cried out and began to move away. He pulled me back to him and carried on squeezing me, his fingers digging into my crotch. He closed his eyes and made grunting noises. He got up, zipped his trousers and was gone. I just stood there. I didn't understand why but I began to feel something I had never felt before. It felt like I had done something wrong. I sat down, pulling bits of grass, not knowing what I was feeling. It felt like I wanted to cry but I didn't know why I wanted to cry. When Mungai called me to help arrest some more prisoners, I felt like he knew what had happened. I didn't want him to know what had happened. It must have been embarrassment and shame that I felt but I could not understand it at the time. When my parents came back, I tried to forget it. Every time I think of that incident, to this day, the same feeling of deep shame takes over. I could never bring myself to tell anyone about it.

Kui's illness persisted. For months, the same symptoms manifested with varying degrees of intensity. Modern doctors seemed clueless and could not help her. They were completely puzzled by the symptoms. They had never seen such a case, where someone appeared to go through moments of madness whilst having seizures and retching to vomit. Sometimes the seizures only took hold of the legs and other times the arms. 'Have you tried traditional healers?' someone asked my parents. They hadn't, and they had nothing to lose. After making a few enquiries, they were referred to a healer in Nyeri, several kilometres away from home. My parents were gone yet again. Kui's illness took our parents away from our lives completely. Baba's business in Kampala began to suffer; he was not delivering the orders. Maitu's section of the farm became overrun with weeds, missing planting seasons. She could no longer sell her produce in Limuru market because there was no harvest. Money became tight. Baba's coffee bushes were now overgrown and infested with pests and disease. Our house fell into disrepair, the damage from the earthquake still visible because all efforts had gone into looking after Kui. Wairimu became our main carer. She was thirteen and having to do all the cooking and laundry whilst studying for her final year of primary school. We did not bath ourselves most nights and hardly saw our parents. Mine and Mungai's feet began to crack like the children of Githatha. We wore dirty clothes because Wairimu could not keep up. Our home began to suffer neglect. There was no end in sight.

It was one Sunday when we were all at church. We were sat in our usual places, Kui now in between Baba and Maitu. People began to turn around when they recognized our singing. We always sang loudly and out of tune. We had not been for a while. They were pleased to see us. After church, everyone came to offer my parents prayers for Kui. 'Jane the healer will be in Banana Hill healing the sick and disabled,' someone told my parents. 'Take Kui to her.' The healing was to take place at the end of January, a few weeks away. My parents were encouraged by this and planned to take Kui to the healer. All month it was all they prayed for. They prayed for the healer who would pray to heal Kui. When the day came, Maitu, Baba and Kui set off before we got up. They needed to be at the front so that the healer might be able to touch Kui with her healing hands. By the time they arrived, there were already large crowds. People had come from all the districts desperate for their loved ones to be healed.

Baba carried Kui on his back so that he could push through the crowds. Maitu held on to his jacket because she did not want to be lost in the crowds and lose the chance of healing for her daughter. They managed to push to the front, standing alongside the disabled and the blind. Baba placed Kui on his shoulders and stood on his tiptoes, being a short man. Maitu held on to him to steady him as crowds swayed from side to side. The radio announcement had said that this was the only time Jane the healer would be coming to Banana Hill. They could not let anything stop Kui from being healed. Jane the healer was dressed in an all-white long dress as if she were a bride. Someone confirmed that she had already married Jesus and was the rightful bride. When she climbed on to the platform the hysterical crowed screamed, 'Amen.' This was the day their loved ones would be healed.

Jane the healer was rumoured to have got her healing powers when Jesus appeared to her in a vision. Now she stood on stage in a school playing field facing a sea of people. She held her microphone and began to pray. She prayed so hard that sweat dripped from her face. After three hours of prayer, she began to heal. She commanded the disease to leave their bodies and one by one the disabled stood up and began to walk. People blew whistles and passed round the baskets for money contributions. The more you put in, the greater the success. Baba dug deep into his pockets. He emptied every note and every coin into the healing basket. Maitu slipped her hand in her bra and took any money she could find, before placing it into the healing baskets. Everyone emptied their pockets and put the money in to help Jane the healer with her healing mission.

After the disabled and the blind, Jane was touching people with other illness. Baba carried Kui high on his shoulders, pushing her forward to be touched by the healing hands of Jane. 'If you feel cured get up,' shouted Jane. People got up and began praising God. Jane's hand came close to Kui but Maitu did not see if it touched her. It was close anyway. The healing power might have had the ability to jump on to Kui.

It was a long day for my parents. When they came home, they were exhausted but hoped that their prayers would be answered. As we sat round the table to eat the supper prepared by Wairimu, the strain on my parents was noticeable. Baba had a few more grey hairs on his temples. The bags under Maitu's eyes seemed more pronounced. They told us all about the healing and we wished we had been there.

Over the next few weeks, our parents could not hide their disappointment when Kui had more episodes. The healing had not worked. Food scarcity was beginning to affect us. Wairimu could not forage much since no planting had taken place. Baba decided he needed to get back to his business before it collapsed and left Kui in Maitu's care. He would help whenever he could. Maitu would look after Kui by herself. She was determined not to give up. She stopped to chat to a woman on her way to the market who suggested the witchdoctor. My parents had a modern approach to life but everything else had failed. Maitu and Kui travelled early one day to the witchdoctor who tied them to a tree and beat them with a branch soaked in cow urine. When they travelled back in the matatu, the other passengers complained bitterly about their stench. Maitu did not care, she was determined to save her daughter. Maitu tried the herbalist too, who prescribed several herbs that needed boiling and the broth straining through sieve. Kui drank it but nothing worked.

Kui's illness became the third of our misfortunes.

Dicing with Death

For a short period, Kui's illness appeared to subside. Baba had begun trading again in Kampala. The morning hadn't started well. Maitu was on edge because Baba had not returned from Kampala. That morning when we woke up, she was clutching onto the hand-held transistor radio, tuning the radio to different bands seeking the news. Finally, she caught the tail end of the news. Many Kenyans had been killed in Uganda by Amin, who was enraged that the Kenyan government had allowed a hijacked Air France plane carrying Jews to refuel at Jomo Kenyatta airport. Amin was doubly annoyed that in rescuing the hundred hostages from their Palestinian hijackers at Entebbe airport, Israeli forces had destroyed a quarter of his air force. In his statement at the airport when the hijacked plane turned up, he had made a speech in which he declared his support for the Palestinian cause. Why wouldn't the Kenyans stand in solidarity when they had suffered the same fate as the Palestinians? 'Kenyans are traitors,' he had concluded. Kenyans trading in Uganda had been caught by Ugandan men and killed. Deeeet, deeet, end of transmission.

Maitu put the radio down, worried sick. It had been a week since Baba was due to return but there had been no word from him. She had spent that last week fretting, biting her nails. She was sure Baba was amongst the dead. She would go to Machakos market to see if any of the traders there had heard from Baba. She didn't want to worry us anymore than necessary and so got us ready for school, but she was very short tempered with us.

Maitu's worries about Baba increased with every passing day. She was restless and decided to go back to Machakos market, where many train traders bought and sold their stock. Many people sympathized and prayers were said for his safe return. One of Baba's friends whom he spent a lot of time with in Kampala called Maitu to one side. He expressed a view that he might be alive but might have a mistress in Kampala who was keeping him there. Maitu was angered by this suggestion, stating that something terrible had happened to Baba. There was a part of her that wondered if there was some truth in what the man suggested. During church on Sunday, prayers were said and worshippers wished us well.

My mother's worries came to head one evening.

She was just locking up for the night when, from the horizon, she thought she saw a figure move. He was calling her, beckoning her to go. The light at dusk was low. She took her torch and made her way to the approach that led to our house. When she got closer, she recognized him. It was Baba. Alarmed, she hurried over. Baba asked her to turn off the torch. He was stark naked. Maitu came back into the house and asked all of us to go to the living room and sit on the sofas. It was a strange request, but we did what we were told. Maitu sneaked Baba through the window into their bedroom without us seeing him. It was only after he had had a bath that he came out in his pyjamas. He had a few bruises but was fine. We were surprised by his appearance without his car, but he told us it had broken down on the way home and that he had got in through the garage.

Idi Amin knew of Baba's success in Kampala. All men like him and other Kenyan traitors on Ugandan soil were to be killed. Idi Amin's men had dragged him out of his lorry, confiscating all his merchandise. They had locked him in the boot, where he remained for several hours. In their killing spree, they forgot Baba was in the boot until the soldier drove his car home. He was not discovered until late that night by the soldier, who was looking for something in his boot only to be confronted by Baba naked and fast asleep. The tired soldier did not want to start killing out of hours. He did not know what to do with him. Baba, seeing the man's predicament, saw the opportunity to bargain for his freedom. 'If you let me go, I will buy you a brand-new TV and pay you a large fee.' This was tempting for a cash-strapped soldier. 'Please drive me over the border and I shall reward you handsomely. The soldier agreed to drive Baba to Nairobi, where he was given instructions to collect a TV and money from a colleague, saying he was sent by Baba who was stuck in Kampala. Baba was in the boot without clothes. The soldier had no time to waste and drove Baba to within an hour of home and left him there to find his own way.

It is not exactly clear why or when or what triggered Maitu's doubt, but it began to creep in. Intuition told her that the illness that had possessed Kui for several years might be fake, but she never let on to anyone. Not even us. She tried to ignore it, but something bothered her. Maitu became more observant with Kui's symptoms. Kui was now too big for Maitu to carry, and her seizures seemed to follow a pattern. They only seemed to happen when Maitu would get somebody to help carry Kui. Her crashing to the ground must have been painful, so Maitu noted they were quite calculated. She seemed to fall in convenient places such as cushioned grassy verges. When Maitu was alone in difficult to reach places, the fits did not occur. Over the next few months Maitu's doubts grew even more but she kept it to herself nonetheless. Coincidentally, Maitu was not the only one with a niggling feeling. Kui, too, must have begun to suspect that Maitu did not believe her illness anymore, but she never let on.

Wairimu was now in boarding high school and Kui would be joining her in a few months. Kui performed very poorly at the end of primary but Wairimu's school took her in anyway because the headteacher knew of my parents' struggle with her illness. By then, Baba had resigned himself, or had begun to lose interest in Kui's illness too. Wainaina and Mungai were now in boarding school and finally it was my turn to transfer to Musa Gitau primary, joining them.

Shopping Galore

I was sat by the same telegraph pole Wainaina sat at when he kicked the stone, watching the children play, when I saw Baba's car approaching. I jumped to my feet and ran to the car. Baba looked happy as he jumped out of the car, hurrying towards me.

'Would you repeat a year down if you got a place at Musa Gitau?' he asked.

'Yes, I would,' I replied without hesitation. 'I really would.' It was half a scream, beaming with excitement.

'In that case, you are going to boarding school!' said Baba, his face mirroring my excitement. 'Let's go tell the headmaster!' His arms spread out, inviting me to run to him. We hopped like two excited children holding hands to the headmaster's office, where Baba informed him that I was transferring to a different school. This was the most exciting thing that had ever happened to me.

The next two days were like a dream. Baba and I rose at the crack of dawn and sat at opposite sides of the dining table. We crunched on buttered toast and sipped our tea, which Maitu had set up on Baba's silver tray. He had poured my tea, which he had never done before, adding milk, and handed it over to me to add my sugar. He told Maitu of our itinerary in Nairobi. He read through the kit list of my boarding school essentials. '3 nightdresses, 10 vests and pants, 1 pair of gum boots, 1 raincoat, 1 rain hat,' my heart melted a little as he read through, '...2 tunics, white shirts, shoes...' and the list went on. I could no longer wait and ran to the passenger side of the car. The ride in the Toyota Hilux was slow, despite it being only half an hour to Nairobi. Baba found a parking space and I hopped out alongside him.

Our first shop was the luggage store. There were suitcases of all shapes and sizes, of every colour. There were red, green, yellow and black. There were backpacks too, hanging all over the walls. We walked up and down until Baba stood by the Samsonite section. 'I like these,' he said, pointing at a few stacked up together. The shop assistant had followed Baba like a mesmerised puppy and now reached for the cases.

'What colour would you like?' Baba asked, looking at me.

'The red one, please, the red one.' I could barely

contain myself. Baba paid for the medium-sized case, which I insisted on carrying, hopping, out of the shop.

'We need to get some things from Uchumi but we will get those at the end.' Our next stop was 'Njiri's fashions'. There I picked out three pastel-coloured nightdresses, vests and panties.

I spotted them the moment we walked into our next shop. Bata shoes. I skipped to a pair of maroon shoes so shiny they sparkled, with a silver buckle at the front and a raised heel.

'Baba, I want these,' I said, lifting one up to my chest and stroking it like a pet. Baba walked over, inspecting the shoes.

'They are not suitable for school,' he advised, 'the heel is too high.' But I was not listening.

'Please Baba can I have these, they are perfect for school, please,' I pleaded. The shop assistant helped me try them on. They were a size too big. Baba was shaking his head; I would not budge.

'Okay, you can have them only if you let me choose the next pair.' I did not care about the next pair. He might as well have bought me bags; I had my shoes. I slid my feet into the cool leather of the maroon shiny shoes with a raised heel and a silver buckle. I was in heaven. The rest of the day was magical.

For lunch, Baba took me to his favourite five-star

restaurant, New Stanley, to the west side of the business district. Baba always commanded impeccable manners. We stood by the polished mahogany stand with a sign 'Please wait to be seated'. Soft music played in the background.

The restaurant was half full of stuffy well-fed Europeans with their napkins tucked into their collars, busy chatting. Some clicked their fingers, their commanding voices full of inflated self-importance. 'Boy,' the over-attentive African waiters tripping over with exaggerated eagerness to please white people was comical.

A waiter approached us, checking out Baba's suit as if to convince himself we could pay our way. 'Table for two?' he asked with uncertainty. Before Baba could reply, the waiter's attention was taken by a European couple who stood behind us. Turning away from us, he smiled so broadly you could see the tonsils at the back of his throat. He walked off, smiling and bowing, 'Where would you like to sit? Sir, madam?' to the couple, leaving us standing there. Several waiters made an attempt to seat us but every time they approached us, we were soon abandoned when white clients came in—'Of course, sir, this way,' 'Goodbye sir, it was great to have your custom.'

When we were eventually seated, the first waiter told us to 'come this way' abruptly and impatiently, as if we were wasting his time. He sat us in a corner by the toilets, and when Baba protested quietly, his lips tight with irritation, the waiter replied that the other tables were reserved for real customers. It seemed that over twenty years after independence the African mind still belonged to the white man. Baba never liked to make a fuss in such an establishment. We ate happily nonetheless, Baba watching my impeccable use of cutlery and napkin with glee. His hard discipline paid off at times like this.

It was nearing dusk when everything on the kit list was ticked off. We took everything to the car. The ice cream bicycle came by ringing its bell. Baba bought me ice cream as we drove home. That night I barely slept. I dreamt of boarding school with all my new things.

This memory would be reignited at Wainaina's wedding and, looking back now, it was a memory to treasure. The excitement of my going to boarding school and the only time Baba and I would ever dine together alone. The one time we shared something special.

At Boarding School

My parents waved, smiling proudly as the pickup truck reversed, skidding, the tyres spraying gravel. Carrying my red suitcase, Miss Martha walked alongside me to the side entrance of a long building. We paused outside the big bottle-green door which made me feel very small. I wandered what we would find behind the green door. Miss Martha fumbled in the deep pockets of the crisply ironed light blue tunic she wore, pulling out a bunch of keys. She flicked a few to the side before inserting one into the keyhole. 'This is your dormitory,' she said in Gikuyu. My parents had told her I didn't speak English. Vernacular was prohibited in the school grounds but talking to me in English would only have contributed to my anxiety.

When the green door swung back, it revealed a small room with several sinks on one side and toilet cubicles on the other side. Next was the bigger room, with showers and large pails on the side. 'This is where you wash after school. Are you a bed wetter?' she asked. My heart stopped. I was a prolific bed wetter. I was thrown by this question. I had the bladder of a cow and the projection of a firehose; I could destroy a mound of red soil with my projection. I believed I had the same size bladder as Jane our cow. Once she and I had urinated at the same time into the soil and I was fascinated to know my bladder kept going the same length of time as Jane's. I said nothing, ashamed of admitting that at my age I still wet the bed. Maitu had not told me what to do about bed-wetting. She must have forgotten. Miss Martha, noticing my silence, asked again. 'Are you a bed wetter?' I looked down and said in a most quiet timid voice, 'No.'

'All bed-wetters have to place their bedding in the large pail and have a shower every morning. Everyone else gets ready and goes for breakfast.'

We walked past the ablutions. She opened another door and began to walk down the cold dimly lit corridor of dormitory no. 3, which was as uninviting as it was dark. The vast hollowness of the room was daunting, with an array of tall iron bunk beds towering over me. The beds were all made up neatly with different coloured bedspreads. A combination of fear and dread began to well up, rising from the soles of my feet through my body to the top of my head.

'Follow me,' Miss Martha said, noticing I had stalled. 'Let me show you your bed,' she said from halfway down the corridor. I followed her obediently, my maroon shiny shoes with a silver buckle making a clicking sound, interrupting the ghostly silence as I headed to the end of the corridor. She stopped just before the end and pointed at the top bunk, which did not have a bedspread on. The bed was covered with a yellowing sponge mattress that had seen better days, which sat clumsily as if trying to escape. The narrow windowpanes reluctantly allowed only a smidgen of light. The thin threadbare curtains were partially drawn, the faint floral pattern wasted in the dark dormitory.

'This is your bed,' she said pointing at the top bank. 'I will leave your suitcase on your bed; others are still in class. If we hurry, you should just about make the last lesson.'

From a distance, the bell rang. 'Too late,' she said shrugging her shoulders. Voices could be heard as the children ran out of the classes and made their way to the dorms. The door burst open and a group of girls came in. 'Oh look, there is a new girl.' They all came running towards me. Miss Martha turned round and said, 'This is my room,' pointing at another door, 'if you need me. I will escort you to supper, just relax for now.' And with that, she was gone.

The girls who were about my size surrounded me. 'What

is your name?' asked one girl with a very posh accent. The only English I had mastered at my old school was to be tested to the full. 'My Namu ais Mary Njambi' Emu A Ara Y,' I replied in a crude peasant accent. I even spelt my name. She shrilled with laughter, ran off and told a horde of other girls who came running and surrounded me. 'Ask her her name,' the girl giggled, and another girl repeated the question.

'What is your name?'

'My Namu ais Mary Njambi' Emu A Ara Y.' Nervousness made me feel the need to spell my name. Laughter erupted. The crowd gathered, all surrounding me. I could not understand this spectacle—after all, in my previous school my reply would have been perfectly acceptable. They repeatedly asked me my name and I told them in exactly the same fashion as they rolled and cried in laughter.

By early evening I had become the main source of entertainment. I did not like this game. I was tired and felt humiliated and on top of that my brand-new red Samsonite suitcase had disappeared with all my new clothes. Miss Martha came out and asked the girls to leave me alone. She escorted me to supper. I did not eat much; I had lost my appetite. After supper, Miss Martha took me to evening prep and I dreaded going back to the dormitory because of those wretched girls. I sat next to a very light skinned girl called Dorothy, who seemed very kind. When the 9pm bell rang, I followed

Dorothy to the dormitory. I felt sad at losing my suitcase with all my things. When I got to my bed, it had reappeared as if by magic. Miss Martha had taken it to her quarters to put labels on my clothes. I was relieved.

I was frightened to fall asleep. Miss Martha's question about bed-wetting had completely thrown me. The thought horrified me, fearing what my neighbour on the bottom bunk would say after a torrential rain of urine if I fell asleep. I put my red suitcase at the bottom of my bed, the only comfort I could get. I dared not fall asleep in case my bladder gave way.

When the lights came on in the morning with Miss Martha calling everyone to get up, I sat up in fright. I had fallen asleep. I panicked. I began feeling my bed to see if it was wet. To my astonishment, it was bone dry. Fear cured my bed-wetting.

No Cure for Homesick

When I said yes to Baba's question of 'would you like to go to boarding school?' I would never have anticipated the hollow, gut-wrenching feeling of loneliness and homesickness that would consume me. It began to creep up slowly as I waved to my proud parents on my first day.

As I walked down the slope to my dormitory with my housekeeper Miss Martha, my feet began to feel heavy making me drag them. The dragging was compounded by my oversized maroon shiny shoes with a silver buckle and a raised heel. On my first night in the dorm, I had lain in my bed, eyes wide open, staring into the black void above me. Everything that was familiar was taken away from me. Maitu's warm smile as she embraced us when we appeared up the hill from our school on the other side of the ridge. My mother tongue that was familiar to me; the comfort of familiar words and expressions were replaced by a concoction of meaningless words. They sounded cold and unfamil-iar. They lacked the warmth of the Gikuyu words. I was worried that my dreams would be inhabited too by this new, foreign language and when I slept, I tried to block out any English words from mind in case they invaded my dreams.

At boarding school, no one loved me. My brothers did, but I didn't see them often, us being in separate classes and dorms. Boys tended to play with other boys and we rarely had contact with them. No one looked at me in the tender way Maitu did, or the way Baba looked over at me as he tried to catch the news on TV. I missed our TV. I missed my bed. I missed our dog Ian Smith. I missed the way Ian Smith and I ran down the hill to the river and back again, Ian Smith trying so hard to overtake me.

Baba had come home one evening with a brown puppy with a black face. He named it Ian Smith after the tyrannical Rhodesian white supremacist. Baba hated the way white people humiliated and emasculated black men. They referred to grown men as boys. Those men had been through the initiation that made them men. They were real men. They had danced all day and gone to the river and remained stoic to be men but the white man ignored the Gikuyu customs. Baba called our dog Ian Smith so that he could say, 'Ian Smith, go fetch my slippers, boy.' I used to sit with Ian Smith on my lap and remove the ticks or fleas on him. He would roll around the grass while I laughed. I longed for Ian Smith.

Boarding school lacked the freedom of my pink pebble-dashed house. There were rules about everything. When to wake up, when to sleep, when to eat lunch, breakfast and supper.

Sundays were all about God. It was as if we had to make up for the days of the week when we didn't interact with him. It began at 9 am when we attended the English service wearing our freshly laundered uniform. It lasted forty-five minutes, after which we returned to school for milk. After our milk, we returned to the Church of the Torch for the Gikuyu service, which lasted a mere four hours, or it seemed like it. The preachers were all monotone. The murmur of their preaching soon became like the soft moo of our cows in their paddock, like a lullaby soothing me to sleep. I slept for what seemed like eternity, dreamt and when I woke up, we still had ages left. After the service, I got a chance to say hello to Cucu Herina, who lived little walk away and attended the church every Sunday. I wanted to spend the afternoon with her but there were rules about that. After the Gikuyu service, we went back to the school for lunch and at 4pm we went to Sunday school. They read us bible stories. After supper, we had social evening where we sang songs praising God. Surely even God needed a rest.

My teacher Miss Maina was kind, beautiful and engaging. I enjoyed being taught by her and the time spent in her class. Out of the classroom, I was engulfed by loneliness. I longed to be back home in Riara Ridge. One day I was walking on the playing field after supper when I looked over to the horizon. Far far away, I saw three trees that looked like the trees one ridge away from my home. There was a mound of building sand that had been left on the corner of the field and grass had grown over it. I climbed on the mound and took a better look at the trees. I became convinced that they were the trees one ridge away from home, close to where Wanyoike *kibubu*—the deaf lived. Every day after supper, I walked to the mound and looked at the trees, thinking about how close they were to my home. Somehow that sight made being in school more bearable.

One day I stepped on to the mound and looked for the trees. They were not there. The horizon was covered with a blanket of fog. My heart caved in. I stayed there until it got too dark to see the trees. By the third day, the fog had not lifted. And that's when I made the decision.

When the bell rung for supper that day, I hurried to the dining hall and ate in haste. I took my plate to the dirty dishes bucket then headed to the table where Mungai and Wainaina sat.

'I am running away,' I told them. They looked surprised.

'Why? Where are you going?' they asked.

'To Cucu Herina's and she will take me to see Maitu

and Baba.' I said my goodbye and exited the hall by the back entrance. I sat on the grass close to some boys playing football. The light was fading and when the 7 pm prep bell rang, I ran in the opposite direction toward the hedge. I crept under the barbed wire, making sure my dress was not caught by the sharp edges. I stood up on the other side in the maize plantation and began to run. I ran, ducking branches of maize until I reached the junction next to Thogoto day primary. On the road, I walked hurriedly until I reached Guka Mwaura's shop, where I stopped to look.

Guka (grandfather) Mwaura was Cucu Herina's youngest brother. When he was a young man, he was recruited to join the Mau Mau. Like many Gikuyu men, their role as men and ability to sustain themselves had been eroded by the arrival of the white man. The Gikuyu were farmers in the Central Province of Kenya. When their land was awarded to the white settlers, Gikuyu were deported to native reserves. With no land to farm and all their goats confiscated, the Gikuyu men had no means of sustaining themselves. The reserves were overcrowded, with no employment prospects. Most young men became vagrants, unable to leave the reserves because all Gikuyu were required to have a passbook. Passbooks were obtained upon verification for a job by a white employer. Most could not obtain them. The white employers could destroy a person's passbook, rendering them incapable of ever acquiring documents to leave the reserve. Guka Mwaura had dreams of being able to marry and have a family of his own. He could not marry without money for dowry. It was hopeless. He decided to join the young men walking by night to the Rift Valley, where prospects for black people were better. That changed soon after he arrived there, when all the inhabitants were expelled because white settlements were expanding. They were now referred to as squatters and forcibly removed. One night he was resting in the squatter hut of a friend, when the door opened. They recognized the purpose of the visit straight away. These were oath administrators for the oath to fight the white man. 'You have to undertake all the jobs given to you,' he was instructed upon joining the underworld of freedom fighters. After the ceremony was over Guka Mwaura was told to await instructions from his boss, who he would meet in due cause.

Guka Mwaura was eventually arrested and taken to the most notorious detention centre, called Manyani. Upon arrival, the new inmates were initiated by being stripped naked and pushed into a cattle dip to sanitise them. Those who couldn't swim drowned. The naked men were then asked to stand in rows. A woman was invited to come in naked and start dancing whilst massaging her breasts and private parts. If any men got an erection, they were taken aside. Their testicles were placed on a bench and bashed until they bust.

They were fed the contents of their testicles. The conditions were so atrocious. There were no provisions for water or sanitation. They used the same pail for drinking water and defecation. Many detainees died of starvation, beatings and dysentery. When Guka Mwaura was eventually released years later he was a broken man. He opened a small shop in Thogoto village as he tried to rebuild his life. When we went out on school trips, I always stopped at his shop to say hello. He always leaned over the wooden counter, a big smile on his face, and would give me a tropical sweet but never a Fanta, which I always craved.

On the night I ran away from boarding school, I walked past his shop but did not stop for long because it was shut. I carried on walking, turning to the left towards Kiamburi where Cucu Herina lived. It was approaching 7:30 pm when I knocked on Cucu Herina's door.

'*Mwana wa mwana wakwa*—daughter of my daughter,' she greeted me. She was delighted, confused and worried. 'Is everything okay?'

'Yes Cucu, I am fine. I have come to live with you,' I replied. She did not ask any questions but pulled a stool over and welcomed me to sit down. She was just heating water on the cooking stones to wash her feet. She poured the water in the basin, removed my shoes and socks. She lifted my legs up and put them in the water and began massaging them. The warmth from the water being massaged into my bones travelled all the way up to my soul. When she finished, she soaked her own feet in the water. We told stories in Gikuyu and when I began to doze, she took off my navy tunic and white shirt, folding them carefully, and placed them on the stool. She carried me to her bed where I slept like a log. For the first time since I went to boarding school, I did not have nightmares. I wanted to live with Cucu Herina forever.

When it was morning, Cucu Herina dug up the sweet potatoes she had buried in the embers. They were freshly baked. She peeled them, blowing them to cool down and handing me one. She was boiling water for *turungi*, to which she then added sugar and began pouring it into a mug until there was no more in the pan, then poured it back into the mug. This is how we cooled tea. She repeated this several times until it was cool enough for me to drink. We were just about to finish our breakfast when we heard a knock on the door. I recognized him straight away with a sinking feeling. It was the school messenger on his bicycle coming to get me.

When Miss Martha did a head count the night before, she had realized I was nowhere to be seen and I had not been to prep. She had run to other dormitories, speaking to the house mothers, but no one knew where I was. She ran to the headmistress, all frazzled, exclaiming that I had gone missing. Mrs Wambugu rang Baba, who said I may have gone to Cucu Herina's house. The messenger was from Cucu Herina's village and he knew her well. Upon arriving at the school, Miss Martha had sent him out to go look for me.

Boarding school for me was the greatest and worst experience. It was great for my education because the quality of teaching was next to none, and it laid a foundation that I would never have achieved elsewhere, least of all at my peasant school. It was also the worst because it took me away from my beloved home and stole time from the early part of my childhood. Looking back now, the term before we went to boarding school was one of the happiest times we ever shared as a family and the last time we would all live together as a family. Several weeks before we were transferred to boarding school, Baba took us to the agricultural show ground for the last time. To this day, I wish everything had stopped there.

Fun at the Show Ground

The agricultural show was the main event for most people living in the Central Province of Kenya. It was almost certainly the biggest event in most people's calendar year. It was when farmers brought out their prized possessions to showcase to the world. Big fat bulls with rings in their noses, draped in the previous year's medals were paraded to adoring show goers. Merino sheep with brushed wool coats trotted around whilst proud farmers displayed large marrows, extra-large onions and other vegetables. Crowds marvelled at their hard work. There were prizes and medals to be won. Entertainment for children and grown-ups alike added to the merriment.

There were exhibitions of the latest farming technology, seminars on maximizing crop, irrigation systems and solar lighting. There were food stalls selling all manner of food. There were ice-cream vendors on bicycles, their familiar bells calling to the children.

Baba's relative Chief Mwangi was a bull breeder, taking home several prizes and medals every year. Every year he gave Baba tickets to bring us all. The preparation to attend the event usually began the day before. Maitu rose early and began kneading dough, rolling and cutting before throwing the different shapes into the boiling oil. As the mandazis browned, she would scoop them out and leave them on the side to drain before dusting them off with sugar. Next, she prepared the chapatti dough, which she rolled, oiled, rolled again then fried on the chapatti pan. When she was nearly done, she gave each one of us a piece of dough to roll out our own little chapattis, which she fried for us. Mungai and I always ran to the back of our house when we had something nice to eat. We would nibble tiny little bits, not wanting to finish, savouring every piece.

With our Sunday best washed and ironed, we all lined up to have a bath in preparation for the early start the following day. On the day, our parents woke us up at the crack of dawn. The corridors were a hive of activity as we dressed excitedly. 'Where are my shoes, I left them by my bedside?' someone would be calling. 'Look under the bed,' Maitu would reply. Before Maitu and Baba were ready, we were at the table waiting for breakfast. Maitu would bring out the tea in a kettle; she would even have added milk and sugar to save time. She'd then place down the tray of sugary mandazi, which we feasted on with the tea. Maitu packed more mandazis and chapatti wrapped in newspapers, and flasks of tea, into the picnic bags, which Baba loaded into the Ford Anglia. Once we were all in the car, we sang excitedly whilst Baba drove to Nairobi showground. At the entrance was a big sign: 'Welcome to Nairobi Show Ground.' Traffic marshals guided people to the parking lot that was already filling with eager showgoers. The showground was a feast for the eyes. We visited different stalls displaying the latest gadgets in farming. My parents moved from stall to stall, looking, talking and taking note of anything that we could use for the farm.

When it was 10 am, Maitu and Baba would look for sitting spaces with benches and tables at the numerous picnic sites. We would all sit around a wooden table.

'Have you seen anything you like yet?' Baba would ask Maitu as she poured the tea into cups before handing out the mandazi.

'I like the irrigation system,' Maitu would note.

'We don't really need one because the farm gets a lot of rainfall,' Baba would observe. At lunch, Baba took us to the hotdog stand. Mungai and I being the youngest, we held on to Baba's hand. Maitu walked with the older children. When all the hotdogs had been paid for, we would walk over to the field with neatly trimmed grass where we ate, played and enjoyed the sunshine. But the day was not done. We had many more stalls to visit. Baba would buy new overalls to wear when spraying the coffee with pesticides. Maitu got new gum boots and when it was 4 pm our parents took us to the merry-go-round, which was the highlight of our day. Our day concluded with ice cream in cups and small wooden spoons which we ate on the way to the car. Exhausted, we'd drive back home, my brothers and I falling asleep long before we got home. It was only the following morning when we realised the show was over.

Forgotten at Half-Term

The school year was divided into three terms. A term was three months in school and one month at home for holiday. We spent a total of nine months a year at school and three months at home. Halfway through the term we had four days for half term. School days were long, beginning at 8:30 am until 4:30 pm when we returned to our dormitories to have a bath and break before going to supper at six o'clock. At 7 pm, when the bell rang, we returned to the classroom for prep until 9 pm. It was exhausting.

We valued and looked forward to our half-term, which was Thursday to Sunday. On the Thursday children got up very early in preparation to see their parents. Breakfast was rushed as everyone wanted to get to the assembly ground to wait for their parents eagerly.

One half-term Thursday, my brothers and I sat on the steps staring at the gate, waiting for our parents' arrival. The assembly ground began to thin out as excited children ran to their parents, calling 'Mummy, Daddy.' We watched in anticipation as more children left excitedly. We sat in the midday sun, our noses sweating, still gazing in the directions that parents arrived from. We still believed they were on their way. Our house mothers waited impatiently with us because they needed to get home to see their own families. By one o'clock, we were hungry but refused to go to the dining room because we didn't want our parents to arrive and not find us, causing them to leave without us. By four o'clock, we were persuaded by the remaining house mother to go to the dining room; the cook would not leave until everyone had left the school. We ate quickly and returned to the assembly ground to wait.

It was now dark but still we waited, still believing our parents were coming to get us. There was no sign of our parents. Miss Martha finally convinced us to walk to our dormitory to wait for our parents. At ten o'clock, Mungai said it.

'They are not coming! Our parents have forgotten about us!' his lips quavering, about to cry. Our hearts sank with disappointment.

'Why would our parents not come?'

'Maybe they died,' said Wainaina. 'My friend's parents both died in a car accident. May be our parents died in a car accident too,' said Wainaina sobbing.

'No children, your parents have not died, I'm sure

206

there must be a good reason. Maybe their car broke down. Cars are always breaking down,' consoled Miss Martha. She was right, I thought. Our car had broken down several times, maybe that was what had happened this time too.

That night I slept in my bed and Mungai and Wainaina slept on the lower bunk beds. When Miss Martha woke us the following morning, I jumped out of bed.

'Are they here?'

'No, they are not here,' she replied, feeling sorry for us.

'Take us to Cucu Herina,' I said finally. 'We know where our grandma Herina lives.' Mungai and Wainaina lit up; even Miss Martha thought it was a good idea. She too longed to see her children. 'Okay, I will take you to your grandma's house,' she said. We dressed hurriedly and made our way to the breakfast hall. After eating our boiled eggs and buttered bread with tea, we set out for Cucu Herina's house.

We arrived at Cucu Herina's house as she was just leaving with her *kiondo* strapped to her back, a hoe on her shoulder and her machete in hand. She was going to till her *shamba*. Miss Martha explained that our parents had not come to pick us up and the school was now shut for half term. Miss Martha was pleased to leave us with our grandmother and hurried off to see her children. Cucu Herina thanked her, waving her goodbye.

'Don't worry, my child's children, I will ask your cousin Ngige to take you home,' she said, setting her tools down. We followed her down the path to Tata(aunt) Wanjiku's house to find her eldest son, who would take us to our parents.

At midday, we waited for the country bus to take us to Nairobi. The dusty journey-in the old bus, coughing smoke-took us an hour. We hurried across town to the station outside Nation Newspapers for a matatu to take us to Banana Hill. Any other day we would have been excited to be in Nairobi, but we just needed to get home to Riara Ridge. It was three o'clock when we got into the matatu that would take us to Banana Hill. From Banana Hill, we took another matatu to Mungai Chengeca Road, the furthest point matatus went to. From there we walked four miles, keeping a steady pace to avoid walking in the dark, especially worried about hyenas and the leopard.

It was six pm when we arrived home. The house was dark as Maitu was outside, locking up the animals. When she saw us, she was surprised, because Baba oversaw school matters and she had no idea it was half term. She had not seen Baba for weeks since he had left for Kampala. She had lost a lot of weight and had shaven her head clean, making her look much older. She was very pleased to see us but we could tell she was sad about something. She had lost the sparkle in her eyes.

That bright face she had when she and Baba danced outside our mud-plastered temporary house to Kamaru's music was gone. Now she looked withdrawn and tired. We only spent Saturday at home with her before setting off again on the long journey back to school.

Baba's Metamorphosis

Baba's business was growing rapidly, making him very wealthy. His friends became ministers and other prominent people, most of whom were farm owners in Riara Ridge and its surrounding areas. He became a prominent member of the PCEA church. He took to affluence like a duck to water, eating out in the finest restaurants, and wore the finest three-piece suits, complete with cravats and the occasional fedora. Being only five-foot-tall, he favoured platform shoes, which gave him extra height. He was always clean-shaven, with a neat afro, Brylcreem glittering in the sun. In his silk socks, he always stuffed thick wads of money which he covered with his flared trousers. He lost all interest in his former friends and family in Thogoto. Baba, unlike Maitu forgot where he had come from. When he left for Kampala, he would hold a big wad of money in his hand, peel off a 100 shilling note and hand it to Maitu, who accepted it begrudgingly.

When we children went to boarding school, Maitu and Baba should have had time to nurture their relationship. The toll of Kui's illness must have been immense and completely exhausted my parents. Whilst Maitu was tenaciously maintaining our home, Baba's life was slowly metamorphosing in the opposite direction. His trips to Kampala brought him money and success. Being only a young man, still in his thirties, with a lot of money, far away from home, Baba faced temptations he couldn't resist. He was gone for several weeks at a time, and when he came back there was a noticeable strain on their relationship. When he eventually came home, he was cold and abrupt to Maitu, and to us when we were home. He lost his temper easily. We were scolded and beaten for minuscule reasons. There must have been temptations for Baba before the height of Kui's illness, but after her illness they became magnified. Home, wife and children were now a tedious concept to him. Try as she might, the seed Baba's friend planted in Maitu's mind of possible infidelity could no longer be ignored. It fuelled her suspicion. Maitu suspected Baba had a mistress in Kampala. As his business trips got longer, the rift between them widened.

The unmistakable hum of the distant car from the other side of the ridge now always cast a cloud of gloom. The sound would disappear momentarily as if to award us a moment of composure. The lining of my stomach would flutter. Even the busy chorus of wildlife seemed to hush in anticipation. When Baba was not away on business in Kampala, he'd come home from Nairobi at dusk. The car would go around the gravel-strewn path, circling the roundabout with the thorn tree in the middle before grinding to a halt in front of the path leading to the front door. When he first selected the seedling from a selection of plants in the back of his pickup truck, instructing Munyau the workman to plant it in the middle of the roundabout, Munyau had raised his eyebrows in doubt but dared not question the boss's decision. Later Munyau and Maitu discussed the poor choice of the centre plant, saying the tree would grow too tall for the front of the house. 'It will be impossible to cut because of its sharp poisonous thorns,' observed Cucu Herina when she came to visit. Despite having a garage, Baba never drove into it; it was now used for storage.

We would all pretend to be excited and ran through the door shouting, 'Baba, Baba!' Unimpressed, he would pat us and stride down the path to the house; even the mighty thighs of the locusts would thrust their light bodies out of his way. The clunk of his shoes on the black and white tiles would soon be cushioned by the deep rug as he found his way to the wall unit cradling the three in one ghetto-blaster TV. He'd push the eject button on the stereo section. With the smile on his face he would look at the cassette with bold writing on it: 'Abba in Switzerland.' He would push it back into its slot, press play and proceed to his yellow velvet chair, shuffle his bottom into a comfortable stance and close his eyes. With a soft pleasant expression on his face, his short stout fingers would tap lightly on the mahogany wooden armrest whilst the room filled with Abba's 'Money Money Money.' Before the next song, he would slide his feet into the sandals placed carefully by either foot by Maitu, who would do so without disturbing his trance. His equilibrium was our soul searching; not even the crackling fire would ease the chill in the room. Even when nothing was said, everything was said. When all was quiet, we wondered what he was thinking. Was he contemplating punishment and if so, who was the recipient? When Baba was in the room, we were filled with fear and anxiety, each one of us wondering if we'd done anything that would warrant a beating. I'd wrack my brain about the comings and goings of my day, wondering if I would be the one sent outside into the hollow nothingness of the dark night for a stick with which I would be beaten. Looking for stick to be beaten with was cruel, and psychological torture. He expected his victim to determine the tool by which he would inflict pain on us, as if somehow making us complicit in our suffering. If your suffering was immense it would be because you chose a stick that was too harsh.

It was a great relief when Maitu slid open the

wooden interconnecting panel, smells of her cooking diffusing the awkwardness of pretending to study. My brother Wainaina didn't even check that his study book was the right way up. When food was served and after saying grace, Baba, tight-lipped, rounded cheeks swollen with food, would swoop his eyes around the table to ensure the correct use of cutlery. Baba always sat at the head of the table, his big head seeming disproportionately bigger than the rest of his body. His intense brown eyes seemed to read bad deeds from one's brain. His face seemed to smile but when he spoke, he was impersonal and unnecessarily harsh. When he coughed, I could feel the sphincter of my bladder slacken. My brother Wainaina always sat next to Baba, looking up at him adoringly, stuffing his food in his mouth until swollen, mimicking Baba's every move. The clink of cutlery created suspense as to who would be the first to self-incriminate. 'Baba, today Mungai fought a standard 7 boy!' Wainaina would cave in. It would all kick off. 'It wasn't me, Wainaina threw the first stone, but the big boy accused me so I stood up for myself.' Both would be found guilty and would walk out into the dark together, grumbling at the other for starting the conversation. They would both go to sleep crying.

The Mould

Our living room was not short of sitting space. When one entered the door by the front entrance, on the right was a row of black fabric sofa sets, one three-seater and two armchairs on either side. On the opposite side was the more elegant, yellow velvet three-piece set on which the visitors sat. The people on the black set were forced to look at the people on the yellow set. And the people on the yellow set could either look at the people on the black sofas or look outside through the window behind the sofas. When the TV was on, the people on the black sofas were forced to turn their heads to the right and the people on the yellow velvet sofas had to turn their heads to the left. When everyone turned to the wall where the TV was, their eyes wandered up the wall following the big crack from when the earthquake struck, which seemed to get deeper day by day as if reflecting our parents' relationship. At the top, black blotches of mould began to form on the walls.

The earthquake had shattered a few bricks which now leaked when it rained. My parents never got a chance to repair the roof due to their tending to Kui's illness. Both were now a reminder of the curse that was playing out before our very eyes.

I do not remember why we, the children, were sat on the sofas when Baba was home, but we just were. We sat facing Baba and Maitu. Baba was quiet. There was a bit of tension but at the time we didn't recognize it as such. Our parents barely had conversations these days. Finally, he broke his silence and spoke. 'Where were you today?' Maitu gave an answer which I do not remember as it bore no significance. Baba repeated the question but received exactly the same answer. Next Baba got up from his chair, walked over to Maitu, reached out, pulled her out of the sofa, and put her in a head lock like Mungai and Wainaina did when they played with one another. At first, we watched with curiosity; we did not understand what he was doing. It was only after Maitu's muffled distressed screams that we realized he was strangling her. We screamed and screamed. Munyau, his wife and the neighbour's workmen ran towards the door knocking loudly. It was only then, as we struggled to unlock the door to let them in, that Baba let go of her head and walked off to their bedroom. From that day onwards, Maitu slept on our bedroom floor.

My parents' relationship seemed very strained from

then. When Baba walked out of the house in the mornings, all smartly dressed, Maitu would use hand gestures to curse him, calling him '*Kaguba*', which I understood to mean one of restricted growth or retarded. She sneered at him and he, observing her from the car's rear-view mirror, seemed to curse her back. When the car disappeared down the hill, Maitu would spread out her hands, her fingers arched like a cat's about to scratch. She would curse some more and make cursing noises. 'Go to your prostitutes,' she yelled as the car got further away.

One night, Baba walked over to his armchair, sat in his usual position, slippers laid in their place, and began watching the news. '*Hamjamboni mabwana na mabibi, hi ni habari ya taila leo*,' began the news reader. '*Mheshimiwa na baba wa taifa Mzee Jomo Kenyatta amekufa*—good evening ladies and gentlemen this is today's news. His excellency and father of our nation Mzee Jomo Kenyatta is dead.' We all froze. Whatever each one of us was doing, we stopped to stare at the small square that was the TV. The news that the father of our nation was dead was chilling. Baba sat bolt upright with a worried look on his face. 'Are they going to fight?' we asked Baba. He didn't hear us. Such news was sure to cause uncertainty, with many wondering if Kenya would disintegrate into chaos barely two decades after independence. We wondered what the implications of his death would be. The newsreader announced that Jomo Kenyatta would lay in state for several days so that mourners could go to pay their respects to the Father of the Nation.

There was deathly silence in the air when Baba finally switched off the TV, which was now playing a mourning song hastily written and sang by Mungaano choir. '*Natazama kilele cha mlima wa Kenya, Mzee Kenyatta sasa ametuacha*—I face the tip of Mt Kenya, Mzee Kenyatta has left us.'

Maitu served dinner as usual. Baba sipped water from his glass, taking a moment to swish it round his mouth. His stare was between the serving dish and the serving spoon. He swirled his food around his plate, hardly eating any. He seemed troubled. There was a knock on the door. We turned around to see Munyau's troubled face, through the glass front door, fearful of the implications of the news.

'They are going to fight like Uganda,' he said worriedly.

'I pray not,' replied Baba unconvincingly.

Baba did not go to Kampala for a while. Although he blended in by speaking fluent Baganda, he was still troubled. He waited to see if trouble would break out. Moi, the acting president, had made a statement reassuring everyone that he would be following in the footsteps of Mzee Kenyatta, his slogan being '*Nyayo*-footsteps.' Moi was the successor and no match to Jomo Kenyatta, who came into power with a cult status after his high-profile arrest, detention and trial by the British government in Kapenguria, a region in Northern Kenya, at the dawn of Kenyan independence. When Moi became the acting president after Kenyatta's demise, he promised to rule Kenya without 'tribalism, drunkenness, corruption and smuggling' which turned out to be his motto masqueraded in a mantra of peace, love and unity. Ironically, his tenure as the second-longest-serving president in Africa will go down in history as the worst for human rights violations. Moi would silence anyone that criticised him by implementing detention without trial and the assassination of opponents assisted by his henchmen, police and militia. His government ensured that public funds were redirected to a Swiss bank account for safe keeping, where it would be laundered into virgin white guilt-free money whilst he bathed in the tears of the poor. Moi's presidential slogan '*nyayo*—footprints, became a note to himself to remember to eradicate footprints from the land he was grabbing.

Kenyatta's death did little to quell the sense of doom in our home.

The Adulterer

During term time, Maitu was at home alone except for Munyau, his wife and their three children, who attended Githatha primary school. His youngest, Kioko, was Mungai's playmate and he enjoyed studying Mungai's insects with him. We had all been shipped off to boarding schools by now, both my sisters in high school and my brothers and me in primary. Baba was often in Kampala but when he was home, he dressed up as usual in his pinstripe suits, leaving a trail of Old Spice eau de toilette behind him. Every morning, he sat waiting for Maitu to serve him breakfast. She browned the toast using the charcoal burner in the kitchen, boiled the tea leaves, poured it into the silver tea pot with the milk in the small silver jug, the sieve sitting on its cradle on the side. After breakfast Baba would walk to his Toyota, stand back to stare at the writing on the driver's door which read: 'Peter N Wainina, Green Gold Farm, Riara Ridge, P.O. box 28737 Tel: 274,' beaming with pride looking at his name in italics. Satisfied, he would get into the car, start the engine and disappear down the dusty track.

This morning nothing was amiss, albeit Baba seemed moodier than usual, but Maitu assumed he had a lot going on with his business and served him breakfast before he drove off as usual. Maitu had just finished giving instructions to Munyau on where he would be digging because she wanted the ground prepared for planting before the start of the long rains. She had offered him a cup of tea with four sugars, which he gratefully gulped before heading down the hill with the hoe on his shoulder whistling a tune. Next Maitu brought out the dirty laundry, transferring the boiling water from the stove into the blue plastic basin and cooling it with water from the hosepipe before sprinkling the Omo into the water. The scrubbing had begun, with each clean garment being flung on her pile of wet wrung out cloths on the grass ready to be rinsed, when Baba drove back up the driveway. She instantly assumed that he had forgotten something but as the car got closer, she noticed he was not alone in the car. When the car came to a stop on the circular drive, she realized that the passengers in the car were my Cucu Herina and aunt Wanjiku, who sat between them. Maitu had stopped scrubbing the clothes, throwing the garment she'd been washing back in the blue plastic basin before drying her hands and fastening her *rithu* around her waist. Baba got out of the car, leaving Maitu to walk over to her mother and sister, who appeared startled as to why they had been summoned to our home. Baba emerged from the house a few moments later wearing a fresh shirt, got into the car and drove off without so much as an explanation of what this was about.

Once Maitu had made the visitors tea, they were just about to start drinking when a crowd of elders from neighbouring farms emerged, all walking curiously towards our house. She had met many at the PCEA church, where the burgeoning middle classes met every Sunday for worship.

'What is going on?' Maitu asked.

'We have been summoned to a meeting by Baba Wairimu,' one grey haired man replied, walking slowly and leaning on his stick. Maitu recognized a lot of them, including Wanyoike who was deaf but could lip read.

'About what?' she asked, rather startled.

'He didn't say, that's why we are here, to find out.' The puzzled crowd found grassy patches to sit on because there were not enough chairs for everyone. The mumbling started whilst they waited for Baba to return. It was not long before the roar of the car could be heard from a distance and to Maitu's surprise, both my sisters were sat in the front seat of the pickup wearing their green uniforms. Baba walked out of the car and headed straight into the house, leaving my eldest sister Wairimu who rushed out of the car to greet Maitu, her aunt and grandmother, who she hadn't seen in a while.

Kui, however, walked out of the car with a rather disinterested demeanour and went and sat separately, saying nothing but donning a rather curious look on her face. Cucu Herina pinched Maitu to attract her attention and pointed to Kui, the only person rather suspiciously unfazed by the morning's proceedings. Cucu Herina, Maitu, aunt Wanjiku and Wairimu walked over to her and asked what she knew. 'Nothing,' she replied rather sheepishly, grabbing a fistful of grass and casting it away from her palm. Whatever it was, Kui knew and the trio hoped she would tell them before Baba returned. She however stood up and walked into the house singing, '*mama kifagio leo ni tatomboa siri yako*—broom woman today I shall tell your secret.' The mystery just intensified.

It was sometime before Baba emerged with his suit jacket off and his sleeves rolled up, walked to the crowd and made sure everyone was comfortably seated. He cleared his throat and began, 'I have called you here today because Wangari is an adulterer,' to a big gasp from the crowd. He had never called her Wangari; it was always her pet name Gakari.

'Not only is she an adulterer but she tried to poison me too,' he continued. The crowd was startled by this proclamation. Maitu let out an audible gasp. 'I have all the evidence I need and she has been to the witch doctor, bewitching me as we speak.' Cucu Herina clasped her hands in disbelief.

'Kui, come out here and tell the elders what you know!' he finished, inviting my sister Kui to speak to the crowd.

Kui made her way to the crowd, discourteously, looking at them directly as she spoke to the now speech-less group. 'I saw her,' pointing at Maitu, 'walking hand in hand with a man, and I have seen her rub witchcraft on Baba's things, she is trying to poison him,' at which she started crying although no tears came out of her eyes.

It is not clear when or where she relayed this information to Baba, but she had managed to convince him of the story. Cucu Herina burst out, 'Kui, please think what you are saying, your mother will be killed.' Ignoring Cucu Herina, Kui carried on with her fantasy but could not name or describe what the man looked like, or which witch doctor she had visited. Maitu spoke of her confusion because she didn't not under-stand what her daughter was accusing her of. After the short meeting the villagers left confused and fearful for Maitu.

For the next two days, Baba said nothing, the suspense nearly killing Maitu. She was on tenterhooks and in her upset-mindedness, when she served Baba his breakfast, she added the sugar into his tea. He always preferred to add the sugar himself. He erupted into a mad rage, tearing off all her clothes as he punched and kicked her. When he tired of punching her, he looked around for a weapon. They both saw it at the same time. The axe that Munyau had left on the side to chop the logs for the night's fire. He ran to grab it, she jumped to her feet and flew towards the back of the house, running down the hill, but did not take the usual path, instead running through the coffee plantation, towards the farm to the left, creeping under the barbed wire and kept running until there was no breath left in her body, when she collapsed into a heap.

Some women who had been harvesting sweet potatoes, seeing her bleeding in her underwear in broad daylight, came to her rescue, giving her a cloth to cover her modesty. She covered herself, scrambled to her feet and kept running until the soles of her feet bled. She didn't stop running for miles, for fear he would find her with the axe. The driver of a Datsun, seeing a distressed woman running down the road, stopped and asked her if she was ok and wanted a lift. The man seemed to know she must have fought with her husband and did not ask her any more questions. He was kind enough to take her to Cucu Herina's house in Thogoto.

The following day, having heard what happened, Ngwiri, my parents' old friend, came to see Maitu, seeing her pain asked if she wanted to go for a walk. It was then they saw Baba's car. He told Maitu he had come to collect her; he wanted her to return home with him and when she refused he attacked her again. After that, there was no turning back. It was the following day that Maitu knocked on my classroom door, interrupting my English lesson with Miss Maina.

Wainaina's phone call to me in London with the news of his wedding reignited so much pain. It was only natural that he should want to invite people the living in Riara Ridge. Those people had sat on the grass as Kui read Maitu's fateful lies. Many had remained Baba's friends after Maitu left. They would be attending the wedding.

The Russian Circus

I don't know what possessed me to ask, or even how I knew about it, but I walked over to Baba as he sat in his yellow velvet chair, composed myself and asked. When I began to speak, he was staring at his toes, spread out as if to allow the warmth from the crackling fire to seep in between. The yellow velvet fabric covering his armchair was discoloured on the side closest to the fire since Baba always insisted that the fire be lit at dusk with his chair very close.

When he looked up at me and I knew I had his full attention, I gathered the courage to ask him: 'Please can you take us to the Russian circus?' He looked at me as if I had said the most curious thing, tapping his fingers on the arm of the chair. I guess I had. Finally, he smiled and replied, 'Yes! I will take you to the Russian circus.' I ran to the kitchen jumping up and down, saying, 'We are going to the circus.' Wairimu, who was busy cooking supper, stopped and began jumping up and down. Mungai and Wainaina heard us from their bedrooms and ran in to find out what the excitement was about.

'What is a circus?' Mungai asked, a look of disappointment on his face.

'It is where animals do magic,' I replied, which brightened his face instantly. We all began the chorus, 'We are going to the circus.' Kui ran in too. We found it very difficult to engage with Kui after what she did to Maitu. We were now all skipping, 'We are going to the circus, not any old circus, the Russian circus.'

'Be quiet!' Baba bellowed from the living room, where he was watching the evening news.

The massive circus tent was visible from the road, with bunting flapping in the April wind. As the car turned into the narrow track off Ngong' road, our excitement was uncontainable, and by the time the car stopped in the busy car park, we were already getting out of the car. Mungai and I walked close to Baba, who seemed quite happy, as we headed to join the queue at the entrance. Circus performances were a rarity in Kenya, in fact the whole of Africa. I don't know how I knew about the circus; it could have been someone from school or an advert on TV. We had no idea what happened at the circus or what a circus was but it sounded very thrilling and we could barely wait for the performance.

Baba must have known we hated him; going to the circus was the nicest thing he did for us after Maitu left. It was as if my suggestion had given him a chance to make it up to us and get us to like him again. He had spoken to us on the day he picked us up from school about Maitu leaving. We all knew because Maitu had visited us at school. He knew we knew because none of us asked where Maitu was or said anything when he told us, preferring to keep quiet instead. We didn't even act surprised when he gave us the news that she was not coming back. If anything, we appeared to become timid around him as if to recoil from his misdeeds. He had reiterated that we were never to see or talk to our mother again. We all knew that we would see her again and we would talk to her again. He was foolish to assume that we would relinquish our relationship with our mother at his say so. If anything, it was he we hated not our mother. It was the first time that we seemed happy again in his presence.

At the entrance of the circus tent, there were hotdogs, candy floss and roasted peanut stands. Baba paid for peanuts and candy floss. An assistant took us to our seats in the theatre-style seating surrounding the stage. It was then that we heard it. The deep roar of a lion. Eyes opened wide, we shivered at hearing a lion roar so close to us. We looked around in fear, trying to see where the lions were. The show began as a tall, skinny white man walked onto the stage, dressed like the dancers on *Soul Train* except his clothes were shiny. He appeared to bounce on his heels as he walked round the stage clapping. The people began clapping in unison.

He cracked his whip and the lions ran in and jumped on their stools. He raised his hand to our gasps of awe. He commanded the lions to sit. Another crack of the whip and the lions jumped off the stools and ran to where there were flaming hoops and jumped through them before running back to their seats. The crowd erupted, going wild with cheers and laughter. The door opened and another trainer walked in, in the same fashion as the first, followed by white tigers who interspersed themselves among the lions on the stools. A crack of the whip and the second trainer shouted something in a foreign language which we assumed to be Russian. The animals, still sitting on their stools, raised their front paws and waived at the ecstatic crowd. The trainers took a bow and commanded the cats to leave the stage.

The grand finale was a few elephants that marched to the rhythm of drums. They stood on big balls and began to roll the balls forward. Everyone clapped wildly. The animals that brought so much terror to us seemed completely tame and cooperative with their commanders. At the final curtain, all the animals ran around the stage taking a bow to rapturous applause.

After that day, we did not see Baba for a while because he left for Kampala the following day. To this day, that night was engraved in our minds as the moment that Baba had a temporary change of heart. It was as if he was taking a little break before destroying everything he ever worked so hard to build.

Broken Time

As far as children go, Wairimu was a gift to my parents. She was modest, obedient and responsible. Whenever our parents were out, she took care of us. She was full of love and duty. When Maitu left, she instantly stepped into her shoes, making sure we were fed, washed and dressed in clean cloths, plaiting my hair despite the trouble I gave her.

When Maitu left, she took no possessions. She had no money, no clothes and no way of starting again. Despite being only a teenager, Wairimu recognized that Maitu was in dire straits and needed her help. The day Baba left for Kampala, Wairimu would go to the pantry and get busy reorganizing the food he bought for the house. She would split the bags of flour in half, rice, cooking oil, bar soaps, beans, everything. She would pack every item into a sack, fasten it with a rope and leave it by the door ready for the following morning. At the crack of dawn, she would carry the load on her back, walking and hitchhiking until she got to Nairobi. Once in Nairobi, she would walk across town to the bus station where she would catch the country bus to Thogoto. She would arrive at Cucu Herina's and Maitu's hut bearing the sack of food and half of the money Baba left us. She would barely have time to have a drink of water before catching the country bus back to Nairobi, walking across town to the bus stop outside Nation Newspaper, getting into another matatu to Banana Hill, where she would walk and hitchhike back home in time to cook our supper. That was how she maintained Maitu in the darkest of her days. Although Wairimu was exhausted when she returned from her mission, she still had to cook our dinner and get us ready for bed.

Wairimu thought of everything. With Maitu gone and Baba spending all his time in Kampala, it became Wairimu's job to handle and think about parental duties. On the first day of the year, she would organise us to be together, playing and singing together, because she believed that if we started the first day of the year happy, it would set a precedent for the rest of the year. On Sunday, she made sure we were up on time to walk the 2 kilometres to church. After church she would herd us back safely home, cook for us and make sure we were clean. She would turn on the TV and we relaxed, watching *Soul Train* followed by *Different Strokes* and other Sunday family extravaganzas.

It took eight long years after we applied to the Kenya Telecommunication for a telephone and we were the lucky ones. There were people who waited for a landline so long that mobiles phones were thought of, designed, tested and rolled out whilst they were still on the waiting list. Our house was so remote, it would take a long time to install the posts and cables, they told my parents. That, combined with the unnecessary difficulties put in place to necessitate bribes, guaranteed it would be an eternity before we got our telephone. Finally, the lorry turned up our drive one afternoon with the remainder of the posts and cabling. Once they were securely in the ground, the phone could be installed. It was a shiny cream dial telephone. It was a great shame we didn't know any telephone numbers, but we promised ourselves we would ask around. That night, however, Baba came home with a padlock, which he secured on the last dial, locking the hopes of ever being able to use the phone. We aspirated our quiet disapproval. Maitu had not been around for that moment to see the phone she craved so much.

It was Wairimu's friend who brought the sparkle back when he showed us how to operate a padlocked telephone. It turns out many parents had no intention of allowing their children on the telephones.

'Instead of dialling a number, just tap the ringer several times to match the number you want to dial,' he said. 'If you want to dial nine, tap the ringer nine times and the call goes through.' He opened up a new world for us. Other children rang our number on the off chance there would be children willing to chat. We rang random numbers and when children answered it, we chatted to them. Some of those children became our virtual friends; we rang each other several times a week but never met them. That is how we met Kim. He would ring our house or we rang his house. He told us they lived in Thika, a short distance from Nairobi, and that his father owned a haulage company. We all spent many hours speaking to him on the phone, he telling us all sorts of stories.

We used the telephone freely whenever Baba was out without having to explain the huge phone bills; after all, the phone was locked with Baba being the only key holder.

It was Wairimu who introduced us to cakes when she did home economics at school. After the first term, she came home and baked the first cake in our oven. It was the most delicious thing I had ever tasted. She began baking biscuits too, but they didn't taste like the ones Baba used to buy in a box to be eaten at 4 pm with tea. What Wairimu baked were cookies, which I didn't particularly like. It was Wairimu who introduced birthday celebrations into our family. People generally didn't care much to remember the dates they were born. Most rarely remembered their age let alone celebrated a birthday. I remember one time, she asked a friend to drive her to my school with a beautiful cake she had baked for me and when she got out of the car, the candles were lit as she sang me 'Happy Birthday'.

It was Wairimu who taught us to make jelly. At boarding school, we had jelly after lunch but Wairimu taught us how to make it mixing it with passion fruit and bananas.

It was Wairimu who backed Kui into a corner and insisted she tell Maitu and Cucu Herina what she knew during Maitu's kangaroo court in front of the neighbours. Wairimu was the one who had to cope with being in the same school with Kui after Kui split our parents up. She was the one who borrowed five hundred shillings from a friend to help Maitu start a little kiosk selling fruit and veg before she got a job in the General Hospital. It was Wairimu who reported a teacher who used to touch young children inappropriately, leading her to be expelled from the Swahili primary school she attended, therefore joining us in Githatha primary.

But even the nicest, kindest, most patient person has a breaking point. Wairimu was only just a teenager when she became our guardian and Baba's maid. She cooked, washed ours and his clothes by hand. When Baba was back from Kampala, she had to iron all of Baba's enormous collection of colour-coded shirts using the charcoal iron, which was impossible to control. You had to start ironing at the right temperature just as the charcoal was turning into embers. If the charcoal was flaming red, you'd burn the clothes to a crisp; if most ash had fallen off the iron, it would be too cold to iron Baba's cotton shirts. When ironing, she was careful to save some of the embers to start a fire later for cooking if the gas cylinder was empty.

When Baba got home, he expected the food to be served to him like Maitu used to, and he'd inspect all his shirts for creases. If anything was amiss, Wairimu would get a beating. It was her job too to plait my hair by force because I hated my hair being plaited, but she didn't want me going to boarding school with unkempt hair.

Wairimu was sure of her place in the sibling hierarchy. In one of his rare relapses of kindness, Baba bought Wairimu a Timex watch, which she loved to wear. He had probably bought it for her so she could do all her chores on time. Mungai and I were busy playing at the back of the house one day when Wairimu called out to us.

'Who dropped my watch?' she asked angrily.

'The screen is broken.'

'It wasn't me,' Mungai yelled as he loaded all the prisoners into his squash bottle, to prevent them from escaping. It took hours collecting different coloured insects, ranging from ladybirds to dung beetles and grasshoppers.

'Was it you, Njambi?' she yelled back.

'Not me,' I replied, capturing a few more escapees.

Hours later Wairimu yelled to come into the house to wash.

'Mungai, you wash first,' she instructed Mungai. She had heated the water on the charcoal burner before transferring it into the big blue plastic basin. There was rarely any hot water because the tank storing water heated by the solar panels was for Baba's bathroom only and we had to heat our own.

'Why do I always have to go first?' he protested.

'Because I said so,' replied Wairimu. Mungai hated washing himself. Wairimu pulled his arm and pushed him into the bathroom. She stood outside the bathroom door waiting for water to start splashing. When the door opened a few minutes later she was still standing at the door, wised to Mungai's tactics.

'Go back and wash yourself,' she yelled. It was barely two minutes of splashing himself with water running down his still dirty legs before Mungai emerged again from the bathroom. Then it was my turn. At least the water was still clean.

When Baba came home that night, everything was as it should be: dinner was ready at the table, we were clean, well, some of us, and his shirts were ironed. He walked over to the TV and felt the back before turning it on.

It was around this time that Baba was walking round his coffee bushes when he heard muffled sounds coming from one of the terraces. It sounded like crying.

Curious, Baba walked to the end of the row, down the path to where the sounds came from. To his surprise, Munyau was crying into his handkerchief, his shoulders heaving up and down.

'Whatever is the matter Munyau?' Baba asked, full of concern. Munyau jumped to his feet, embarrassed at being found in that state by Baba. He took his hoe and carried on digging.

'It's nothing, Baba Wairiumu, please forgive me.' Baba walked over to him took the hoe from him.

'It takes a lot to make a grown man cry. What is wrong, maybe I can help?' That made Munyau stop crying, thinking about what Baba said.

'It's my boy, Kioko. He passed his CPE with top marks,' he wept.

'That is great news, I cry when my children fail but you cry when your boy does well,' Baba conversed.

'That's the problem. He passed with the highest marks in the country and has been called to attend Alliance High school,' he cried even louder. Baba was now totally lost. Alliance was the best school in the country, Munyau should have been very proud of his son, not heartbroken.

'Please explain why that makes you so sad?' Baba queried. Munyau could not control himself.

'I am a peasant, I will never afford to pay the school fees for my boy, let alone buy him the uniform.' He wept very loudly now. Baba now saw the problem.

Baba would have given anything for his children to go to Alliance High school and he had the money. It was ironic that it was his worker whose son got into Alliance yet he had no money to educate him.

'Don't cry, good man, your son will go to school.' With that, Baba paid for all Kioko's education fees.

* * * *

It was a few days later at dinner when Baba's gaze fixed on Wairimu's stretched-out arm with a frown on his face.

'What happened to your watch?' he barked.

'I left it in the bathroom and when I went back it was on the floor with the glass shattered,' she replied, placing the serving dish on the table to explain herself. Baba's lips tightened, like they always did when he was angry, but he carried on eating, stuffing big portions of food into his mouth. Worms and butterflies crawled and fluttered in my stomach. We all became very stiff. We knew how situations like this ended. A deathly silence in the room, the clink clank of the cutlery adding to the chill in the air. When he finished eating, he pushed the chair back with such force the scraping on the floor made us jump. He walked to his chair and sat down for a minute without switching the TV on. We carried on eating, listening to his heavy breathing.

'Mungai!'

240

'Yes, Baba,' Mungai answered, his voice quavering.

'Come here.' Mungai took the long way round the dining table, walking slowly, hoping to delay the inevitable as much as possible, before standing at my father's feet.

'Who broke your sister's watch?' Baba asked in a stern voice.

'It wasn't me, Baba, I have never even seen the watch. I don't even know what it looks like.' He hurried his defence. Silence.

'Njambi, come here.' I nearly jumped out of my skin. I froze. I could feel warm liquid trickling down my leg. I hesitated, deciding on whether to go to the toilet or go to Baba.

'I said come here!' he barked, full of irritation. I walked slowly, following the route Mungai took, rubbing my thighs together to stop the warm liquid trickling down my leg. I knew I was innocent. I had not seen or touched Wairimu's watch.

'Did you break your sister's watch?'

'*Cha tinie*—its not me,' I replied.

'One of you must have dropped it! The watch doesn't have legs. Which one of you did it?'

'It's not me, I haven't even seen the watch,' we both protested our innocence tearfully.

'Shut up,' he yelled. 'Mungai, it was either you in your curiosity to find out how it works, or it was you Njambi because of your jealousy,' he concluded. I

241

swallowed hard, feeling angered at being called jealous. I had not yet experienced jealousy as an emotion but I knew it was a very bad thing. I had heard Maitu and Cucu Herina speak of jealous women or men and the destructive acts they performed. I was not jealous.

'Go get a stick!' he interrupted my thoughts. My lips arched downwards, tears streaming down my cheeks, whimpering. We headed to the door and into the night in search of a stick. Stemper, our dog, came outside whimpering too, joining in our misery.

Despite our fear of the dark, the fear of going back into the house was greater. 'Hurry up!' Baba howled from inside.

We handed him our sticks, stood back and waited for instructions. He stood up and walked closer to the lantern to inspect the quality of the sticks. Satisfied, he bent over, moved the coffee tables out of the way and pointed to where we should kneel down. He placed one stick down and began to walk towards me. My heart thumped so loudly, although I could not be sure if it was mine or Mungai's. I could feel his fear as if by telepathy, his prepubescent face scrunched up pitifully. I wanted to hold my little brother's hand and pull him away from the pain and the hurt.

'On your knees!' he barked, his red eyes glaring like he had been drinking. He was teetotal. In the dark light, the protuberances of his forehead looked like the peaked horns of the devil, the shadow of the stick with its branches taking the shape of a pitchfork. I closed my eyes so tightly for fear of seeing the ferocity of Baba's fury. It was ugly and spiteful, as if he was possessed by hellish demons. I refused to look the devil in the eye. I wanted the ground to open up and be sucked in by the molten lava deep beneath. He raised his hand and swung his arm, the stick making a deafening swash sound as it travelled at lightning speed on to my back. The force was so much, it wrapped itself round to my stomach. Hot scorching lava enveloped my body, leaving my back raw. The burning came in waves, spreading down the cheeks of my bottom, down to my thighs, calves, even my feet. The reverberation from the back of my throat came with so much force, I made an indescribable noise between a scream and a surprised shriek. It felt like forever until Mungai's scream came. He alternated between Mungai's back and my back, going back and forth as if fairness was the important element of his wrath and cruelty. Mungai's screech was distant and muffled, as if he was miles away. The room was spinning faster and faster, swallowing Mungai's scream into the molten lava.

'It wasn't me, please believe me.' His pleading got fainter and fainter as I floated on the magma, my body the colour of charcoal. Only involuntary whimpers escaped when no more noises came out of us.

Our ear-shattering screams must have echoed across the ridges and beyond. Even Stemper wailed. With every stroke of the cane came a wail, back and forth, until the first stick was spent. He paused to get the next stick. The biting sting now shifted to my calves because my dress was beginning to soak through with blood. We writhed on the floor, trying to shield exposed areas of our bodies. Even our feet stung. He was frenzied like a mad dog. Wairimu and Wainaina were crying, 'Baba, don't kill them.' A loud bang on the door stopped him. It was Munyau, the dim light only picking out his teeth and eyes, making him look like a squirrel behind the glass pane.

'*Ithe wa Wairimu, ni chau,*' he asked, begging in his native Kamba. Only then did Baba come out of his frenzy. He stopped, looked around the room as if he was in a trance, looked at the stick. The stick looked like a sugarcane after all the juice had been wrung out. It was a splintered mess. It was no longer green, but red. Covered in our blood. Mine and Mungai's blood. It was spent. He threw the stub on the floor and walked to his bedroom.

We lay on that floor for eternity. Too painful to move, every bit of our body biting with pain. We could not hear Wairimu's voice begging us to stop crying. We had no more breath left in us. That was when I felt it from deep within, welling up in my body. The deep, seething, raw hatred. Every sting, every burn was pure and concentrated hatred. Baba was a monster!

Wairimu's Wish

Photographs; a snapshot of a moment in time. A reminder, re-telling the story of that particular moment. When Wairimu arranged for the travelling photographer, Martin of Martin Photos, to come, she could never have predicted that that would be the last time we would ever have our pictures taken as the famous five. All Maitu and Baba's children together. That morning she had woken us up early, as she did on Sundays since Maitu left. It was as if by sticking to Maitu's tradition, she kept her around us. She made breakfast before setting off on the journey to the PCEA church on foot. The week before Christmas, Baba had taken us shopping for clothes. It was the first time he had taken us shopping for clothes for a very long time. It was as if he knew his days of responsibility for us were coming to an end and he wanted to buy us goodbye clothes.

On that day, I wore my new grey corduroy trousers, which were slightly flared at the bottom. Flares were in fashion. Kui and Wairimu wore matching corduroy flared trousers although in different colours: Wairimu's were black and Kui's were brown. They wore baggy shirts with drawstrings in the middle. Wairimu's shirt matched her black trousers whilst Kui's shirt was a duck egg blue. Mungai and Wainaina wore smart grey trousers and shirts. Wairimu and Kui carried their high-heeled shoes whilst I wore my clogs. The journey to church required sensible shoes because it was an obstacle course or triathlon. There would be a lot of walking, sometimes getting wet and sometimes, if we were lucky, we would get a ride. We would walk down the hill away from Githatha, leaving the road used by Baba whilst driving for a path that headed to the river. After crossing the river, we would walk up another hill all the way to the top and walk for about a kilometre before the next river and up another hill before emerging at the back entrance of Nazareth hospital. From Nazareth, we joined the tarmac to the small church made of corrugated iron. They were about to begin building the new church sometime that year having held several fund-raising events.

As if predetermined by the gods of fate, that would be the final journey to that church for all of us siblings. It was also important that we had made the journey in our brand-new Sunday best clothes. We sat in the usual place in the second row where we sang loudly, always out of tune. Singing was our favourite. Reading of the scriptures was usually quite boring—that was about the time when I nodded off. The collection hymn was jovial. The thinking was that happy people were likely to donate more. When the service was over, we walked out, checking out everyone's Sunday best whilst others took in how stylish we looked. Baba was not with us because he had gone to Kampala. Maitu's departure had divided people: some felt sorry for her, but others wanted to remain friends with Baba, so refrained from asking of her. Most people ignored Kui, preferring to speak to Wairimu, who was doing a good job looking after all of us.

After church, we set off on the journey back home. Wairimu insisted we be extremely nice to each other since it was the first day of the year. When we arrived home, we ate food from the previous evening. Soon after lunch, we saw the familiar figure approaching from the horizon carrying his camera cases. It was Martin from Martin Photos. 'Quick, the photographer is here,' said Wairimu, jumping to her feet. We greeted him excitedly as he began to unpack his camera equipment. 'Get the sodas, quick,' called Wairimu. Each one of us ran to the house to collect our preferred soda to use as props for the pictures. I chose a Sprite, Kui and Mungai chose Fantas, whilst Wairimu and Wainaina chose Cokes. We had pictures taken at the front of the house by the veranda, at the back of the house by the steps leading to the kitchen and on the grass. Click click

click went Martin of Martin Photos; several rolls of film later we had exhausted every conceivable pose. When he was satisfied, he packed up, promising to come back the following week after developing the pictures. We spent the rest of the day watching Sunday night TV, which was the best all week. Apart from *The Famous Five*, *Soul Train* and *Different Strokes*, there was *Good Times* followed by the news and *Hart to Hart*. The day ended how Wairimu hoped it would. Laughter, love and family. To this day I am so grateful for those pictures, a bitter-sweet memory.

Mungai and Wainaina decided that photographs of his wedding would be taken by Martin of Martin photos. This was going to be a lovely touch and sure to bring back memories of how he captured our lives under Wairimu's loving guardianship.

Bus Stop Fracas

Wairimu reached her limit when Baba started bringing different women to our house. One woman in particular, who was only slightly older than Wairimu and who he eventually married. She slept in Maitu's side of the bed. Covered herself with Maitu's blankets. She even wore the clothes Maitu left behind. She began to befriend Maitu's friends. She walked around the house that Maitu built having counted the breeze blocks one by one on the 7 ton lorries. Wairimu had enough. She asked Baba if she could reside in the student halls of her college, to which he agreed.

One day when she was at the bus stop, she saw the woman whose-name-refuses-to-leave-my-mouth. As she walked past her, the woman said something rather sarcastic which left Wairimu blind with rage. Wairimu exploded. She told the gathering crowd 'that the thing in front of you is the one sleeping with my father in my mother's bed.' There were gasps of outrage. 'She uses the same bed sheets; I doubt if she washed them. She wears my mother's clothes, and she has no shame,' she continued.

'Shame on her,' shouted a woman from the group.

'That's not all, she treats my young brothers and sisters like orphans.'

'What a terrible woman,' yelled a mother with a baby on her back, twisting her lips in disgust. Other people spat with scorn.

'My father picked her up from the streets and lured her with chicken like a stray cat,' Wairimu continued sneering to laughter. She-whose-name-refuses-to-leave-my-mouth was green with embarrassment. She cowered, looking for an exit, but there was nowhere to hide from the accusing eyes. Wairimu, the prosecutor carried on.

'I hear she has sold my mother's plots which she paid for with money from her women's guild.'

'Aiii!' exclaimed the crowd.

'She is the definition of a slut.'

'You say it, sister,' helped another woman. Finally, Wairimu's friend ushered her away.

'She has learnt her lesson,' she said, walking off with her head held high as the crowd cheered her.

Exactly two days later, a policeman handed Maitu and Wairimu a subpoena to attend a hearing at the chief's office. When they arrived, both were very smartly dressed. Baba was already waiting with the chief.

'Mr Njogu, please tell us why you are here,' beckoned the chief.

'I am here because this girl abused my wife,' he replied, sounding rather lame.

'What's your relation to her?' enquired the chief.

'She is my eldest daughter.'

'And who is this?' the chief asked, pointing at Maitu.

'That's my wife, her mother.'

'Let me get this straight, you brought you daughter here because she abused her mother?'

'No,' corrected Baba. 'Her mother and I are separated, and she abused my girlfriend who lives with us now.'

'You brought a girlfriend to live with your teenage daughter in her mother's house and you are surprised your daughter abused her?' asked the chief.

'No, I would like my daughter to respect my girlfriend.'

'Let me stop you right there,' said Wairimu, standing on her feet. 'I have been a good daughter all my life. I have looked after your children, your home, cooked for you and done all your ironing and you bring me to the chief to get me to respect that rug you brought to Maitu's house, the house she built counting every breeze block on top of 7 ton lorries?' she paused. 'From today onwards, I am no longer your daughter because today my father died.' Baba drew a big breath in stunned disbelief. She turned round to Maitu and said, 'Come,

251

Maitu, let's go. Your husband is dead.' They walked out and shut the door behind them. The chief shrugged his shoulders, saying, 'I have real work to do. Close the door on your way out.'

The End of Term

Baba's lunacy did not end there. It extended to each one of us, at home and everywhere. It was the end of the term; all the children were packed, waiting for their parents. My friend Wanjiru spotted Baba's Toyota Hilux. I ran to one of the many windows of my dorm to see for myself. Sure enough, Baba was outside talking to Mungai's teacher Mr Job. 'He is always very playful in class,' said Mr Job. 'If he begins to focus, he will do well. Have a happy holiday.' With that he was gone.

Baba's mood had changed after talking to Mr Job. By the time Mungai and Wainaina ran to hug him, he was cold and angry.

'Your teacher says you play all the time in class.' Mungai froze.

'It's not true, he sees on me all the time and he doesn't like me.' Mungai did not finish his protestation before the slap knocked him off his feet. Baba was walking to the bushes to look for a stick. Breaking a branch from a plant and peeling off all the leaves, he commanded Mungai to lie on the grass. A few children and parents began to watch. Mungai was crying and protesting, his close friends looking on in horror. 'I said lie down,' ordered Baba. He lay on the grass, face down, as Baba began to whip him as if no one was watching. Seeing our parents was supposed to be a happy time. Baba's idea of fun became when we were sat in the corner trembling.

A Poisonous Game

Looking back, Kui's wickedness had always been there, but like a niggling symptom of a cancer, we simply ignored it. Mungai and I loved walking around the farm shirtless. We were investigators, studying every creature that moved in minuscule detail. We collected creatures, mainly insects because anything bigger was likely to do us harm. We knew to run away from snakes and avoid lizards, and as for safari ants, we had already learnt the sting of the bite and so kept well away from them. We collected different types of leaves for the potions we created for our prisoners. Mungai and I understood our game. Kui used to observe us from her bedroom window with interested curiosity. We discussed our theories with each other and did not seek anyone's opinion. One day Mungai and I were dipping our prisoners in the potions when Kui appeared out of nowhere, towering over us.

'Do you know this is the most powerful potion?'

she asked, holding two leaves, one in each hand. That captivated our interest, jumping up to have a look at the new leaves.

'What is it?' we asked curiously.

'I will give you one each if you say I am the queen.' 'You are the queen!' we said in unison, dying to take the new leaf.

'I am going to give you one each. Be careful, it's very strong, once you hold it you need to close your eyes immediately,' she instructed.

'Okay.' We held out our hands to receive the leaves.

'Hold it at the stalk, carefully.' We did as we were told. 'Now close your eyes, I am going to count to three. When I say three you rub the leaf on your breast quickly, at the same time. One, two, three,' she said, running away as we rubbed stinging nettles on our breasts, a sharp scream and crying from coming from us both.

Then there was the time she tricked us into climbing into the sisal basket. She placed the basket on the second step at the back of the house by the kitchen door. She instructed us to climb into the basket whilst she sat on the bottom step, supporting our weight. Once we were in the basket, she put the strap on her head like the women carrying heavy baskets to market. She stood up, her feet unstable from the weight, making her wobbly and stepping side to side. When she was steady on her feet, she began to walk down the hill towards the section of the farm we rarely went to because it was too steep and always felt secluded. She took us to the top of the terrace and offloaded us there. Once we were off her back, she ran in the direction of the house saying the *irimu*—the giant—was coming to get us. She knew we would panic and it would take us a while to get out of the basket. We struggled to get out, causing us to fall down the terracing. We ran home crying, fearful of the giant.

After Maitu's departure, Kui's affection for Baba increased tenfold. At dinner, she sat in Maitu's chair. She told Baba stories of her day and how she felt she was getting much better. Baba had completely lost interest in the family, least of all Kui's illness. Nothing she said would make him look up from his newspaper. Having witnessed Kui's actions at the meeting Baba had called during Maitu's trial, during which Maitu was condemned as an adulterer, he, like most people ignored her. They talked about her in gatherings as the evil child that condemned her own mother. 'She is possessed,' some concluded. Cucu Herina had rebuked her for her cruel act of betrayal against her own mother: 'You do not belong to the *mbari ya Herina*—Herina's clan,' she told her. Word of Kui's actions travelled far and wide. The whole of Riara Ridge knew that she stood up and spoke to the elders without reservation or shame in her accusation of her mother as an adulterer. Some began to speculate that she might have been in love with her own father and it was jealousy of her mother that drove her. The rumours reached Thogoto. All our relatives and friends and anyone that knew us who heard of Kui's action despised her. Most spat at the mention of her name and wished she would never return to Thogoto. She the bearer of evil. Cucu Herina said Kui's mouth would convince a new mother to hand over her newborn baby due to the composed way in which Kui had stood and denounced her mother. Everyone hated her.

Baba completely ignored her. It was if she was an object. He went past without so much as a glance. It was not clear whether Baba believed her lies, or they had come at a convenient time for Baba to have a legitimate reason to get rid Maitu, no one knew, but Kui's actions did little to endear her to Baba. Baba was now a free man without a wife to stop his womanising. Every night for months, Baba had brought home different women until he settled on She-whose-name-refuses-to-leave-my-mouth. She soon learnt of Kui's action which ended our parents' marriage. She viewed Kui as a threat to her relationship with Baba and she wanted to have nothing to do with her.

At her school, everyone knew what Kui had done. They called her *mukoma na ithe*—she who lays with her father. She got completely isolated by everyone. It was Wairimu who felt sorry for her and occasionally talked to her.

It's not clear whether she meant to do it or not, but speculation remains that she faked it. It was the beginning of the school holidays. Baba was in Kampala and She-whose-name-refuses-to-leave-my-mouth was now living with us. Her presence had taken the warmth out of our pink pebble-dashed house, creating a chill in the air.

It was mid-morning and everyone was busy doing one thing or another. Mungai and I were in the back, looking after our prisoners in the pink torso. We got distracted by Jane, our cow, who was grazing close by. She stopped and did a big splatter of poo, which led us to jump and run to the poo, sitting down around it like we always did. We loved watching the steam rising from the poo. Then we would listen for the familiar buzz of the dung beetles as they flew into the dung. We loved watching dung beetles at work. The boy beetles would get straight to work whilst the girl beetles sat on the edges watching. The boy beetles would begin to roll the dung into big balls.

It was big balls that girl beetles find attractive in boys. The boy with the biggest ball would attract his mate and they would begin their journey as a couple, using the Milky Way for navigation, living and lay their eggs in the poo. We were so engrossed in the dynamics of dung beetles that when we heard a huge crash coming from the direction of the garage, we jumped up in fright.

We ran to the garage but the garage door was locked. We ran round to the front through the living room door and to the corridor that led to the garage. Everyone arrived there at the same time. She-whose-name-refuses-to-leave-my-mouth was the first on the scene; Mungai, Wainaina and I next. Munyau had run with us but had waited at the door because he never came into our house.

The garage looked like it had been burgled. Everything from the shelves was on the floor. It looked like the top shelf had collapsed and everything come crashing down. We could not figure out what had caused the commotion. We turned round and looked in Wainaina's and Mungai's bedroom. There was nothing. We feared it might have been a thief. We looked in Baba's bedroom, left unlocked because She-whose-name-refuses-to-leave-my-mouth was sleeping there. Nothing. We looked in Wairimu's bedroom followed by Kui's and my bedroom. Still nothing. We went to the bathroom, kitchen and living room. There was nowhere else. It was then we looked at Cucu Nyambura's door. It was the room that was separate from the rest of the bedrooms.

Munyau, who was stood by the living room door, looked on curiously. Our faces told him we were too frightened to open the door for fear that a thief might be hiding. He being the man opened the door, kicking it in like an action hero. On the floor we saw someone lying motionlessly and when we moved closer we saw it was Kui. We stared at her, wondering what she was doing on the floor. It was a long time since she'd had a seizure. As a matter of fact, Kui had not been ill since Maitu had left. Now we stared at her full of panicked concern. Next to her was a jerry can of pesticide which Baba used to pour into his pump before spraying it on the coffee bushes. We stood there trying to figure out what had happened.

'Oh no!' said Wainaina. 'She has drunk poison like Kinuthia. Look it's on the floor!' he shouted in a panic.

A few months prior, some children from Githatha had trespassed through our farm in a great hurry.

'Where are you going?', we had asked them.

'To a funeral, do you want to come?' We had never been to a funeral before and actually did not know what a funeral was. Our curiosity led us to say yes and we followed the group to the funeral. The funeral was on the northern ridge. We hurried down the hill and climbed up to the northern ridge where we could see a crowd already gathered. They were staring at a box when we arrived. Kui had told us that in the box was a dead body. Mungai and I were a bit frightened. We walked forward holding hands and leant over to have a look. It was the body of a boy probably the same age as Wairimu. He was dressed in a dark suit and his eyes were shut like he was sleeping. His skin was not the usual glossy black colour but a chalky white. There were white things in his ears and in his nose. Someone had sprayed a can of perfume popular at the time called *binti el Sudan*, which they kept spraying. Kui told us that the white things were cotton wool to keep maggots out of his body.

Now Kui lay motionless on the floor, her legs spread out with the occasional twitch. She-whose-name-refuses-to-leave-my-mouth just stood there, a sinister smile on her face. 'Let's take her to the hospital please,' cried Wainaina, full of panic. 'Our Kui is going to die.' She did not flinch. She stood there smiling. 'Help, Munyau, please help,' we called to Munyau to do something. He looked about timidly; farm workers were not permitted to enter the house. Wainaina opened the door which had swung back as if closed whilst Munyau lifted Kui into his arms, calling her name, 'Wangui, Wangui.' When she was securely in his arms he walked out of the door and began running as fast as he could down the hill to the neighbour whose car we always borrowed when Baba was away in Kampala. We watched him disappear down the hill and waited until we could see him walking up the hill on the other side of the ridge.

We heard no news about Kui. When Baba returned from Kampala, we told him about Kui's suicide attempt and how Munyau had taken her to Nazareth hospital. He walked calmly to his yellow velvet chair and sat down, closed his eyes and began to hum to the tune of

'If you change your mind' by ABBA, blaring out of the three in one ghetto blaster, but said nothing.

Kui was in hospital for months with no visits from anyone. She had recovered a long time ago, there just wasn't anyone interested in going to visit her or find out about her wellbeing. I guess she had cried wolf for so long, draining people's sympathy and patience. Some people speculated that she had not drunk the pesticides and was only seeking attention. None of my family members cared to verify the truth. People in Thogoto had no compassion for her; in Riara Ridge people thought she got what she deserved for backstabbing her mother who had struggled for so long with her 'illness'.

As always, it was Wairimu who felt sympathy for her and seeing that Kui could not continue to stay in the hospital. She asked a friend to drive her to the hospital to check on her. Wairimu found her looking gaunt from lack of food. The hospital wouldn't release her until the humongous bill was paid but there was no one to pay the bill; Baba's words were 'let her rot in there.' Wairimu knew that Kui could not live in a hospital endlessly and so came up with a plan to get her out. Wairimu would keep watch on the nurses, and when there was no one around Kui would jump out of the window and run behind the kitchen and exit the hospital from the back gate. She would trespass through people's farms and find her way to the front by the main road, out of sight of security, where she would find Wairimu waiting in the car with her friend. The plan worked and finally they were driving off with Kui in the back seat. That was just the beginning of Kui's problem. Where would she go?

Wairimu asked her friend to drive her to Chief Mwangi's house in the hope that he could persuade Baba to forgive her and take her back; besides, they could not think of anywhere else to take her. Chief Mwangi was in no mood for housing a traitor as he called her, stating that his was a Christian family and there was no place for a devil child. Thogoto was out of the question since everyone there had expressed their hatred for Kui. Wairimu sat in the car trying to find a solution; her friend was getting impatient and needed to go.

'We have no choice but take you back to Baba's house,' she said finally.

It was dusk when Wairimu and her friend dropped Kui at Baba's house. She stopped briefly to say hello to us but did not want Baba to find her there, so they sped off. It was the first time we had seen Kui in months. We did not know how to be with her. She had brought so much pain and suffering to our family but in a strange way we still loved her, she was after all our sister. We didn't talk much but she ate supper hungrily then waited to face her predicament.

The tension was immense as we waited for Baba to return. She-whose-name-refuses-to-leave-my-mouth had gone to her mother's and we had been left under the supervision of Munyau. Our ears pricked up when we heard the distant drone of the car from the other side of the ridge. All our hearts thumped loudly as we waited in anticipation. Kui was sweating profusely, sweat dripping from her temples. As the engine sound got closer and halted, our fear of the repercussions of Kui's presence grew. Everyone and everything was frozen. We heard keys in the door and Baba walked in.

For a moment, he tried to figure out why we looked like the sunken hull of a ship. And then he saw her. His eyes reddened. His nostrils puffed out, his fists clenching in a robotic fashion.

'I said I never wanted to see you again. I am going to close my eyes and count to three and by the time I open my eyes, I want you out of here forever.' He closed his eyes and we watched to see what Kui would do. She was frozen on the spot and did not move. Upon opening his eyes and seeing her still standing there, he strode to her all tensed up like the Incredible Hulk. She jumped and cowered under the table, crawling to the opposite side. Baba threw the chairs out of his way one by one. Kui sneaked from under the table and bolted towards the open door, running as fast as she could in the direction the car had come from, disappearing down the hill. Baba threw a few more chairs out of the way and headed towards where Kui had gone.

'Do not ever come back here!' he yelled. That was

how Kui left Baba's house for the last time. With that he closed the door, turning the key. Like Cain, whose jealousy led him to slay his brother Abel in the bible, Kui's selfishness and jealousy of our parents' attention had led her to destroy herself and her family. Her actions had led her to be cast out into the wilderness. Like the cancerous tumour that lies deep in the body, she had unleashed her malignancy leaving no one unscathed. Like a severed tumour, she was discarded to rot.

We walked to the table and began arranging the chairs. Not knowing what to do, we sat at the table with our books pretending to read. Baba watched TV, breathing heavily. Since Wairimu and Kui had left, it was I who had taken over the role of housekeeper. I had completely forgotten to cook with all the events of the evening. I only remembered when Baba yelled, 'Where is my dinner?' Then I ran to the kitchen and began to cook ugali, because he liked his ugali freshly cooked.

That night, I lay in my bed wondering what would become of Kui. No matter how angry I was with her, I still wished her well. She had lost all her family and I wondered where she would live.

My Crime

Our pink pebble-dashed house lost its mojo. It felt cold, like the morning chill of the month of July. Crickets and grasshoppers seemed to have taken a vow of silence. Even the sun's rays couldn't penetrate the blanket of gloom in our home. The whole place was awash with melancholy. Every time I saw her walk out of the bedroom that Baba and Maitu used to share, I felt my body transpose into a ghostly form which would lift me from the ground. I would feel my hands circle round her throat, slowly throttling the life out of her until she collapsed on the floor. It was only when she slammed the door shut that I would emerge from my reverie. I despised everything about her, even the air she breathed out of her nose; I could sense it long after she left. Her legs were fat. Fat all the way from her ankles, leading to her arse, which was too flat for an African woman. The only protrusion from her back was the girth of her shoulder, which appeared to carry the weight that should have been on her arse. At the front, the most prominent feature was her nose. It was a big, fat, long nose, which looked like Pinocchio's after he told too many lies. I am almost certain the reason her nose was so long was because of the lies she told. She even forgot to mention to Baba that she had other children, pretending they were her siblings when they went to visit her family. It was only when she was sure that she was pregnant with Baba's child that she came clean, about one child.

After Wairimu and Kui left Baba's house, I was now what Wairimu used to be. I looked after my brothers. I didn't like the way she scolded them, especially Wainaina. So I stopped speaking to her. I remained in my room most of the days when I was home from boarding school. We also had a new maid who tried to befriend me but I was now a hormonal teenager. I had no interest in talking to the maid.

One day, I was busy looking for something. I looked everywhere but it was nowhere to be found. I went into my old room, which I had shared with Kui but was now the maid's room since I slept in Wairimu's old room. I looked everywhere but I could not find what I was looking for. I was about to exit the room when I thought I should look under the bed. I knelt, lifted the bedspread and peered underneath the bed. My attention was immediately drawn by seeing the sleeve of my favourite turquoise jacket with Kawasaki stickers on it.

It had been given to me by Wanjiru, my best friend at primary school. I frowned, wondering how my jacket had got into the suitcase under the bed. I pulled the suitcase out to take my jacket. When I opened the lid of the suitcase, it was a treasure trove of stolen items. Baba's shirts were in the suitcase, She-whose-name-refuses-to-leave-my-mouth's bras and petticoats, Wainaina and Mungai's trousers, my shoes and other miscellaneous items. I gasped in disbelief. I ran to Baba's door, knocking loudly. I was expecting She-whose-name-refuses-to-leave-my-mouth to answer the door because I knew Baba was in Kampala. I could hear her coming, her heavy feet stamping as she walked to the door, then the door swung open. I was the last person she expected to see. She stared at me, a confused look on her face.

'Come look at the maid's case,' I told her urgently. She reached in her pockets and pulled out a rock, broke a bit which she put in her mouth whilst stuffing the rest in her pocket. I had noticed this peculiar behaviour; she collected soil and rock which she kept in her pockets to crumble under her teeth throughout the day. It was also making her fatter. I had noticed she had put on a lot of weight. Now she followed me to the maid's room with disinterest where the suitcase still lay open. She peered into the case, her eyebrows rising at the realization of the findings.

'She is a thief!' she exclaimed, leaning over to shuffle through the find. 'Go call her,' she said. I ran outside through the garage door, where maid was bent over a basin washing clothes by the tap. I asked her to come inside. She straightened up, wiped her hands on her dress and followed me through the garage doors, down the corridor to the room that she slept in.

When she saw She-whose-name-refuses-to-leave-my-mouth standing over her suitcase, overflowing with our things, her face clouded over with embarrassment. She had been caught stealing. She began unwrapping her *rithu* because she must have known the punishment for stealing was loss of job.

'You must leave at once,' She-whose-name-refuses-to-leave-my-mouth announced. We emptied our things out of the suitcase and she was gone.

It was a few days later, when Baba and She-whose-name-refuses-to-leave-my-mouth arrived home to find we had fallen asleep on the sofas whilst watching WWF. She had read the letter in the post box addressed to her, which stated that everything in the suitcase had been acquired legitimately and that I had sold the items to her. And, seeing an opportunity to get rid of me, she had taken the maid's word. I had protested to Baba about my innocence before he began punching and kicking me. It was then I saw an object hurtling towards me then blacked out.

* * * *

270

After I ran away, Mungai and Wainaina were questioned about my disappearance. They denied any knowledge, claiming they woke up in the morning to find I was gone. They continued to live with Baba and She-whose-name-refuses-to-leave-my-mouth. Mungai began to take education very seriously with astounding results. He was no longer the carefree playful child he had been. Our family breakdown seemed to have matured him. There was no one to mother him and this must have made him responsible for himself. He also began playing tennis, becoming a top seed in the under 18s. He passed his A levels with top marks, securing a place at Moi University. At a different time, Baba would have been overjoyed with Mungai's achievement, but She-whose-name-refuses-to-leave-my-mouth had done everything to discredit us so Mungai's achievement was met with disinterest. As for Wainaina, She-whose-name-refuses-to-leave-my-mouth made sure she stopped his education, claiming he would not benefit from further education. There was a time when this would have been unthinkable to Baba but now it seemed we were not the most important people in his life anymore. To this day my bitterness for Wainaina's loss is as raw as ever. All those years Baba had bribed the headmistress of Musa Gitau, it was his dream that his children should get the best education money could buy. She had not only taken away Wainaina's future, but also took away a bit of Baba's dream. Wainaina became a workman like Munyau, tilling the land until one day Wairimu sent someone to the farm to call Wainaina, who was busy digging terraces. The stranger told Wainaina that someone in a car on the other side of the ridge wanted to speak to him. He washed his hands in the river before following the stranger. When he got to the car, he saw the person in the car was Wairimu wearing a wig and sunglasses. 'Get in the car, bro, I am taking you to London.' And with that, all of Maitu's children were gone leaving our pink pebble-dashed house behind.

The Grass Gets Greener

In the meantime, Maitu and Dr. Okello from the General Hospital had fallen in love. He was posted to London to further his medical specialism. He was kind, loving and looked after Maitu and me well, and when the time came, we all boarded a flight to begin our life in London.

PART TWO

PART TWO

The Reunion

I looked forward to Wainaina's wedding with cautious trepidation. The wedding threw chaos into all of our lives, reigniting all those memories we'd suppressed. We had moved on in the best way we could but now were forced to delve into our past; opening old wounds. We were like unexploded dynamites that could go off anytime threatening Wainaina's big day. I, for one could not trust myself. The memories of our lives, the fear I felt at the start of every day hoping I had not done anything wrong. This haunted me to this day. First thing every morning I search my brain as to what I did the night before that would cause me trouble. Never allowing myself to really be happy because I would be awaiting retribution. Every time I thought of the wedding, I felt like I would spontaneously combust. My anger grew by the day. Baba's mistreatment was beyond reprieve. He had destroyed our lives leaving deep trauma which had no cure. No one had ever made him accountable for his actions. I needed justice or at least some sort of moral compensation for all the pain and hurt he caused. I felt unable to deal with my emotions. That's when the thought came to me. If only I could meet Baba, I could look him in the eye tell him of the pain, fear of the beatings, the image that haunted me of the object hurtling towards me. He had to be accountable for his actions. I was now a grown woman full of anger. The least he could do was give me my answers. This became my objective. We had to clear the air before the wedding. I flew to Nairobi the week before and procrastinated about ringing him. I finally summoned up courage and made the call.

The conversation with Baba was strange but better than I expected. I had carried the burden for so long with so much anger and when I finally spoke to him, words failed me. I wondered if he would agree to meet up and discuss what we should have discussed a long time ago. I arranged to meet him three days before Wainaina's wedding in the New Stanley, the place he and I had shared a meal when he took me shopping for my boarding school kit list, one of the few happy memories I had with Baba. I must have subconsciously hoped this would recapture that moment so many years ago. The other reason I booked a table at the exclusive restaurant was to show my father that this girl—this girl he had nearly killed—was doing just fine. I longed to make him feel insignificant. I had to prove to him that despite his neglect, I was doing well for myself. Yet another part of me craved his acceptance. I wanted him to be proud of my achievements. I wanted to say that although I did not become a lawyer working in the highrise buildings in Nairobi, I had acquired a degree and had worked in a highrise building in London. Not only that, I had become a comedian traveling all over making people of all backgrounds laugh. Yes, I was as daring as he had been traveling all the way to Kampala in uncharted waters far away from home. I wanted to tell him of my beautiful daughters, of their father and how we were as a family. I would have done anything to see the beaming smile of pride, he had every time he read my report card.

After the phone call, I felt nervous, but hopeful, encouraged by the conversation. I had waited so long for the moment I would come face to face with him. The call went some way to diffusing my anger. During our years of estrangement, I sometimes went over in my head what I would say to him if I ever came face to face with him. I would yell and scream at him as no words ever came to my mind that would encompass my anguish, but during the phone conversation I just mumbled my words and ended up informally inviting him to meet up. I never imagined in my wildest dreams that our paths would cross again. In my minds eye, I thought my father had realized what he had done to us was wrong. The only reason he had never reached out to us was because he was busy and never had a chance. I was now giving him a chance. I felt that he would apologise, gather me into his arms and weep for the loss of our relationship like he wept for his dead baby son. Only this time he would apologise for all that he did to me. To us.

On the day, as I stood waiting to be seated, that meal during my shopping trip with Baba was all I could think about. I had been so excited but now I felt like a nervous wreck. I was angry and fearful at the same time.

A disinterested waiter showed me to my seat when he was certain no important white people needed serving. Little had changed since I stood there waiting with Baba. There were still white people being fussed about whilst I was barely getting a look in. The only noticeable difference was there were now more tables occupied by smartly dressed black people. I was shown to a table in the corner where I waited for Baba to arrive. The thought of seeing him made my palms wet with sweat. Bob Marley was playing on the speakers, 'Everything's gonna be alright', and why wouldn't it be? My father had had a lifetime to reflect on his actions and by now, surely, he would be sorry. I was deep in thought when I saw him walk in through the door. He looked older, balder and darker than I remembered him. He had not lost his sense of style, wearing a three-piece grey suit. He had half a smile as I stood up to go and meet him but froze on my tracks when I saw the unmistakable nose behind him. He had thought it necessary to bring Her-whose-name-refuses-to-leave-my-mouth. Even her sister tagged along. They were followed by five other unmistakable noses, *their* children who I had never met. The sheer sight of Her-whose-name-refuses-to-leave-my-mouth with her entourage made me queasy. I could not believe my eyes. Of all the scenarios that had played in my mind, this was not one of them. I had not prepared myself for this scenario! I looked towards the door contemplating my escape.

I had booked a small table in the corner, out of the way in case Baba and his apologies got too loud. The clones rushed towards me before spreading their tentacles around me.

'We are very pleased to finally meet our older sister,' one snorted. 'You look younger in person, Wainaina showed us your pictures. You are very light skinned; do you bleach your skin or is it lack of sunshine in Scotland?' I felt suffocated, weighted down by the same foggy gloom that masked the three trees one ridge away from our home in Riara Ridge, when I run away to Cucu Herina's house. It felt all consuming. Claustrophobic! I tried to see clearly but it persisted.

'I live in London and no! I don't bleach my skin,' I muttered under my breath, struggling to pull myself away from their grip. The air around me was thinning and I couldn't breathe. Everything was becoming blurred and I was sure I could collapse at any given moment. The waiter found us a big table for our 'family reunion.'

I could not believe Baba would be so inconsiderate. The man had the audacity to bring them to our reconciliation meeting. I sat down as my knees felt weak. The daughters scrambled to sit on either side of me. Baba chose to seat two seats away from me so he couldn't look directly at me. She-whose-name-refuses-to-leave-my-mouth sat next to Baba. She stared at me with great interest. Unable to help herself she reached over the table, stretched her hand out and felt my hair. 'Is it all your hair?' I recoiled. The waiter handed out the menus. All I could do was lift my finger and point without much thought. Everything was whirling around me. At one-point Baba's eyes and my eyes locked. For a split second, I thought I detected a small sign of remorse before he was interrupted. 'What do you want,' she nudged him. I had told Baba on the phone that I would be treating him to the meal. 'My treat,' I had boasted. Now they were taking advantage of the free meal, ordering the most expensive things on the menu. Someone wanted T-bone steak, others wanted sea bass, since they didn't fancy tilapia, the local fish. Someone was asking for a wine list. 'Bitch, you've never even drunk wine before,' I thought to myself. I barely ate. I felt ambushed, cornered and resentful. This was not what I had in mind. How could I have been so naïve as to imagine that Baba had acquired some decency? How could he be so insensitive? All I wanted to do was get up and run. Run and never stop. Like the night I ran away from his home, never to see him again. But what about Wainaina's wedding? I couldn't bear the thought of seeing him again. And them. The waiter handed me the bill. I knew that meeting up with my father would make me cry, but not as much as I did when I paid for the bill.

The Wedding

The cock crowed a little louder, waking the hills surrounding Riara Ridge. The skies were clear. The roads were lined with banana plants. The butcher's knives were sharpened. Goats bleated solemnly, their big yellow teeth grinding sweet potato leaves loudly as if to hush the honing steel. The rolling pins flattened the bread. Wrappers fastened tightly around the generous waists of the cooking women. The stew in large pots bubbled away. It was promising to be quite a feast. Today was a big day. Wainaina was the last of the Pathetic Three to be getting married. Mungai, his brother's keeper had organised the wedding with meticulous precision. As always, he had risen to the occasion. Trying to keep things together for his older brother. There were to be armed guards at the venue not because he feared the tensions would get out of hand, but there had been reports of armed robbers targeting weddings and funerals. The wedding guests naturally assumed it was to stop the family tearing each other apart. We had all been briefed on where we would be seated and that we should refrain from anything that would ruin Wainaina's day. Wairimu was heart-broken by the decision to invite Baba and she could not reconcile herself to attend the wedding. I, on the other hand, felt incapable of missing Wainaina's wedding. I had prayed for resilience. 'It's about Wainaina,' Mungai had urged. It was not what I would have imagined Wainaina's wedding to be. She-whose-name-refuses-to-leave-my-mouth had found a way to manipulate Wainaina. Not only was she coming to the wedding, but her daughters were bridesmaids too. She was on the wedding organising committee. It pained me to see how involved she was with Wainaina's affairs when she had shown nothing but disregard for him when he needed her most. She had treated him like an orphaned farm boy, giving him scraps of food.

The flight from London to Nairobi had been long and I fell asleep in a bad position. When I woke up in Nairobi my back was in agony, but there was no chance I'd be able to see a physiotherapist before the wedding. On the morning of the wedding I got up at five am to do my yoga stretches, took a dose of paracetamol and things were holding up. I was managing just fine.

Our car arrived as the buses of boisterous women from the groom's side came to claim the bride at the entrance of the bride's house, as was the custom. After months of negotiation, the bride price had been agreed and the wedding could proceed. The elders would be provided with copious amounts of alcohol; there would be livestock and money. An immaculate white Range Rover decorated with orange and yellow ribbons waited at the side of the road to drive the bride.

Orange and white roses were arranged neatly and fastened to the bonnet. The driver listened to gospel music, turning it down as the women alighted the bus, singing, '*Muhiki wanyu mwega mwega, ehubite mahua, na nguo yake njega njega, na nyumba yake njega njega*—the nice nice bride, with her flowers and nice nice dress, and her nice nice house,' signalling our arrival to the bride's family. The women now gathered and crowded around the gate. The chorister began.

Huti guku—knock here.

The others joined in.

Huti guku—knock here.
Kwa nyina was Maritha ii—It's Mama Maritha's house.
Huti guku—knock here.

They took a few steps forward, stopped to gyrate their hips, then moved forward singing the wedding song, urging the bride's family to let them in. The calling

286

song was repeated, accompanied by the horns of the waiting vehicles. The gates opened and the bride's women greeted them by gyrating their hips to the chorus but not joining in. After several calls the bride's women welcomed their visitors, who gyrated in, each carrying gifts which were handed to the bride's women. The bride's women and the groom's women were in agreement. The stockpile of gifts looked respectable. The bride was ready. Now it was the turn of the bride's women to sing their gratitude, with permission for the groom's women to take their bride. She was now leaving home. She gyrated to whistles and cries of encouragement. Her maids clapped, joining in the dance. *'Arrririririririiririririririrrriiiiie!'* went the cry of celebration. The party danced victoriously to the waiting vehicles.

As our car sped down Riara Road, I caught a glimpse of the PCEA church in the cloud of red dust created by the wedding motorcade. I remembered the last time we had attended the church under the guardianship of Wairimu on the first of January all those years ago. If only time had stood still. I felt a pang of bitterness at what our lives had become. I remembered how we had posed for the photographs as Martin of Martin Photos had clicked away. Then, I could never have predicted that the next time I entered that church I would be full of indescribable pain and bitterness.

The loud onslaught of horns approaching notified

the guests of the bride's arrival. They had come in the hundreds. When I asked Wainiana how many guests were expected, he had replied, 'Approximately one hundred to four hundred and fifty.' I had laughed, replying that was not an estimation but a calculation of high interest from an unscrupulous moneylender. He was way off the mark, it was more like seven hundred.

* * * *

The compound was already filling up when our car pulled up at the gates flanked by armed guards. Several coaches were already parked in the vast gravel carpark, having ferried guests from Thogoto, Nakuru (the bride's home) and Githatha. Guests had filed out and many were chatting in the compound, some hugging one another. The driver of Maitu's car was just parking when we arrived, having come straight from accompanying the women collecting the bride. I walked over to Maitu, complimenting her on how beautiful she looked in the red wool skirt and matching top I had brought her from London. Her maid squeezed out of the car, running to the boot to collect her wheelchair. Once Maitu was in the wheelchair, her maid walked round to the other side of the car and assisted auntie Wanjiku, leading her to where the wheelchair stood. She then took auntie Wanjiku's hand, placed it on the wheelchair, then placed her hand on top of auntie's hand and began to push the wheelchair.

'Is Tata alright?' I queried, puzzled by the maid's actions.

'She lost her marbles ages ago,' the maid replied in a matter of fact way. I stood back at the shock of the news.

Auntie Wanjiku had seemed very odd to me when I saw her at Maitu's house the day after we arrived from London. She had been cold towards me, as if she had not recognised me. I had been surprised by her indifference but I had become distracted with chatting to my cousins and hadn't thought any further on the issue. As a child, I was always struck by her beauty. She was tall, dark, very slender and elegant. Although she was a modest woman wearing cheap clothes, she had the type of beauty that made her radiant even if she wore a sack. Now her beautiful face was transformed by the mask of dementia that had also afflicted Cucu Herina.

I was overcome by great sadness at the thought of Cucu Herina. I had not seen her for several years after moving to London. Maitu and I had been shopping when we got a call from Thogoto telling us of her death. We were distraught at the timing as we were unable to attend her funeral, because it was on my graduation day. It was bittersweet that she would be buried on the day I completed my education. She was an educated woman who read her bible confidently. She would have been very proud to see me graduate. It was as if she had lived long enough to know I would be ok. Maitu and I had held special prayers on the day of her funeral, wishing her a safe journey. The last time I had seen Cucu Herina she too had not recognised me and lived in a perpetual parallel reality, only engaging with those from her past, most of who were dead. I had taken photos of her with my Nikon but found those photos to be heart-breaking because it was no longer Cucu Herina the comedian in them. Now auntie Wanjiku wore the same mask that I had seen on Cucu Herina. It filled my heart with sorrow.

Unlike auntie Wanjiku, Maitu was physically frail, her neck and limbs stiff from the medication she took for her Parkinson's tremor. What Maitu lacked in mobility, she made up for in sharpness of mind. She had the mind of a detective. Nothing missed her eye. She often attracted my attention by tugging on my dress and pulling it down. Once I leaned over, the grip of her hand encircling my wrist was of steel and nothing would prise it off. Not even handcuffs matched her grip. From her low position in the wheelchair, her hawk's eye missed nothing. It was her stiff finger that highlighted a few wedding guests who arrived in Chief Mwangi's bus, smirking at how all the children bore the same striking resemblance to the chief. It was her finger that pointed out her old colleague the Cook from the hospital, who sat her big thighs very close to the undertaker,

Mr Mbugua. I smiled knowingly at the thought that my guardians had finally got together.

Now Maitu's stiff hand encircled my hand, pulling me down. I leaned over to hear what she had to say, '*Ngui icio nicikinyite?*—are those dogs here?' she stammered. Sensing the acid in her tongue, I laughed, adjusting her dark-rimmed spectacles, hoping to neutralise things.

'They are everywhere Mum, but this is going to be a celebration not only for Wainaina's wedding but for us. We survived, despite everything,' I reassured her. I felt my heart constrict with sadness, wishing Wairimu had come to the wedding.

'It was too painful,' she had said, bitterly. 'I don't think I will be able to contain myself if I see that devil,' she had stated angrily.

* * * *

The sun shone unblinkingly as if to dry out the animosity amongst the guests. We congregated around the entrance of the wedding venue. The gardens were beautifully manicured enclosed by neatly trimmed hedges—a glorious location indeed. There were white marquees on either side of the field. The plethora of ushers and bridesmaids brought colour to the lush green grass and shrubbery that surrounded the wedding field. The ushers wore navy suits with crisp white shirts and orange cravats. The bridesmaids wore fluorescent orange chiffon and satin dresses held in at the waist by olive green satin bands. Overworked hairdressers whose swollen feet cried for rest had worked late until every head was braided with skilful Maasai twists, their oiled scalps now glistening in the sun. Their olive eye shadow shimmered, drawing one's gaze to their thin, kohl-lined eyebrows.

The bride was now in the possession of the groom's family, who brought her to the grounds singing loudly. The drivers in the car park responded by honking their car horns, creating an air of jubilation. The dancing women from the groom's side now merged with the maids and ushers. We danced to the corner of the gardens where there were rows of chairs arranged neatly draped with white fabric, with orange and olive bows. The bows matched the orange flowers on the arch that marked the entrance to the chapel-style seating and bridesmaids' dresses. That was where the exchange of the rings would take place. She-whose-name-refuses-to-leave-my-mouth was amongst the women shaking her humongous hips in a way that only a hypocrite would, gyrating down the entrance towards the makeshift chapel. Seeing her there amongst the other women filled me with anger but still I gyrated my hips, seeking inner peace. She smiled broadly. Her daughters fussed busily in their bridesmaids' dresses, referring to Wainaina as their brother.

We stopped at the arch. Then women sang proudly.

> *Ukiona njukite guku muthenya uyu ni munene*—if you see me here today it's because it's a big day.

Everybody joined in.

> *Ukiona njukite guku muthenya uyu ni munene*—if you see me here today it's because it's a big day.
> *Ukiona Muthoni guku menya in muthenya munene*—If you see Muthoni here know it's a big day.
> *Hanini*—a little,

sang the crowd.

> *Tucoke thutha*—let's move back,
> *Hanini*—a little,

replied the crowd.

> *Nitugue na urio*—lean to the right
> *Hanini*—a little,

replied the crowd.

The line of women from the groom's side edged

closer, stopping at the arch that led down the satin corridor. The bride moved forward. She was joined by her parents linking arms on either side. They were giving her away jointly. Little bridesmaids wearing white chiffon dresses, holding baskets of flowers followed them. A little bridesmaid walked over holding the bride's train as they walked down the white satin carpet to the front where Wainaina waited. He had urged Mungai to keep an eye on him in case he fell asleep. We laughed heartily to see Wainaina joking on his wedding day.

The dutiful ushers led the older bridesmaids to their seats at the front. When all the bridesmaids were seated, I walked with Maitu's wheelchair towards the front. Everyone had already taken their seats, now placing hats, umbrellas and newspapers on their heads to shield themselves from the intensity of the Kenyan sun. Cousin Ngige, his brothers and their families were all seated. Auntie Wanjiku seemed to have a moment of clarity when she saw her son Ngige and walked towards him, her tall elegant lean body defying her age. The only giveaway to the severity of her condition was her inability to see the objects she walked into. It was as if auntie Wanjiku's soul had died, leaving her body to wander aimlessly like a zombie. We walked on the other side of the chairs, careful not to ruin the arrangements with Maitu's wheelchair, parking it next to her maid and auntie Wanjiku. I sat next to Maitu.

Wainaina and his best man wore pristine white suits,

their heads turned, waiting anxiously at the makeshift altar. I wanted to stand up, not to miss anything, but I remained seated. He was now a man about to take a bride. He looked handsome and I was proud of my older brother. He tried hard to appear confident but for a fleeting second he gave Baba a quick look as if to seek his approval. I felt his vulnerability. Everyone stood as the bride strode hand in hand with her parents. I turned to look at the bride, and my eyes locked with Mrs Kimani's. Suddenly, I could hear Wairimu's lone voice at that sports day, '*jugu karanga ni moja kwa penni*—the peanut is one for a penny,' the humiliation I felt for her that day still fresh. My lips tightened uncontrollably, the ends curling down. It is the non-verbal way of saying 'f*** you'.

The wedding guests sat according to the order of arrival or their loyalties. It appeared that people took sides a long time ago, establishing their allegiance: those that supported Maitu and those that supported Baba. The people from Thogoto sat on one side, with people from Riara Ridge sitting on the opposite side, resembling rival football fans kept away from each other. Maitu and I were surrounded by our close family and friends from Thogoto and her colleagues from the General Hospital.

'Njambi!' A big slap on my back. I let out a scream, thinking things were kicking off. The whole time I had been on edge expecting violence to erupt at any minute, it was almost laughable. Mungai, who was at the front, turned round with a troubled look on his face. The group from Thogoto all turned round, expecting trouble. It was Maitu's sister auntie Kabui, who had arrived late and could not wait to talk to me. She was delighted to see me after so many years. She hugged me tightly, swaying from side to side. Tears welled up in my eyes, partly from joy but mainly from the pain of being slapped on my bad back. She held me tightly. Tears rolled down my face; I definitely needed more paracetamol.

When I met up with Baba at the reunion, I had brought him a gift. Baba loved beautiful clothes and I thought it might be a way of opening our reconciliation. The gift was a beige suit with a matching waistcoat and pink cravat. I had chosen it with nervous expectation, remembering the suit he wore when we went shopping for my boarding school kit list. After our bitterly disappointing reunion, I had merely handed him the present before walking out, fighting away tears. Now I looked over to where he sat, guided by the huge yellow headdress worn by She-whose-name-refuses-to-leave-my-mouth. Baba's bald head was visible, glistening in the sun as he turned to face Wainaina and his bride, who had now joined him. Baba wore my suit. For some reason this surprised me. I don't know what I had expected. I wished I would have been happier or prouder to see him wearing the only gift I have ever bought him. Instead I felt conned. I had seen him briefly when we arrived. I was planning on avoiding him, but he had seen me. I hadn't even tried to see him again after that disastrous meal. 'I am the best dressed man at this wedding,' he beamed. I said nothing.

* * * *

The priestess wore a garish crimson pink outfit with a matching hat with flowers on the rim. She was a stranger who had been introduced to Mungai and Wainaina by Baba. She was accompanied by her husband, who was a preacher too. These days' husbands and wives team up to preach, usually in assembly halls full of thousands of people. They are now the celebrities in Kenya, with most commanding more wealth and fame than politicians. No self-respecting preacher or priestess travels in a cheap car, with most choosing top spec Range Rovers, which is surprising because to the Gikuyu, the Land Rover—the Range Rover's predecessor—represents our oppression, being the vehicle that was driven by the colonialists as they beat, and ran over locals or carried them to jails. For the older generation this must add salt to the wounds. Higher profile preachers and priestess usually opt for helicopters—after all, they are burdened with delivering prayers to God, hence the appropriate mode of transport.

'Let us pray,' she began, necks creaking to bow. She

began by thanking God for Wainaina and his bride, her husband shouted, 'Amen.' She thanked God for the beautiful day he had chosen to bring together everyone in the name of love. She clearly did not know of our family history.

After the first hymn, the priestess called for Wainaina's mother to come forward and the bride's mother too. I got up, ready to push Maitu's wheelchair to the front. I heard gasps of astonishment and when I looked up, I felt like I had been hit by a hammer of steel across my face. I blinked to have a better look. Stood next to Wainaina was none other than She-whose-name-refuses-to-leave-my-mouth. Like a bull provoked by a daring matador, I could feel my body puffing up in rage. In the motion of an enraged bull about to charge, I kicked off my nine-inch Kurt Geiger shoes. I unlocked the brakes of Maitu's wheelchair and taking long powerful strides on the warm grass I charged forward. How dare she disrespect Maitu in front of all the guests? The people from Thogoto gasped with their mouths wide open. I pressed forward, seeing red flashing before me. All the pent-up anger I had suppressed over the years now emerged in waves, like the boiling water sprayed out of a geyser rising from the hot earth. I got to the front row, turned the wheel and was about to charge when I saw the horror on Mungai's face. He had the look of fear I'd seen the night Baba beat us for breaking Wairimu's watch. He shook his head at me beggingly to stop. I looked at Wainaina. Suddenly the little boy hopping around the school playground after kicking the stone with all the children dying with laughter pointing at him flashed before me. My head was about to explode. I couldn't move. Ngige, seeing the impending disaster, had rushed up behind me and now put his hand on my shoulder, nudging me away, guiding the wheelchair back to our seats. I turned round to look at Maitu. Her face was defeated. She wore a grimace, big round tears streaming down her face. The sound on the loudspeaker brought us back to the ceremony.

'We are gathered here today,' the priestess began. I felt Maitu's hand twitch as she went on to mention the witnessing by Wainaina's parents on this glorious day. I felt Maitu's pain. It was as if a razor was slicing through her heart slowly. She looked like a broken woman. Like the woman who sat in my school field under the *mugumo* tree on the day she knocked on my class door all bruised up. Like that day, I lacked words to console her. Then I remembered. '*There was once a man who travelled a long distance in the blazing hot sun,*' I whispered into her ear, masking the proceedings of the wedding. '*By midday of his third day on the road, he was very thirsty and could not walk any further to find a stream,*' Maitu listened, squeezing tightly on to my hand, I, sensing the helplessness she felt.

The gods had colluded to humiliate Maitu in front of all these people. This was compounded by her disease which had crippled her making her incapable of fighting like she once did. This was a cruel twist of fate seeking to degrade Maitu. I wanted to fight Maitu's battle. Like she had fought for me when I ran away from Baba's house. I wanted to champion her cause, but I couldn't ruin Wainaina's wedding. This was the only moment he had ever had to shine. I would not be the one to take it away from him. I was overcome by bitterness.

The woman who had mistreated Wainaina as a child now stood up as his mother, knowing that Wainaina's mother was present. Baba did not have a moral compass to hold his wife back or he simply was oblivious to what causes human suffering. Despite of all the pain he inflicted on us, he still had no self awareness of the misery he brought us. Still I carried on, willing all the strength in my body. '*He sat by the side of the road trying to catch his breath,*' I spoke in unison with the priestess as if possessed by prayer. '*When he noticed a drop of water coming from above. The traveller could hardly believe his luck at finding water,*' I spoke louder, people of Thogoto tuning in. '*He quickly reached for his gourd and held it out to trap the water. Drop by drop it began to fill up. With every drop, he got thirstier. When he had collected enough, he raised the gourd to his lips, about to take a sip.*'

'If anyone here knows any reason why these two should not be wed in holy matrimony, speak now or forever hold your peace,' carried on the priestess, everyone holding their breath. 'Aah,' a voice came from the back. Heads spun round, Mungai jumping to his feet. The armed guards stood to attention, ready to lend their services. 'Chiow!' went the sneeze. But I persisted. '*Just then a big crow swooped down, knocking the gourd from his hand. It fell on to hard rock and broke into small pieces.*' As if hearing my chanting the priestess's husband said, 'Amen,' wiping his forehead which was beading with perspiration. She was about to proceed when the police chief jumped to his feet. Deathly silence. Mungai was on his feet again, looking like he was having a heart attack. Everyone held their breath. I carried on. '*The traveller wailed as the liquid quickly evaporated in the hot sun. "Noooo, you damn bird," he cursed, "what I'm I to do now?" When he looked up, he had an idea. He would climb up the rock face to the source of the water and there he would quench his thirst.*' The police chief reached into his pocket, pulling out his phone, and began to take pictures, a big smile on his face. Relief. I did not stop. '*He got up and began to climb the rock face using every ounce of his strength until he was at the top.*' The priestess, sensing the tensions in the room, spoke very fast and so did I. '*When he got there, he saw a huge serpent spread across the rock, its mouth wide open, venomous saliva dripping out of the mouth. He stopped, realising that the bird had saved his life.*'

'No one objects.'

'Whilst he was up there, he saw down below on the other side an oasis plenty of water and beautiful plants.'

'I now pronounce you husband and wife,' finished the priestess. Just like that Wainaina was married. People clapped, if only to release the tension.

The Phone Call

I was back in London soon after the wedding. I was angry at Maitu's humiliation at Wainaina's wedding and Baba's refusal to address the issues I wanted to speak about. He had brought his entire family to the reunion to act as a shield. I tried to convince myself that the anger in me would recede. My encounters with my father both during the reunion and the wedding had opened the deep wounds that lay weeping, begging for acceptance. For years, I prayed that one day our family would be reunited again. Someone definitely answered my prayers and Wainaina's wedding certainly brought our family back together again, albeit with baggage. What I now felt was profound anger and resentment at Baba's lack of remorse or even understanding of what his actions had done to us, his children and our mother. I had to find a way of living with the bitter anger that consumed me for the days that followed. I tried even harder to push all the feelings back into the

Pandora's box where they lived before the wedding but to no avail. There was no way out. Everything that had happened both during the reunion, wedding and in my childhood swashed around my head like dirty laundry in the washing machine. I decided to confront Baba; it was the only way I could finally get the truth from him. Why had he treated us with such contempt? Why did he neglect his duties? Why could he not control his anger like a normal human being? Why had he destroyed all our lives, ruining our ability to be normal functioning humans? If I loathed him before, I loathed him tenfold now. All these questions rang around in my head. He was a grown man who refused to take control of his destiny. His refusal to acknowledge his deeds left me seething. It was his life choices that had brought me to this predicament. Like a zombie, I picked up the phone and rang his number.

The phone rang only once before he picked it up. 'Hello, can I help you?' I hadn't thought exactly how the conversation was going to go. Like the girl I was many years ago wearing my pink nightdress, my heart was pounding. I wiped my sweaty hands on my denims.

'Hello?' he said again.

'Hello,' I replied with hesitation. 'It's me, it's Njambi.'

'Gacambi wa Maitu.' His voice transformed into something deeply warm and soothing. He always called me Gacambi, daughter of my mother, when he was in a good mood. This confused my emotions. I was ready to explode but his tone neutralised my anger. The day a long time ago when he took me shopping for my boarding school kit list, he had held my hand and called me 'Gacambi Wa Maitu.' I was named after his older sister Tata Njambi, whom he nicknamed Gacambi. My whole body relaxed. It was like nothing had ever happened between us. Baba was talking to me, referring to me by my pet name. I had to remind myself why I had rung him. We spoke about my flight back to London and the weather.

'I would like to talk to you, privately,' I added, gathering courage and careful not to ruin the harmony between us. It was important that I do this. The last weeks had been of wretched bitterness and self-destructive thoughts. This was going to be the therapy I needed.

'I would like that,' he said much to my surprise.

'I am coming to Nairobi at the end of the month and I would like us to sit down and talk.' Somewhere cheap, I thought to myself. He would be paying his own way after the last time.

'Save the 24th in your diary,' I said finally.

When I hung up, I was pleasantly surprised and relieved at the course the conversation had taken. It was nothing like I expected. In a strange sort of way, I was overcome by a sense of peace. Maybe my father and I would find peace again. Maybe he and I could

have a relationship like we were meant to have before
Kui's illness and before the wealth and success changed
Baba and took him away from us. Maybe Baba and I
would become foodies together, just like we did that
day in New Stanley restaurant. That night, for the first
time since the wedding, I slept soundly.

Wairimu's Interruption

It was Wairimu who informed me. I was in the middle of teaching my antenatal class and thoroughly enjoying the group. It was my first session with them and we were just warming to each other. They wanted to know everything about having a baby. I was making my mark. They laughed at my usual jokes: 'When the midwife says to you, let me have a look at your cervix, I don't want you to panic and say I haven't got one.' They laughed. '...obviously I will not be able to demonstrate perineal massage.' They laughed again, but don't be fooled, these groups tend to be highly intelligent individuals. I had already established that one of them was an actress, and would find out later that morning that one man had been posted to London three weeks earlier as a foreign correspondent for the *Washington Post* and his wife was very close to giving birth to their first child. There was the woman whose father was born in Naivasha and who travels to Kenya frequently. She had come over to me during the break and we had a lovely chat about Kenya. She did PR for a tour company based in Northern Kenya. We talked with disgust about the licence that had been purchased in Texas which would allow rich Americans to shoot the black rhino in Namibia. We despaired about King Juan Carlos of Spain and his love for hunting elephants. Elephants that will probably become extinct during our lifetime, we shrugged. This group was going to be fun. After having my daughters, I couldn't bare to leave them in the care of anyone else. My time in boarding school had taught me so much. The value of childhood and the need to maintain the parental bond. I remembered the indescribable feeling of missing Maitu, the longing to be in her arms, having to wait months to see her. I couldn't do that to my children. I had found myself unable to work before finally quitting my IT job. I retrained to work as an antenatal teacher which meant I could see my children all the time apart from the Saturday when I left them with my husband whom they adored. They loved playing football in the park with him, having late breakfast in Starvin Marvins before cycling back home in time for my arrival.

It was about 12:15pm, a cold Saturday in January in Finsbury Park. The group was engaged, keen and eager. They had a multitude of questions already. 'Are you saying it's okay to ask a doctor or midwife questions about procedures they suggest?' asked one man. I was just about to respond to his question when the phone rang. It was only 2½ hours into the session. I hesitated, but I had decided a long time ago never to ignore a phone call. The last time I had ignored a phone call a few years ago I had learnt a great lesson. Maitu had fallen whilst going for a walk in the park and could not get up and was in great distress. We were to learn later that this was the onset of her Parkinson's disease. I decided then that I would never ignore any calls whilst teaching, irrespective of the caller.

I walked over to the table where the phone was vibrating. It was Wairimu calling. 'Are you ok?' I asked her in English, a signal that I was teaching. Our conversations are usually in Gikuyu. She mumbled something. Not the usual, 'Ah, you are teaching, I will call you later.' I repeated the question, reinforcing the signal that I was in front of a group, teaching. But this time she very flatly stated, 'Njogu is Dead.'

I must have understood what she said because I let out a noise that I cannot describe. I hung up and walked to the board as if to carry on teaching. I didn't think the group had noticed anything. But one of the men asked me, 'Everything ok?'

'No,' I replied and burst out crying. And then I just said it. 'My father's died.' The group stood up, not knowing how to react to my news. No one really knew what to do. I could not compose myself. Someone suggested that we take a break and I said, 'Good idea.' The actress walked over to me and hugged me. Up until now I had been in charge; now the class were like lost sheep, walking about in disarray. They had relied on me to give instructions but now I was weeping away. It was then that someone suggested going to lunch. I thought that was a good idea too and it would give me an hour to compose myself. I ran to the toilet and was now crying very loudly. I grabbed some tissues and began walking back to the room I was teaching in. The American man was waiting for his wife, who had popped into the toilet. He put his hand on my shoulder. I cried even more. His wife came over to me and I shifted into her arms. I buried my face in her coat and wept.

'I will stay here with you,' said her husband. They walked me back to the room and offered me a seat and some water. It was then that he decided that the class was finished and I was in no fit state to teach. From then on, he took charge, ringing my husband and asking him to come and collect me as they would not let me drive home. His wife informed the rest of the group of the decision and contacted the course organiser for a replacement teacher. I was touched by this American couple and the way they dealt with my grief. The British couples had been concerned but they politely kept their distance as though they did not want to interfere. It seemed like hours before my husband arrived. I waived the couple goodbye and they gave me a sympathetic wave. They emailed me later that evening to see how I was doing. I will never forget their kindness.

I wanted to go straight to Wairimu's and my husband understood. She would be the one to console me as she had become like a mother figure to me. I sat in her small and comfortable if not too crowded flat and cried and talked and cried. I could not decide whether to go to the funeral or not. By the time I got home, Wairimu had checked the diaspora website for the death announcement and she quickly informed me to check it out as she and I were not mentioned as his children. She was ok with that; as a matter of fact, she had already told my brothers she wanted no part of it. But no one had bothered to check *my* views on it. I guess I wouldn't have cared if Wainaina's wedding had not happened. I was furious and I immediately rang Wainaina, reprimanding him for placing the advert. Did he not know I was just about to find peace with my father? Now he had died, presumably to get out of talking to me.

By the following morning, I was all over the place. I decided to ring She-whose-name-refuses-to-leave-my-mouth. To this day, I have trouble referring to her as my stepmother, let alone speaking with her. Everything changed following this conversation. I was hysterical. She handed the phone over to her daughter, who had moved into our house in Riara Ridge soon after her mother began living with Baba. She was not my father's daughter. She cried as she told me the details of Baba's death. He had suffered a brain haemorrhage. He had gone to work on the farm, walking around his coffee bushes. I thought of him as a young man, full of hope that his green gold would bring him untold riches. It had been a bitter disappointment, just like the break-up of our family, living in our pink pebble-dashed house on top of the hill in Riara Ridge. His financial decline began soon after I left home. His business in Kampala became obsolete as everybody began to trade. Selling essentials was no longer lucrative. He had collapsed whilst pruning his coffee bushes, his escape, and was rushed to Nazareth hospital where was Kui once admitted after her suicide attempt. They moved him to Aga Khan teaching hospital for emergency surgery. He woke briefly when his surgeon came on the ward round. 'Ithe Wa Wairimu,' the surgeon had addressed him. 'I don't know if you remember me? My father is Munyau, he worked on your farm and you paid for my education.' Baba smiled with recognition of Kioko. 'You did well, my son.' His eyes closed. It was Kioko who held Baba's hand tightly as life twitched out of his body. Like his father Munyau, he was there at a profound moment in Baba's life. If it wasn't for Munyau, Baba might have killed anyone of us. It was like he was a guardian angel for Baba and now he had sent his son to guide Baba into the next life.

The Eulogy

The Pastor eulogised Baba's life. It took the best part of an hour, Maitu and her children barely getting a mention. I listened intently, resting my chin on the palm of my hand, wishing my throbbing headache would go away, as he recounted my father's early years. The usual embellishments followed, exaggerating his love and kindness to his fellow humans. I could not see Maitu's face but could only imagine her sneer, dying to spit at the niceties. Her head stooped low as she sank into her wheelchair. The illness had shrunk her body, now barely recognisable. Her head always drooped nowadays, reminding me of my daughters—who were very small as babies in their car seats when they could not hold their heads up. Thankfully, Maitu's brain was still as sharp as ever. I could almost hear her snigger as the Pastor talked of my father's life at his relative Chief Mwangi's home and what a great family they were.

'There was a time when Njogu would never have

been allowed to set foot in the place he called home,' the Pastor continued. 'Who could have foreseen that one day his children would be sat face to face with the aggressor, as equals?'

'Just what did he mean?' I began to ask myself. Who were these aggressors? And why wouldn't Baba be allowed to come to Riara Ridge? I promised myself that I would speak to the Pastor after the service, but the proceedings overtook me. I watched thoughtfully as they loaded my father's coffin into a matatu, whose main job was to ferry harassed passengers to and fro, but today it served as a hearse. Maybe it was symbolic of the chaotic way Baba had led his life.

Baba's face was a ghostly grey when I peered through the glass of the coffin earlier that morning. His coffin had rested on a trolley in the courtyard of the mortuary, which created privacy for the mourners. Through my swollen, tear-filled eyes, I spotted a scrawny grey kitten whose faint meow was wasted on this group. I felt sorry that it should be condemned to a life in the mortuary compound. A woman came over to me and patted my shoulder and hugged me. Together we cried.

I placed my hand on the glass and stared at his face. He had a moustache, which I found to be curious because he had never grown a beard all the years I knew him. There was no need for the glass to shield the living from the dead. There is already an invisible barrier between our world and one which we mere mortals will never understand; no matter how much we try, we can never comprehend death. His eyes were wide shut, almost symbolic of the finality of death. *That was convenient, wasn't it?* was all I could think. His stature appeared even smaller, unlike the devil that had towered over me that night, wielding a stick as he beat Mungai and I to oblivion. Now he looked pathetic and frail. We must have stood there for more than a minute because Mungai came over, put his arm around me and ushered us away. He was keen to keep the line of mourners filing past the coffin. Nothing must mess this carefully planned day. I was shocked by the intensity of my grief; so was Wairimu and indeed everyone else.

The drive back to Riara Ridge to bury Baba was bumpy. The dusty track had remained the same. When I got out of the car, I surveyed the home of my childhood. Mungai's and my play area was now surrounded by people—gravediggers. That was the site where Mungai and I had dismembered the imitation baby, the place we released our prisoners, the place we planted our pork sausages. They never grew, like our family they didn't possess essential ingredients to thrive. The grave diggers were already waiting for the coffin, still holding on to their shovels, the red soil forming a round mound clearly visible. I used to love moulding the red soil before I destroyed it with my urinary projection. That thought made me need the toilet. I looked across to the other side of the ridge to the place where Mujarewa had frightened us. It was the route we took when going to the peasant school and the way I climbed the night I left home.

I walked towards the main entrance of the living room, stopping to take it all in. I paused by the flowerbeds where we had posed holding our soda bottles, smiling at Martin of Martin Photos. I looked at the door leading to Cucu Nyambura's bedroom, the amalgamation of furniture, the cream phone still in the corner. Then my gaze became fixed. The black armchair. That black armchair that I sat on that night. The night Baba lifted the object that came hurtling towards me before I blacked out. I turned round and began to run.

'Njambi, hello, I guess we never met but I am your next-door neighbour. I saw you when you were very small after the fire that killed our workman's goat.' I stopped and spoke to him. I looked like a frightened animal. He guided me to the crowd gathering round the grave.

'The soil will go back to the soil,' the Pastor said, sprinkling soil into the coffin. Other close members of the family lifted the freshly dug soil, repeating 'the soil will go back to soil'. The man put soil in my hand and encouraged me to do it. 'Soil will go back to soil,' I mumbled. The blurred vision from my teary eyes of the acacia tree across the ridge made me wonder what had become of the leopard. Had it been caught and moved to a game reserve, or did the villagers take revenge for all the killings he had committed? I wondered what he thought of the comings and goings of our pink pebbled-dashed home as it disintegrated. The colour pink had faded, leaving bare concrete with steely coldness, just like our family.

The Pastor was already performing the last rituals, a few men pouring concrete on the casket. 'Wait!' I called, but my voice was drowned out by the women who began singing. *'wihoke mwathani rugendoini—* trust in God on the journey.' They didn't hear me! The shovels were already throwing heaps of soil onto the cemented coffin. I had a few questions that I needed to ask my father before they buried him, now swelling up with anger again. How could he? An old woman seeing my distress put her arm on my shoulder.

'Did you know him?' she asked.

'No!' I barked. 'I did not know him; he was after all my father.' What was wrong with me? She was just being kind. But Baba had taken the answers, what hope did I have now of gaining true peace? True understanding? I stood in dismay and mental exhaustion as the concrete cemented any hope of reconciliation.

'Why the concrete?' I asked Maitu's maid later as food was being served. Apparently grave robbers usually trolled the obituaries column looking for funerals and would dig up bodies to steal the coffin and the deceased's clothes. For the rest of the day, I felt nothing but numb resentment for my father. He was an egotistical, selfish, unpredictable bully, who had showed no remorse for the way he had treated my mother and us. What possessed him? Was it the witch doctor Kui spoke about? Was there any truth in it? I twisted my lips as I thought of Kui's role in breaking up our family. How I hated her!

PART THREE

Maitu and Baba

After Baba's death, my brain became a medley of old films of my life replaying in my head. I had to stop doing whatever I was doing to re-live the worst bits. Every time my brain landed on a happy memory of Baba doing something nice like taking us to the circus, the bad memory of the night of my trial would emerge. Images of Baba lifting the object which came hurtling towards me remained etched in my mind. I re-lived that moment, feeling the stifling fear I felt that night. The terror that compelled me to run for my life in the dead of night returned with every vision. It was as if there were competing forces taking control of my mind, and all my reality transporting me down a dark tunnel.

My nights were full of recurring nightmares, in particular the night Baba whipped every bit of mine and Mungai's bodies. I could see Mungai's little body writhing around on the floor. I would see his body going stiff and blood running out of his ears and mouth and before I knew it, I was drowning in Mungai's blood. I would scream, 'Mungai, wake up,' but he wouldn't wake up. I would wake up drenched in sweat, unable to move. The images were like a Saturday matinee replaying loudly in my head, refusing to let me go.

As months went by, my craving for answers grew like a mutating virus. I needed to find a resolution or some sort of closure. I needed the answers that Baba had taken to his grave. I needed to know what had made him such a monster. I hardly knew his relatives because he never spoke of them. Who were his parents? Why did he never mention them? Why would he not have been allowed to visit Riara Ridge, as the Pastor had said? For my own sanity's sake, I needed the answers.

That was when I began my research. The only relatives I could think of were Chief Mwangi, Baba's sister Tata Gacambi and his aunt Cucu Nyambura. I began by searching for their contacts, but that avenue went cold before I even began. Chief Mwangi and Cucu Nyambura had died soon after Wainaina's wedding. I contacted Tata Gacambi's son, who informed me that his mother was senile and did not recognise anyone, even him. I never expected it to be easy. It was going to be a long road. I resorted to contacting relatives in Thogoto who knew Baba in his early days. This turned out to be a hive of information. An interesting theme began to emerge. The villagers spoke of the conditions of the time, of Muru Wa Itina and *gatis*. What were those conditions? Who were Muru Wa Itina and *gatis*? It soon became clear that I needed to undertake wider academic research to understand the political and economic climate of the time. I realised the history of Kenya is well documented but only to interested parties such as the military and academics. The second generation Kenyans and subsequent ones seemed to be completely in the dark about how close the Gikuyu tribe came to being completely wiped out. I was lucky to find an old distant relative of Baba's who was 100 years old. Maitu, always a detective, became my main source of information. I began to ring her every day to collect information. During the night, I tried to process what Maitu and the villagers had told me. The Parkinson's disease that afflicted Maitu for ten years was taking its toll. She was frail and her speech was deteriorating very fast. Time was of the essence. Our conversations were recorded on my phone and on paper.

In my quest to discover Baba's life, I found Maitu's.

Making of a Poor African

Deep in the ridges, in the heartland of a district called Kiambu, in a place called Gatukuyu, Githunguri, a well-to-do man called Muhota celebrated the birth of his second son to one of his two wives around 1874. The boys, Ngige and Waiharo, grew up in the footsteps of their father, learning the trade of herding, crafts and land-clearing in accordance with the Gikuyu tradition. The Gikuyu were Bantu and industrious agriculturalists whose sole pride was farming. They were accomplished farmers and practised land-resting and crop rotation to maintain the integrity of the soil. Farming was in their blood; they knew and understood their land. They were mainly vegans, cultivating a plethora of provisions such as yam, cassava, arrowroot, sweet potatoes, greens, stinging nettle, green cabbage, pumpkin leaves, pumpkins, bananas, mangoes, loquats, wild berries, black eye beans and maize. Their societal structures and daily lives revolved around farming activities. Their seasons were defined by planting and harvesting. Major dance festivals, circumcisions, weddings and competitions took place after harvest.

The Muhota boys partook in the essential Gikuyu ceremonies but little did they know theirs would be the last generation to enjoy a way of life that had remained unchanged for centuries. By the age of eleven, whilst Waihairo and his younger brother Ngige tended their father's goats—which were used as currency and rarely eaten—on the rich highlands of the Central Province of Kenya, their future was already being carved out by European noblemen, thousands of miles away.

* * * *

At the behest of Portugal, Otto Von Bismarck the German Chancellor oversaw a hastily organised conference which began on 15th November 1884 and ended on 26th February 1885. The Berlin Conference sought clarification on European spheres of influence in Africa. These few aristocratic men gathered round a table late into the night, dwarfed by a huge map of Africa, and with a pen they superimposed borders on over three thousand tribes, dissecting whole kingdoms and binding arch-enemies, with indescribable repercussions. The borders determined the fate of Africans for centuries to come. None of these men had ever been to Africa. In attendance were representatives of fourteen countries but the key players were Germany, France, Italy, Spain, Britain, Belgium and Portugal. During the 'Scramble for Africa', as it became known in a gentleman's agreement, it was decided that France would take the countries in the West of Africa, Germany three countries in sub-Saharan Africa, Italy two countries in the north of Africa, Spain two countries in the north-west of Africa, Britain mainly the middle strip from Egypt to South Africa, Belgium the central Congo and Portugal two countries to the south of the equator; thus Kenya was declared a British protectorate. Her Majesty's agent and Counsel General A. H. Hardinge made a proclamation on the 1st July 1895 that he would take over the Central Province of Kenya as well as the coastal areas. Soon after, work began to build the Kenya–Uganda Railway. It was predicted to bring fortunes as they looted African resources when its construction began in 1896, but by its completion in 1901 had become a laughingstock branded as the Lunatic Express, having cost a total of £6.5 million. A workforce of eighty thousand Asians had been brought in from India, Pakistan and Bangladesh to build the railway, a quarter of whom died due to disease, exhaustion and the man-eating lions of Tsavo.

Having only become a man by way of circumcision in 1891, by now seventeen-year-old Waiharo was an eager-eyed teenager with an adventurous streak. He decided to go on an expedition, visiting relatives in Dagoretti and Thogoto, where he remained for several years. Whilst he was in Thogoto a ship docked in Mombasa, bringing several missionaries sent by the East African Scottish Mission. They set up a base in Kibwezi, 260 miles off the coast of Mombasa, an unfortunate choice due to its inhospitable climate and disease. All the missionaries died of disease except Dr Thomas Watson, a Scot from Dundee. Watson was weakened by disease and almost in despair because the Akamba people further south refused to believe his teachings of the gospel, declaring it a most improbable story. He made his way inland to Dagoretti. It was at that time that his and Waiharo's paths crossed at the new base in Thogoto. Watson employed Waiharo as a guide and watchman. This chance encounter would have long-lasting implications for the Muhota clan, to which I belong.

In order to marry, a Gikuyu man, with the help of his father, had to clear a plot of land, which would be given to his bride as an engagement present. Without land, a Gikuyu man could not marry, so Waiharo returned to his father's homestead to begin the process. The brothers both took wives around the same time. Ngige had one and Waiharo settled on three. Misfortune hit the family when Ngige died suddenly soon after his second child, a girl named Herina Wangui, was born. It was Muhota who discovered his son face down, dead. At the time, there were no burials; the Gikuyu believed in leaving the body out in the forest to nourish another life. Hyenas were tasked with hoovering up corpses all over the Gikuyu countryside. The Gikuyu tradition stipulated that if a woman's husband died, his brother would marry that woman, offering her protection and stability. After the cleansing ceremonies, Herina's mother Wanjiku, now a young widow, was assimilated into Waiharo's family, becoming his fourth wife. They bore a son, (*Guka*—grandfather) Mwaura, whose shop I used to visit in Thogoto.

Although other tribes were affected and had significant struggles against the British colonising mission in Kenya, it was the Gikuyu who bore the full brunt of it. Their fate was sealed by Sir Charles Elliott, the Commissioner of the British East Africa Protectorate in 1902 when he was sent to Kenya to conduct an assessment of the territory and the people. His conclusion was that the Central Province of Kenya, with its bright red soils and perfect climate, was easily the most beautiful and fertile place on earth, and therefore perfect for British habitation. His conclusion of the people was that 'Africans were lacking in each and every way,' and only useful as servants.

* * * *

The death of her young father Ngige was tragic but

330

a more sinister catastrophe loomed as Cucu Herina was being born in 1905. Her birth coincided with the arrival of five thousand white settlers in Mombasa following Elliot's proclamation, heeding to the British government's call for white inhabitants to occupy the Central Province of Kenya. Advertisements had been placed in London and South Africa. The respondents were disgruntled right-wing whites from South Africa, disinherited minor aristocrats from Britain and war veterans, all headed to claim their stake in the Central Province, whose very existence would make Cucu Herina's life and the Gikuyu impossibly impoverished. At the time, her family lived in the vast ridges of Githunguri in a traditional homestead. They had plenty to live on and life was beautiful.

Upon the arrival of the whites, the Central Province was renamed the 'White Highlands'. The White Highlands and the Rift Valley were also nicknamed the Happy Valley, which became a hedonistic haven for white settlers, many of whom were Eton- and Oxford-educated, and gained quite a reputation for their wild swinging and drug-induced orgies. The Gikuyu were expelled from their land to accommodate a handful of colonisers, losing nearly 60,000 acres of land.

From then henceforth, the Gikuyu were condemned to a life of destitution after being dispossessed and confined to the poorer, low-yielding lands in the reserves in Kiambu, Murang'a and Nyeri. These three districts were considered the Gikuyu heartland and were to become the home of the fiercest fighting during the Mau Mau uprising. Remnant Gikuyu farmers left in the Central Province were now to be referred to as squatters, settling 'illegally' on European lands.

The settlers, having learned of Gikuyu superstitions, spread rumours of a curse, which uprooted the Muhota family and many Gikuyu farmers. They fled, leaving their land to rid itself of the curse but intending on returning after several seasons, as was the tradition. When the Muhotas returned to their farm after a couple of seasons, they were chased away by the settlers, who claimed it to be their land. Cucu Herina and her family found themselves dispossessed and landless in Thogoto, now at the mercy of a Gikuyu landowner, Wabureti, who granted them a small plot to restart their lives only to evict them later. Without access to land, food became scarce.

The native reserves were now overcrowded, housing over a million people, most of whom were destitute. Disease spread like wildfire due to unhygienic conditions. It was in the Kiambu Reserve near the town of Kikuyu, in a place called Thogoto, that my parents made their home. By making the Gikuyu destitute, the white settlers now had plenty of desperate cheap labour to be abused and mistreated. All food crops were cleared from the Central Province to make way for cash crops and there was restriction of movement, with all Africans requiring passbooks. The colonial government put restrictions on food movements too. Everyone was required to hold a food permit, without which no food could be purchased. Acquiring a permit was an impossible task, and once acquired, strict limitations on what one could purchase were imposed. Only flour was permitted because Negros did not need complex foods. Any African farmers producing food in the reserves or anywhere were to sell it directly to the colonial government agency, which shipped the food to Britain to help with war rations, leading to mass starvation amongst the Gikuyu. The Gikuyu became vagrants, which was made illegal and a fineable offence. Africans would no longer be permitted to purchase land. All these factors, combined with natural disasters such as disease and famine, contributed to the deprivation of the poor Gikuyu. The Gikuyu, who were now starving became the poster image of African hunger with the British public being asked to donate to the help the starving Gikuyu via the Red Cross, creating the image that has come to define Africa.

Bad luck struck the missionary too. Dr Watson died within a year of moving to Thogoto, paving the way for his replacement Dr John William Arthur of the Church of Scotland Mission. He bought a vast tract of land in the already overcrowded reserve, which he used for charitable means, offering the now starving people bits of food and clothing.

Cucu Herina's mother died too, leaving her an orphan at the mercy of her stepmothers. She was required to look after them and run all the household chores on their behalf. Waiharo made contact with the new missionary, Dr Arthur, hoping for similar employment as with his predecessor. That was how Cucu Herina and her brothers met Dr Arthur. As Arthur's apprentices, Cucu Herina learnt to read and write and her older brother Guka Robinson learnt how to perform simple medical procedures. It was Dr Arthur's profound belief that Gikuyu customs were morally repugnant and he saw it as his duty to correct these objectionable practices. Amongst them was the significance the Gikuyu attached to dancing—which was rich coming from a white man—mode of dress, witchcraft, polygamy, burial practices and sexuality, indeed everything.

Gikuyu girls pierced their ear lobes and cartilage, enlarging the holes over time, and wore ear ornaments. They were ordered to remove the ear ornaments and looped lobes were stitched together so ornaments could not be worn. Arthur employed Guka Robinson as his helper. Cucu Herina, who faced intense hardship at the mercy of her step-mothers, ran away to the mission, where Dr Arthur offered her a bed, food and clothing. This was the very room that my brothers Wainaina and Mungai called their class with the music teacher Mr Job. In return Cucu Herina was to abide by the mission rules. The mission rules were that church members like Cucu Herina were forbidden to wear tribal costumes or practise their customs or beliefs, or anything that was identifiable as Gikuyu. Gikuyu women traditionally wore carefully finished suede over their shoulders and fastened it at the waist with cowrie shell belts. Cucu Herina was introduced to western dresses. She was fond, fascinated and terrified of Dr Arthur in equal measures. In his regular bible studies, he told her about Jesus, who would save her soul, which guaranteed her place in heaven. She thought the White man was referring to Glasgow. She wanted to go to Glasgow. She thought Glasgow was heaven. She wanted to find out how she could get to this heaven—in Scotland.

By far the biggest issue that drove Dr Arthur to evangelise was female circumcision, which became a hotly contested issue. Church officials and members were forced to sign a pledge against female circumcision otherwise they were dismissed. Writing in *The Times*, and his classic ethnographic book *Facing Mount Kenya*, Jomo Kenyatta called female circumcision the essence of the Gikuyu, without which a girl could not marry. Arthur vehemently disagreed, petitioning the British government, who banned it in the 1930s. The Gikuyu were livid and protested outside churches with lurid songs and dances. They showed just how incensed they were by circumcising an old white woman who bled to death in a village in Kijabe. When the British government made it illegal to be a circumciser, the girls protested by buying razors and began circumcising themselves. Female circumcision was the reason the missionaries lost their influence in Gikuyu lands, leading to their demise and the emergence of different factions of the Church.

Dr Arthur was a complex character and had a bad temper. He had his ear to the ground through a network of informers. Any woman who circumcised her daughters or practiced cultural activities would be taught a lesson on Sunday after the sermon but before the collection. Clenching a piece of paper in his fist, he would squeeze through the rows of benches, walk over to the woman frozen in fear, grab her by the neck, drag her all the way to the back of the church, yell at her at the top of his voice for bringing sin to his church, then he'd proceed to throw her out of the door rather unceremoniously, because that's what Jesus would have wanted. Terrified, Cucu Herina did not dare circumcise Maitu for fear of being thrown out of the church. She was forced to stitch up her ear lobes erasing her cultural footprint. Her interaction with Dr Arthur, put her in a predicament when the time came to fight for independence because she felt a duty to the Gikuyu but also the white man.

Women who sinned were required to spend hours if not months in the basement of the church repenting, a process called cleansing which Maitu had to go through for walking out of her marriage years after the death of the architect of the doctrine Dr. Arthur.

Dire straits brought the Gikuyu to Dr Arthur with his self-proclaimed Jesus status. He fed, clothed and took care of illness in return for absolute obedience. One day he was stood at the door after the service, bidding the congregants goodbye, when he selected a few men to run an errand for him. Kinyenje, Gitundu, Nguri, Wanjangiru, Karuru, Githegi, Thiribu, Muhindi and Njoroge. They were to follow him back to his home. Once in his house, they were taken to the back and shown a huge object that weighed about half a ton. He explained that it was an oven for cooking which was to be taken to another *mzungu*—white person—in Tumutumu Nyeri, a journey that would last thirty days. There were no roads at the time and the men were to carry it on their backs, all the way, for a fee of two shillings.

The men began their journey, surviving on wild fruit and bananas and sleeping in the forests. After fifteen days, two men suffering from exhaustion returned to Thogoto, only to run into to Dr Arthur. His fury at their disobedience was indescribable. He stripped them naked. Each received 10 lashes from his whip and were ordered back to catch up with the others and deliver the oven to the settler. Word spread, causing fear amongst the congregants. Cucu Herina, compelled by gratitude and fear, joined the women who hauled bags of rocks

337

from the quarry for the construction of a new Church of the Torch, which was Arthur's dream of building the biggest church in Africa. This was the same church that we spent several hours in every Sunday when we attended Musa Gitau school.

* * * *

The Gikuyu were underemployed, demoralised and hungry. They had lost everything they owned, their livelihood, their customs and dignity. They had nothing to live for and nothing to lose. By the late 1940s tensions in the native reserves were reaching boiling point. The conditions were so dire; it was just a matter of time. There were talks of a Land and Freedom Army that was gaining momentum by the late 1940s, and by the beginning of 1950 it was an unstoppable force. Their plea to the colonial government to grant more land and better conditions fell on deaf ears; in any case, Africans had no authority to petition the government directly and all matters relating to African affairs would be represented by a white missionary. The Gikuyu misery turned into anger encouraging ordinary Gikuyu to join the fight for freedom. Visionaries turned to their customs for guidances. One important Gikuyu tradition was to take a binding oath if undertaking some commitment. Due to the Gikuyu superstitious the oath was unbreakable. They saw this as a way of persuading

338

reluctant Gikuyu to join the revolution. The Land and Freedom Army's resolve hardened with mistreatment of the Gikuyu. They demanded return of their stolen lands using any methods necessary. Oathing administrators toured the countryside by night giving every Gikuyu an oath. Once an oath was taken, all orders must be curried out including killing the settlers and any Gikuyu propping up the British colonisers. Servants turned on their masters killing 32 settlers. This caused great para-noia amongst the settlers who were rather unnerved because all relied on African servants but could not trust anyone. The Land and Freedom fighters finally commanded the world stage. The British govern-ment began a big propaganda campaign condemning the freedom fighters as terrorist and ordinary villages branded as terrorist sympathisers. The paranoid settlers threatened the British Government with vigilantism.

Left with no choice, on 20 October 1952, Sir Evelyn Baring, the Governor of Kenya, declared a State of Emergency, making Kenya a police state. Troops were brought in from the Royal Northumberland Fusiliers and the Lancashire Fusiliers to join the Kenya Police Force and the Kenyan Regiment—a vigilante force made up of white settlers, home guards, Gikuyu loyalists and the King's African Rifles, which was the black East African branch of the British Army in which Idi Amin was a soldier. Their enemy: the Gikuyu, who just wanted land to feed their families. Britain conducted a bombing campaign, killing many people as well as introducing draconian laws, imposing a curfew between six pm and six am and anyone caught out during those hours was to be shot on the spot. Crucially, all villagers were to be moved into internment camps. It was a desperate fight for the colony. This was the environment in which my parents spent their formative years.

The Lone Tree that Weathered the Storm

*'If fighting for our land and freedom is a crime, then we shall fight
to the last drop of our blood, we shall never give up until we have
driven away these foreign murderers from our beloved country.
We reject colonization in Kenya because it has turned us into
slaves and beggars,'*

Dedan Kimathi, Freedom Fighter

Cucu Herina was the lone tree, with torn leaves and broken branches, that is left standing after a hurricane, wounded and shaken but still standing. She was in so many ways a fighter. Not in a heroic and noble sense like the people in the Land and Freedom Army, who were prepared to give up their lives for the struggle for *Githaka na Wayathi*—Land and Freedom for their people, armed with little else than hope, machetes and reconditioned AK 47s; nor was she like the women who braved the wrath of the objectionable home guards to arm the forest fighters, smuggling weapons in their under garments; nor did she join the masses of women who volunteered their children for the causes of freedom, bravely and dutifully smuggling food to the forests, providing a life line for the freedom fighters. Cucu

Herina was not like that. She was rather cowardly. As a matter of fact, she did everything humanly possible to avoid conflict or confrontation. She always chose the path of least resistance but in a determined and tenacious way. Hers was a difficult path beset by several tragic events in several episodes of her life.

As far as tragic events go, the declaration of the State of Emergency had to be the most significant. Cucu Herina was fast asleep with her three daughters, Wanjiku, Kabui and my mother Gakari, in their hut.

'We were sleeping one night when we were woken up by loudspeakers. There was a lot of screaming, shouting and dogs were barking. Herina grabbed us and our sacks that we slept in and ran outside. Someone had set the village on fire. There were Johnnies and gatis everywhere. They had big dogs. It was very scary. I was holding onto Herina's dress,' explained Maitu during one of our daily phone conversations when I began my research.

Outside was sheer carnage. They were hit by a wall of intense heat and toxic smoke, blinding them momentarily. Huts burned ferociously, spitting orange flames and crackling sparks which lit up the scene. There were people lying on the floor, some coughing from the effects of the fumes. Men, women and children were running in all directions in the ensuing pandemonium. No one knew what was happening. An old man ran outside from a burning hut carrying his goat on his shoulder, his clothes ablaze. Someone doused him with water from a small gourd, a futile attempt as he collapsed into a fireball. Mothers were frantically yelling for their children. Cries for help could be heard from those trapped in the inferno. Some villagers were running back to their huts to rescue their loved ones and their goats; after all, this was their only wealth. Fierce guard dogs barked wildly, exacerbating the hellish hysteria in the chaotic scene.

'Oh no! That must have been terrifying,' I said.

'It was. Some people lost their children and elderly relatives with all their belongings, never to be found again,' Maitu recounted. In fact, the majority of Gikuyu people don't possess photographs or any personal belongings from before the emergency. They were all burnt to the ground. The British destroyed not only the artefacts and architecture of the traditional Gikuyu homesteads, but also the functionality of the Gikuyu as a tribe.

Cucu Herina and her children ran in one direction but the British white officers—or Johnnies, as they were commonly called—were shouting commands which they did not understand, so they carried on, causing a furious Johnny to crack his whip, narrowly missing her. The furious Johnny repeated the command, pointing in the opposite direction. The home guards (the specially created Gikuyu militia) were responding to commands by hitting people with the butts of their guns, cursing them as they did so. Others were brandishing whips, herding the frightened villagers into a holding bay, like cargo awaiting transportation. The Johnnies shone torches on the villagers' faces. Women and children were sifted and loaded into the back of a caged lorry. The men were marched to another holding bay, which was surrounded by rolled-up barbed wire, guarded by dogs. They were ordered to squat on their heels with their hands over their heads.

What Cucu Herina lacked in bravado, she made up for in determination and her long strong arms served her well on the night of their forced removal.

'They whipped us to get into the lorry. Herina held on to us tightly. We were squashed like fish,' explained Maitu as we talked on the phone.

The overcrowded old Leyland lorry tipped backwards with the weight. The women and children complained they couldn't breathe. The old engine roared alive, spitting smoke from the rusty exhaust like an old man on his last legs. The impatient driver revved the engine, drowning the screams of women, who called their children's names at the tops of their voices. Their harrowing screams could be heard for miles. The realisation that the lorry was driving away into the night without their relatives was too much to bear. As the lorry pulled away, the screams of those trapped in the inferno faded, their lives evaporating into nothingness. Women sobbed despairingly as they glanced unto heaven, crying to 'Ngai Wa Kirinyaga' to relieve them of this nightmare unfolding before their very eyes. No one knew where they were being taken. My grandmother held tightly to her children, grateful they were all together.

The Screening

'If we are going to sin, we must sin quietly,'
Attorney General Eric Griffith-Jones, 1953

'Where did they take you?' I asked Maitu in disbelief during our phone interview.

'They took us to a field that was all fenced off with barbed wire.'

As they stood there, huddled with hundreds of other women and children, all brought in from the neighbouring villages, Cucu Herina tried to comprehend what the white man wanted to do now. It had been nearly morning by the time the lorry dropped them off in a field in Darogetti, 10 miles west of Nairobi.

'We were ordered to go into the field surrounded by barbed wire, watched by *gatis*—Gikuyu guards with ferocious dogs. Some *gatis* were in *kanyumba ka iguru*—a small house built on high stilts.'

'Like a watch tower?' I asked.

'Yes. They could see everyone on the field.'

'What happened in the field?' I pressed.

The field, which they called *ciugo*—paddock—was

fenced off with barbed wire and surrounded by African guards dressed in black overcoats and black berets, poised ready to use their AK 47s. Dotted around were their superiors, British white officers, all dressed up in crisp Khaki uniforms with their trademark whips and pistols, holding on to their Alsatians. As the morning wore on, the lorries bringing in hordes of women and children ceased. There were a few old and disabled men joining them. The field was now rather crowded, with the confused and scared-looking villagers unsure of what was going to happen to them. By midday everyone was getting hungry, frustrated and agitated. Nobody told them anything. There were no ablutions and anyone needing to relieve themselves were ordered to do it on the spot. Most just sat on the grass, stomachs rumbling, children and babies crying. My mother, 8 years old, howled from hunger as the hot sun beat down on them.

Finally, a voice came over the tannoy ordering the villagers to stand in rows. A Land Rover drove up to the entrance and two white officers helped someone out of the car, but no one could tell who the person was, for he was covered from head to toe with a specially adapted sack that made an all-body balaclava. The top of the balaclava was pointed and the face had holes crudely cut out for the eyes, reminiscent of the Ku Klux Klan. All that was visible from behind the hood was the man's steely evil black eyes, which stared ominously.

The hooded person was assisted through the gates, past the rows of women who stared at the spectacle with increasingly despondent curiosity. These hooded people would become a familiar sight and became nicknamed *Gakunia*—sack.

The *Gakunia* was helped to a chair behind a desk next to a uniformed Johnny. The villagers were instructed to form orderly queues and step forward when ordered. They were to walk to the desk and turn to face the *Gakunia,* whose chilling eyes would scrutinise the frightened villagers, sometimes squinting to get a better look. The eyes focused on the face for a few minutes, causing great anxiety. Audible sighs of relief could be heard when the Johnny called the next person.

There were several women in front of Cucu Herina. The queue moved very slowly. *Gakunia* remained still as the villagers filed past. There were now three women in front of Cucu Herina. A short, stockily built, flat-footed woman with a clean-shaven head and *hangi* dangling from her ears, her decorative cowrie shells glistening in the sun, was next in line. She walked clumsily to the desk, turning awkwardly to face *Gakunia*. *Gakunia* scrutinised. Squinted and then nodded. The home guards pounced on the woman with the speed of lightening, blows raining, others kicking and punching her. She fell backwards, letting out a harrowing scream. The home guards dragged her by her arms to the back of the waiting Land Rover. She was branded with a black sticker stuck on her shoulder.

Cucu Herina could not understand the point of the exercise. What did the woman do? Maitu and her siblings shook with fear. Cucu Herina was frozen with terror. The commanding voice of the officer called my grandmother to come forward. She couldn't move, her heavy legs laden with trepidation. She forced herself to edge forwards, walking very slowly, afraid to make a mistake. The thought of looking at the eyes terrified her. She couldn't bring herself to do it. She feared she would accidentally do something that would trigger a beating. 'Look up,' growled the white officer. She could have jumped out of her skin. She forced herself to look at the eyes momentarily, the piercing evil causing her gaze to drift downwards as if pulled by a gravitational force. Her eyes wandered down the stitching of the roughly sewn up sack before finally settling on his feet. He wore *nginyira*—sandals, freshly cut out of old car tyres. Something caught her attention. Her eyes enlarged as she stared. She knew those feet. There was a small extra toe sticking out on the prominence of one foot. Her eyes moved swiftly to the next foot. She could feel the hairs on the back of her neck rising. He had six toes on each foot! The right foot was covered with an unmistakable birthmark, a black mole. Adrenalin pumped round her body furiously as her eyes shifted back up to look at *Gakunia's* eyes. She knew that he

349

knew she had recognised him. She knew who the traitor was! My grandmother's fear turned to anger and then horror. As she stared into the menacing, cold, demonic soul of the traitor, she could feel her body begin to tremble. She was convinced he would nod at her. She stood there waiting; *Gakunia* did not move a muscle. She walked past, her heart still thumping.

Her encounter with *Gakunia* left her numb as she stood in front of the District Officer Muru Wa Itina, who scrutinised Cucu Herina's face with a sneering expression on his face. He claimed to be able to sniff the resistance of those involved in the Land and Freedom Army. He got nothing from my grandmother.

'Where did you go after you left the field?' I asked Maitu.

'We never left the field,' she replied.

'What? What do you mean?' I questioned.

'We slept in the open field for a long time, until Herina built our house in the patch of the field allocated to us,' replied Maitu grimly.

'What do you mean? How did you sleep on the open field?' I pressed.

'We slid into our sacks and slept in the open. Sometimes it rained but God is great because it didn't rain every night. There were frogs and snakes, everything.'

'How long did you live like that for?' I carried on.

'We slept outside for weeks.' Silence.

'Maitu, hello, Maitu, is she okay?' I asked Maitu's maid. 'Speak, Maitu.' The maid urged my mother to speak. She explained to me that distress sometimes rendered Maitu unable to speak. We were done for the day, but our conversations continued.

Lessons in Building a Concentration Camp

'There is only one way of improving the Wakikuyu and that is to wipe them out; I should be so delighted to do so,'
Francis Hall, Imperial British East Africa Company

The weary women were still sleeping on the dew-laden grass when the District Officer walked in through the gates accompanied by Johnnies and home guards. The children's lethargic whimpers were barely audible, too hungry to cry as mothers cocooned their infants in their chests, wrapped in filthy rags in their desperation to keep warm. It had been several days since they had been brought into this field, kept like cargo and left in limbo. They had sacks, which served as sitting mats by day and sleeping bags by night. They slid into the rough embrace of the sack, which unlike a sleeping bag begrudged them any comfort, for they were neither warm nor big enough. The temperatures in the open field plummeted by night, and by morning the women and children shivered, awaiting the early morning sun which was barely enough to dry their weary souls. The field was reminiscent of the aftermath of a hurricane, except devoid of hope. It was littered with personal belongings strewn everywhere, soggy from the unrelenting rain, as if the gods had colluded against the Gikuyu. Each soggy mess represented their future.

The home guards carried finely chiselled, freshly cut sticks as they made their way amongst the groggy women. The field had been their home since their arrival, with no shelter, sanitation or means to prepare food. They had finally been escorted at the end of the second day, after their encounter with the *Gakunia*, to the *shambas* close by, to collect food. The women had scrambled, collecting what they could for their hungry children, hurriedly eating what they could in the process. With no means of cooking they ate raw sweet potatoes, sugar cane, fruit and anything else they could ingest without cooking. They were dirty and unkempt, with no provision for personal hygiene. Menstruating women just reached through the barbed wire for leaves, which they also used as toilet paper. As time went on, the stress on the women was so severe that they stopped menstruating altogether. A growing stench of urine and faeces began to litter the field.

The District Officer marched down, giving orders to the women whilst their children cowered behind them. They were to shift all their belongings to make way for a clearing, revealing half of the field. The home guards followed their commander like puppy dogs. Those women who were still asleep were woken by cracks of the whip and ordered to stand in rows. Many anticipated the news that they would be returning to their villages now that the screening was over and persons of interest had been taken away. The District Officer spoke in broken Swahili. No one was returning to their village. From then on, they were to remain on that field, the officer explained. The women just stood there, trying to comprehend what he was saying. How were they to live on this field? No one was making head or tail; it just didn't make sense. He carried on explaining that each woman was to be allocated a patch of ground on to which they were to shift their children and belongings. That patch of ground was to be their new home and it was up to the women to construct the houses. The bewildered women listened intently. They had no equipment or other means of constructing homes.

The instructions on the building of their new homes came next. All huts were to be in neat, straight rows, with all the doors facing the watchtower, from which the guard on duty had a perfect bird's eye view of every woman and every woman would have a perfect view of the evil that hounded them. All the walls were to be plastered with the red mud but finished with a white clay from the river. Until their new homes were built, the women would continue to sleep, cook and go to the toilet on the ground in their allocated space.

After the speech, the home guards began allocating

the ground, the women obeying the orders for fear of being beaten. Everyone shifted their belongings to their patch. Suddenly a commotion erupted in one corner; everyone was scrambling to move away from a hunchbacked woman rumoured to be a witch. No one wanted to be the 'witch's' neighbour. It was survival of the fittest.

The building of the huts began in earnest the following day. Each allocation was circular, drawn out on the ground using sticks. The home guards escorted some women to the forest to cut down trees in order to start the construction of their huts. They had no building tools and after their allocation, Cucu Herina pleaded to be able to walk back to their old home in Igajo to salvage anything she could. It was a miracle that their old home had not burned to the ground, as most did. Cucu Herina was instructed to start demolishing her old hut, destroying her home and freedom. It took her two days to dismantle it, helped by Maitu and her sisters. They gathered all the posts, sticks and grass, all tied with ropes on their backs, making several trips to rebuild their new home. Anything else left behind, the home guards confiscated, and any structures still standing were burned to the ground.

Like all women, Cucu Herina worked at a ferocious speed because the short rains were in full swing and the cold that enveloped the Highlands by night was unbearable. The torrential rains that once brought jubilant laughter and the promise of bounteous harvest now spelt untold misery. Only frogs now leapt with glee. The women would just lie there, soaked to the bone, shivering through the night whilst comforting their disillusioned children. Some women were pregnant and others had newborn babies with no way of sheltering them from the elements. The colonial government viewed this as something to incentivise the women, desperate to create shelter for their families, therefore making them work harder.

Once all the material was on site, Cucu Herina started building her house. She dug the holes for the pillars first, which was a great effort on an empty stomach. The home guards supervised the building projects, overseen by the White officers brandishing whips. They would whip anyone who was not working fast enough. The home guards had become the machines of evil, the engines on which the colonial power depended to drive the oppression of a helpless people. They turned on their people in order to win favour with their masters, who viewed them as a weapon to be manipulated at will. It is in these desperate times of need that human beings revert to primitive selfishness, each doing whatever is necessary to survive, even at the peril of their brothers.

Once the pillars were firmly in the ground, Cucu Herina nailed smaller pieces of wood to the pillars, and when she ran out of nails, she used stringy bark to bind the sticks to them. Those sticks would criss-cross the pillars, packed close together so that when the plastering began, those pockets would hold the mud in place. By the time she got to plastering, a few women were grouping together to finish one hut and would all spend the night in the newly built hut, therefore keeping dry for the night. Real camaraderie and teamwork began to emerge as soon as the women got the hang of it. Some would dig the earth and mix the freshly dug soil with water in a pit and slosh the mud around with their feet. When all the mud was smooth, others took handfuls of the smooth plaster, filling in the gaps. Once the gaps were all filled, an outer, smoother layer was needed to give the hut a good finish. When that was dry, they had to whitewash the exterior walls with whitish grey clay, which they had to dig out from the river. It was back-breaking work, carrying all the wet clay in *kiondos*—woven baskets from the river, climbing uphill and walking to Dagoretti, at least half a mile away.

As the women busied themselves with house-building, they began singing empowerment songs as positivity and defiance set in. They changed the words to well known songs and replaced them with abuse and derogatory words aimed at shaming the colonial enforcers. The songs became contentious due to their insulting nature to the white man, which led to them being banned. No one was allowed to sing or talk in public. One such song was constantly played on the radio when I was a child, especially on Independence Day but I never understood the meaning of it.

Kanyaga nchi yako kwa nguvu na raha (step on your land with strength and happiness)
Hili ni hakikisho la rais wetu (this is the promise by our leader)
Zamani tuliwekwa eti namba four(Long ago we were held at number 4)
Sasa abautani tuko namba wani (Now what a turnaround we are number 1)
Kenya, Kenya
Kenya taifa letu Kenya, Kenya (Kenya our country Kenya)
Kenya nchi Yetu (Kenya our country)
Wako wapi wabeberu waone haya (Where are the colonisers they have no shame)
Tuliyoyatimiza kwa miaka chache (We served under them for years)
Ni wao walisema hatuna akili (They are the ones that said we had no brains)
Na huku watunyonya afadhali kupe (And here they suck us dry we would rather have ticks)

When the house-building was finished, the real hard work began. Woken at the crack of dawn by a siren, the women had half an hour to feed their children and congregate at the gate. They were frogmarched to spend their days digging endless trenches surrounding the villages and forests to keep out the Land and Freedom Army, who had sought refuge in the forest. The intention was to starve the freedom fighters, who it was hoped would give up the struggle. The work for the women was exhausting, without breaks, food or water. The trenches, they were told, would ensure that freedom fighters could no longer come to the village for food. The only men in the village were the elderly and their job was to sharpen sticks, which would be planted in the trenches, a further barrier to keep the freedom fighters out.

Whilst the British were busy designing European convention on human rights, in 1954, they were busy eroding the Gikuyu human rights. In total, over a million people had been arrested and detained in either detention centres or concentration camps. 804 to be precise. All men were detained in detention centres and all women and children were held in concentration camps. All were engaged in forced labour. They introduced hanging: 1090 people were hung by the end of the emergency. Countless more were killed in the detention centres and in the concentration camps, all buried in mass graves which remain in situ to this day. Any property or belongings they had were confiscated and distributed to loyalists, and animals fed the soldiers.

Independent Women

'What do you remember most about your child-hood?' I asked Maitu.

'Hunger! Painful desperate hunger, when Herina went out to communal (the term used for forced labour) with Wanjiku and Kabui, I was left behind. We ate nothing all day and when Herina returned, she would have no food, so we slept hungry,' she recounted.

Before the Emergency, Cucu Herina had been a fiercely independent businesswoman. On Mondays, Wednesdays and Thursdays, she woke at sunrise and tied her baby with the *rithu* to her bosom. Stop-and-searches were prevalent and any officials stopping her would insist on seeing her documents. Anyone caught outside of their village without a passbook would be flogged at the chief's orders. Most people loathed the wretched identification documents and thought it a daily reminder of the oppression of the Gikuyu. It had taken Cucu Herina months to apply for a passbook, disadvantaged by her single status. She had to make constant visits to the chief, begging that she be granted a passbook to leave the village so she could support her family. She carried the heavily laden *kiondo* on her back, joining other women traders heading to the wealthy suburbs of Muthaiga and Kileleshwa. They capitalized on the laziness of the European women, who never went to market, and began a business selling eggs and vegetables at their doorstep. Her friend Wanjira, another tradeswoman, had loaned her twenty-five shillings to start the business. Once their *kiondos* were empty, the tradeswomen walked the three-and-a-half-hour journey back home in preparation for the following day. The journeys were shorter on Tuesdays and Fridays, these being market days.

Cucu Herina was a single mother of three, which was unusual in the early part of the century. Gikuyu tradition dictated that everyone had to be married. Some women opted to marry other women whilst others preferred men. Speculation was that Cucu Herina, being a staunch believer in women's freedom, possibly chose this model of family because it suited her, or possibly the political climate, having children, and fighting for survival gave her little chance for romance. 'Cucu, where is your husband?' Cousin Ngige had asked her once. She had reprimanded young Ngige, telling him that it was grown-up business. Cucu Herina had received a marriage proposal from a young

Mswahili man called Hassan from Mombasa, who was Maitu's father, which she declined. It was therefore presumed to be her choice rather than circumstance. There were numerous Gikuyu women who chose not to have a conventional marriage, some even marrying other women. As a matter of fact, my great-great-great-grandmother Ndiko had four wives, which commanded a lot of respect and she had a town named after her.

Tainted Love— Lunatic Express Years

For many years after Maitu left home, I prayed to God every night before I went to sleep. I closed my eyes tight and prayed for my parents to find love with one another again. 'God, please let Maitu and Baba get together again. Let them love one another like they did once a long time ago, like when we went to the show ground. They loved each other very much. Amen.'

It was one of those perfect London days in May that are so rare. I was sat in my garden, enjoying the coolness of the freshly cut grass tickling my feet, my skin soaking in the warmth of the generous sun. My garden was in full bloom, in rare synchronicity with Maitu's three thousand miles away in Kenya. An amalgamation of different smells of blossom and cooking wafted through my nostrils, reminiscent of my childhood garden when we lived in Riara Ridge. I watched two yellow butterflies choreograph their dance to the tune of bumble bees buzzing around the lavender bush and dogs barking excitedly in the park on the other side of my garden. I waited for Maitu to return to the phone from the bathroom. Finally, her maid spoke, letting me know she was back. We had spoken happily, as we did every day now. She recounted the times she spent with her childhood friend Njeri, whose mother was Cucu Herina's next-door neighbour when they lived in *Mihari*—rows. I soon learnt that *mihari*, which I always assumed to be the name of a place, was what they called the concentration camps because the huts were all in rows.

'And how did you start dating Baba?' I asked casually. I would never have asked that question if Wainaina had not got married or if Baba had not died when he did.

* * *

The Lunatic Express puffed ringlets of smoke, like an ageing madame whose heyday was long gone. The majestic bellowing commanded full attention as she greeted the residents of Kikuyu and its vicinity. The once mighty dragon that had seen too much jostled its passengers this way and that way as it snaked round the hills. Like a river that runs deep, she held many secrets. The man-eating lions of Tsavo must have had premonitions of the havoc it would wreak, devouring those that lay the tracks in a bid to halt its construction. It brought fortunes for many and sheer misery for others—for my parents it was both.

Baba possessed incredible insight into opportunities that others simply missed or were unwilling to put effort into. He was fearless, undertaking projects that most considered too risky. Baba's business endeavours began in adolescence on the Lunatic Express.

For most, the overcrowded train felt like the final tip towards insanity but to Baba it was an abundant sea of fish begging to be caught. He was a train hawker operating between the Kikuyu-Nairobi train stations. His hawking skills were invented and perfected on the train, where he marketed sweets and handkerchiefs relentlessly to weary passengers who had no choice but to part company with their money so that Baba would move on to his next victim. He was a good salesman who connected with his customers by telling them stories and jokes, even learning different languages so he could converse with them. The most important lesson Baba learned from the streets of Nairobi was that a good punch would get you out of a tricky situation. Sometimes. But a smooth talker always got away with murder and that he did, very often, although if the need arose he was not afraid to stand his ground, despite his minuscule stature. In the streets, where small matters escalated very quickly, one needed to be well equipped with essential survival skills.

Baba spent all his waking hours pushing and shoving

his way, charming his customers with compliments and greeting other passengers of the Kenya-Uganda railways. By the mid 1950s the Lunatic Express was a hive of activity, packed with commuters and providing a lifeline for impoverished young Africans in search of work. Children made up the majority of commuters heading to Nairobi because their parents were all in detention or labour camps or had no permits to travel. The only people with permits were those working in British households or organisations. But where there was a crowd, there were hawkers selling everything from handkerchiefs to sweets, flip-flops, batteries, torches, anything. One minute they would converge on unsuspecting passengers, the next they were gone, disappeared like a flock of birds when policemen appeared. For Baba, it was his bread and butter. Being caught without a licence meant confiscation of one's stock, so vigilance was crucial. Hawkers like my father had no licence to trade. One needed to have connections at the municipal council to get a licence. He and the other illegal hawkers spent their days playing cat and mouse, ducking and diving and occasionally jumping off the train when the ticket inspectors or police came aboard.

Baba was an eager, agile and smooth-talking teenager with unparalleled vision. Whilst many of his compadres turned to a life of crime, the only option for most, he had no desire to spend the rest of his life in the squalor that was Kenyan prisons. As a matter of fact, he could not wait to leave it all behind. He watched the smartly dressed white businessmen wearing tailored suits with matching waistcoats and colourful cravats that hugged their neck lines with great admiration. He would stand outside the Thorn Tree sidewalk café, which was part of a swanky five-star hotel, and watch as the rich people indulged in lavish dinners, captivated by their laughter and mannerisms. He observed how they used their shiny cutlery, with crisp, starched white linen napkins tucked into their collars, in case their fine food should escape on to their opulent clothing. They sipped alcoholic beverages with such finesse whilst over-zealous African waiters fussed around them. He would look down at his tattered, filthy clothes, which fuelled his desire all the more. That was where he belonged. He just had to figure out how to get there.

He travelled the length of the train at various times of the month. To Mombasa, Kisumu and Kampala, he went at the end of the month when city workers returned home with their pay packets. The rest of the month, he did short trips between Kibera, Kikuyu and Nairobi stations. People returning home were happy to buy a few sweets for their children from Baba, who drove hard bargains, convincing them that his sweets were the cheapest on the market. His voice could be heard from different carriages shouting, '*Bei Raiithi, Bei Raiithi*— cheap prices, cheap prices.' He became nicknamed Bei

Raiithi, which is how his friends referred to him in their funeral tributes. His was a hand to mouth existence, his profits minuscule.

It was on one of these journeys that he saw her. My father knew he was hopelessly in love with my mother from the very first moment he laid eyes on her. She was the most beautiful girl he had ever seen. Her dark flawless face and large brown eyes lingered in his imagination long after she was gone. Every morning she hopped onto the train, chatting and laughing with her friend Wandugu, and every day he'd vow to talk to her but every time he tried his confidence faltered. It was exactly two years after her first commute on the Lunatic Express that he finally summoned the courage to talk to her. The train had just left Kikuyu town station, bellowing noisily, leaving a trail of thick smoke behind, jostling its passengers from side to side, when my father lost his balance and went flying across the aisle, falling on to my mother's feet, as if an external force came to his aid. He got up, looked straight into her eyes and said, 'I really, really like you.' Embarrassed, Maitu averted her gaze, her slender hand clenching even tighter around the knotted handkerchief containing her 25 cents return train fare, mumbling inaudibly that she did not like him. He reached deep into the pockets of his rather shabby khaki shorts and pulled out a tropical sweet and 1 shilling, which he handed to my mother. Maitu turned away, embarrassed.

'Please take it, it's for you,' he pleaded. She, not wanting to make a scene, accepted the gift and then looked away, shrugging her shoulders indignantly, hoping he would go away. Humiliated, my father croaked out his usual sales pitch, '*Bei Raiithi, Bei Raiithi*,' pushing and shoving, '*Bei Raiithi, Bei Raiithi*, get your tropical sweets here. A handkerchief for you, sir?'

Every day he saw her on the train, he'd smile at her—'I really like you'—to a blank stare from Maitu. Everyday she ignored him. Whenever Maitu heard him on the train, she would shrink behind people, hoping he would not see her. She had no interest in talking to him. She avoided him like the plague. His hellos and goodbyes were ignored. He, on the other hand, developed the biggest obsession with her. He pursued her, looking in every carriage to catch a glimpse of her. She was all he thought about. He offered her sweets and handkerchiefs, but she was having none of it. Frustrated by her arrogance and refusal to talk to him, he decided to send his friend Ngugi to her with a message. Ngugi was a loyal friend and so set out on his mission. Upon passing the messages of greetings to Maitu, Ngugi was rebuffed with a stern 'I do not want his greetings' before she returned to her hut, slamming the door shut.

Every few months my father would send his friend with new greetings, only to be met with the same answer. Undeterred, he continued his pursuit, finding out where she lived—much to Maitu's annoyance when she found him sat drinking *turungi* and chatting with Cucu Herina. Maitu had simply walked in then straight out again, leaving embarrassed Baba to finish his black tea and leave empty-handed. He tried everything. She was unattainable. After months of pursuit, it was clear that his love would go unrequited; Maitu simply was not interested in returning his love.

The constant rejection pained Baba deeply and knocked his confidence, so he decided that my mother was a proud peacock and that his undying love was wasted on her. He told Ngugi that he was giving up on her, but the more he resisted, the more his love grew. Seeing her on the train every morning was now a bitter-sweet experience.

* * * *

At fourteen, the purity and innocence of Maitu's character was surpassed only by her flawless beauty. Her eyes, nose and mouth were framed perfectly by her soft round face, giving an impression of frailty, but underneath that exterior was a woman of iron resolve. In the early days of their internment, Maitu spent her days with all the other small children left behind in the camp, singing, clapping and drawing on the red mud with sticks. She was too afraid to stay in the hut. Their favourite song was:

'baba nia thire—my daddy is gone
Riria agacoca—and when he comes
Akadehera mugate—he will bring me
bread.

Singing distracted from hunger. Food at the camps was impossibly scarce. So they sang all day and when the evenings came, Cucu Herina and her older daughters returned empty-handed. They were prisoners and had no permission to leave the camp for any reason other than hard labour. The shambas which they visited weekly under the supervision of the guards, did not yield anything anymore. They slept on empty stomachs. All grown-ups had been extracted from functionality; there was no one left to till the land, or plant any food. People were dropping like flies. Bodies were littered everywhere. It was the job of the women to collect all bodies of people found dead from either starvation or being shot for breaking the curfew, or just because the soldiers were in a bad mood.

Since the internment of the Gikuyu, life had become one of mass starvation and dysfunction. One morning Cucu Herina asked Maitu to do the unthinkable. She instructed her to catch the train to Kibera in search of casual labour. On the brink of starvation, twelve-year-old Maitu was forced to become the family breadwinner.

'That's your fare home if you don't find any work,' Cucu Herina handed her a grubby handkerchief twisted around an octagonal coin and tied into a knot. 'Make sure you don't get caught without a fare,' she warned sternly. Every day, Maitu dutifully walked to the train station clutching her handkerchief tightly. Wandugu, whose hut was a few doors down, called for Maitu every morning to walk to the station, and that became their daily routine for the next few years. They spent their days with hordes of other children going to Kibera slums, knocking door to door offering their services of fetching water, washing dishes, plastering houses with mud, or any other handy work. Kibera was inhabited by the Sudanese Nubians and WaSwahili. The Sudanese Nubians were resettled in Kibera after fighting for the British during the First World War. They were unwelcome in Sudan, leaving the British with no choice but to find them housing, and that was the beginning of Kibera slums. To this day, the Sudanese remain stateless as they are not considered Kenyan citizens. The Kenyan government always insisted they were a British responsibility.

Being a girl, housework was plentiful for Maitu. Dishwashing became a necessity to their very existence, work without which her mother and sisters would slowly have starved to death. She could barely wait for her employer to leave her alone with the pile of dishes. She would roll up her sleeves slowly and wait until the employer left. As soon as she was alone, she would scoop leftover food with her grubby hands, stuffing it into her mouth. Whatever was left behind, she licked the plate until it was clean. That meant that the food she bought for her family had one less mouth to feed. Only then would she begin to wash the dishes. At the end of the day, her handkerchief would contain several more coins as she received her wage after every job. After work, Maitu rushed straight to Kibera station and hopped on to the train home. She alighted at Mutuini station.

Maitu's work in Kibera also provided an escape from the macabre entertainment that children were invited to watch at the police station. Lining them up at the barbed wire fence, the guards invited children to watch naked Gikuyu men being marched up and down singing 'sisi Mau Mau, we are Mau Mau' whilst carrying buckets of excrement on their heads. Anyone who stopped or fell from exhaustion was whipped, whipped, revived with cold water then whipped some more. They watched people being clobbered to death. Those that died were loaded into lorries for mass burial in trenches.

When I was little and Maitu spoke of her childhood, I always assumed it was a happy one. Many times, I heard her mention mihari, Wandugu, the trains, Kibera, gati. These were just meaningless words to me. I could never have been able to link the dots to make a full story. I found Maitu's accounts too harrowing and I began to regret my whole research. I questioned whether this process was healing or adding to my already existing trauma.

'Do you feel better for finding all this out?' queried a black American PHD student at Edinburgh University, when I was considering doing a PhD on the subject of trauma on subsequent generations of genocide or concentration camps.

'No!' I had replied. I felt bitter and angry with a system I trusted, with people I always respected and always thought to be decent. I got angry at my husband because his people did this to my family. I screamed at him. He lived through my trauma unable to comfort me. He was unable to process the cruelty with which the British dealt with the Gikuyu. In the depths of my despair, he would just walk away. I screamed at him. 'I know it wasn't you!' but he remained unable to communicate with me what or how he felt. I wanted to run away to a place where I would never hear anything or see anyone. This was how racism manifested itself. It harmed people and destroyed lives. I had always assumed it was people chanting monkey noises at foot-ballers in a field or when people used the N word. I wished that was all that racism was.

We are not taught history in Africa and I never got it. White people are always sold to Africans as the ones who are there to do good, the ones that are there to condemn the abuse of people by unscrupulous dictators, the ones who turn up during disasters, the ones that

Africans look up to as models of good governance, the ones who *save* us. We are told they are exemplars and champions of human rights. I believed in that system but now I realise that system is only for white people. Some white people! Human rights is not awarded to the black race. Ours was to be abused, seen as subhuman. I began to lose the will to live. For the first time in my life I began to contemplate suicide! I thought of rats; Maitu always told me that when a rat bites, it blows to soothe the sting of the bite before it inflicts further bites. That was the only analogy that could come to mind. White people bite Africans and when it hurts they blow to soothe us before biting us some more. This was too much for me to bear. Everyone had colluded to hood-wink us. I wanted to run to the place I had been before Wainaina ruined my peace. I thought of Cucu Herina, all her life wasted; she was denied humanity because of the colour of her skin, because she was born in the wrong continent at the wrong time. She spent years of her life working, sustaining white people, the people who told her about a God who loved the poor whilst they took all the wealth and drained their sweat. Jesus said, 'Bring all the children unto me.' I remembered the days I spent at church learning of Jesus and his love for children, but not black children. Not the children who perished in the days of emergency, babies just going limp on their mother's backs. My research pointed me to King Leopold II of Belgium, who killed ten million people in Congo, to the little children whose arms he chopped off because they could not pick enough rubber for him. All the kidnapped children in West Africa harvesting cocoa so that a little white child can have a delightful Easter. That was when I lost my faith. I could not comprehend it or accept it. It doesn't exist.

Unfortunate
Encounter

By midday one day, Maitu had concluded there wasn't much work, it being the middle of the month when most people held on to their pennies. She had her return train fare, which Cucu Herina always insisted she carry, tied to her grubby handkerchief for days like today. She hadn't made enough to buy *guruthas*, a type of pancake she always bought when she had surplus for her family. She decided to pay a visit to her good friend Wahu. They had a great afternoon chitchatting, laughing, and completely lost track of time. Realising that Cucu Herina would be on her way home, she made her way hastily, deciding to take the short-cut through the secluded eucalyptus woodland. From afar she noticed a figure walking up the path, but she was preoccupied with getting home on time for Cucu Herina and only recognised him when he got very close. It was the annoying boy trader from the train. He was a pest, she had concluded. He was on the train every morning and evening, his voice always filling the carriage as he advertised handkerchiefs and tropical sweets. He irritated her. He told everyone how much he liked her but she had retorted that she did not care for his advances and wished he would leave her alone. Now he stood in the middle of the path, blocking her way.

'You refused me!' he said, staring in her eyes as if trying to make her see reason. Irritated, she turned away, sticking her bottom out rudely which was a way girls usually told boys they didn't care for them. Maitu began to walk past him, annoyed that he was wasting her time and Cucu Herina would not find her at home. She hated making Cucu Herina cross because she was always so exhausted when she got home. She was about to take the next step when Baba put his foot out, tripping her and causing her to tumble on to the grassy verge of the secluded path lined with fragrant eucalyptus trees. Before she could protest, he knelt on top of her, ripped off her clothes and raped her.

And so the very basis of my origin began with the single act of rape, by my father, against my mother. The family that should have been my moral compass began with the ultimate sin. Even after his death, my father's actions still had the ability to strike at me with such ferocity, rendering me a shivering wreck.

This revelation shocked me greatly, but it must be viewed in the context of the environment in which my parents spent their formative years. Rape was a key weapon of war and became rampant and sadistic. Mothers were ordered to watch their children being raped. Children were ordered to watch their mothers being raped. Why would my father know any different? It was what grown men did to women and children. My parents were the children who had been forced to watch people being beaten and tortured, who had witnessed women and babies being mauled alive by the German shepherds guarding the camps. That would mess anyone up.

The Wolves

The wolves came by night with blacked-up faces. The nights brought no reprieve; it was when the menace began. Cucu Herina and her daughters ate half-cooked food in great haste. Their sacks rolled up underneath their dresses, the teenagers followed their mother like a cat crosses the road with her brood. The houses were all the same and very close together, the ashen clay giving them uniformity. All the doors faced the hawk in the watchtower. The timing had to be absolute. A decoy would walk over to the guard and plead for something. Whilst he was distracted, the women ducked to the back of the houses, remaining under the cover of the thatched hood, listening and moving to the next one. It had to be done after dusk and before the curfew. The decree stated anyone caught outside during curfew hours would be shot on the spot. Cucu Herina had a duty to keep her daughters safe. The wails from the jailhouse by the watchtower were a nightly reminder of the consequence of being caught. Everyone heard the wails as the women were tortured before being thrown into pits filled with ice-cold water containing cactii, snakes and vermin. Other women were poisoned with kerosene mixed with ground chilies, which was planted in their vagina and anus to poison them from within. Others had sticks and guns inserted into their orifices. But Cucu Herina watched her three daughters like a hawk. She would give her life for their safety. The details of their nightly arrangements were finalised by song whilst digging the trenches. There were no breaks, just work. Song was their food for the soul, and their only mode of communication.

Cucu Herina was expecting them. She had received a tip that a *hyena*—a traitor was seen following her daughters' home. He was one of the snitches. The *wolves*—white soldiers knew, from informants, which houses the *spring chickens*—young girls lived in, and women played a cat and mouse game, moving their daughters from house to house. It was just before midnight when they arrived. They didn't knock; they kicked the door in. Cucu Herina had gone to bed early, smearing her face with ash before covering the smouldering embers with rest of the ash to save them for the morning. Covering faces with ash was a desperate attempt to conceal femininity. She had lain on her sack, her mind racing. She jumped to her feet, her hands in the air; '*ndukandathe*—don't shoot me please.' There

382

were three wolves and two hyenas, shining their flashlights in her ghostly face.

'Where are the *chickens*?' asked the lead wolf menacingly with his rolling accent.

'*sijui unasema nini*—I don't know what you mean?' she said, looking surprised. 'There is no one here.' They shone their torches around the room, one spitting, 'Bloody niggers live like rats.' They were gone.

* * * *

Cucu Herina had dreaded the day it would happen. Maitu ran into her arms, sobbing uncontrollably.

'Not you, Gakari, not you,' exclaimed Cucu Herina, her heartache palpable. 'Who was it?' she asked in despair, expecting it to be the wolves or the hyenas. Muffled noises came from Cucu Herina's chest where Maitu buried her face.

'Njogu.' Cucu Herina pushed her away from her bosom to look at her face.

'Which Njogu?' she enquired curiously.

'Njogu from the trains, Bei Raiithi.' Cucu Herina could not recall the name.

'The one who came to see you with his friend when I found you drinking *turungi*.'

'That weasel,' cried Cucu Herina.

It was dusk and everyone was busy preparing their supper. Cucu Herina, holding tightly onto Maitu's hand, led her to a hut at the end of the row. The door was ajar, an old man bent over his cooking stones whilst sitting on a *jungwa*—a man's stool.

'*muthuri uyu*—old man,' called a flustered Cucu Herina. 'I require your services. I would like you to find the weasel called Njogu who defiled my daughter.' The services of elders were obsolete since the troubles. All men were held in detention centres away from the women. He was one of the few men in the women's camp, being old and infirm. He was glad when women of the camp sought his help. It was the least he could do. Using his cloth, he lifted the porridge he had been stirring on the fire with a wooden stick, placing it on the side. He tapped his tobacco pouch, pinching a little of the brown substance, which he brought to his nose and sniffed. Fastening the traditional sheet he wore over his shoulder, he was gone.

It was barely half an hour later when old man Muraguri walked into Cucu Herina's hut, clipping Baba by the ear. Baba stood ashamed like a rabbit in the headlights.

'Explain yourself.' Cucu Herina blurted.

The Arsehole

'I was very young when I met your father in the train, the State of Emergency had just been declared, it made everything hazy. It was the definition of hell. Things were very bad for everyone,' Maitu began during the next phone call. I had been shocked and upset by Maitu's revelations. I began to doubt the wisdom of my digging. I questioned if I was capable of handling the truth. Surely it would have been better to carry on believing that my parents met and fell madly in love with each other. That is what we are taught to expect from the Mills and Boon books I read, the romantic comedies I watched, the love songs I had listened too. There was no story line of how a woman married the man who raped her. I felt betrayed. I felt like a fraud for living my life assuming my origins were anything but noble and good. I was a phony, like my parent's union.

'I remember Herina was sat outside peeling potatoes with Wanjira.' Maitu did her best to console me. I felt it was the first time anyone had ever listened to her. It was the first time anyone was ever interested in her life. It was like she was offloading all the luggage she had carried on her shoulders all her life. I had given her the opportunity to shed her burden. I was not going to abandon her now.

'Who was Wanjira?' I asked. I would be there for her. All her life she had had to be strong and carry on.

'Was she Cucu Herina's friend?' I interrupted.

'She was the most beautiful woman in the village of Igajo. People said she looked like a gazelle. She had the smoothest skin and had the complexion of the sun. There was no one as beautiful as her. She had only just got married. So they were sat on _giturwa_ outside,'

'Remind me what a _giturwa_ is, Mum,' I interrupted.

'They are the traditional stools. After circumcision Gikuyu men were permitted to sit on three-legged stools called _jungwa_ and women sat on a four-legged stools called _giturwa_ if they were married or had children. Herina and Wanjira were sat outside Herina's hut peeling potatoes when they saw Muniu, followed by Muru Wa Itina. Both he and his father were very bad men. Everyone knew and feared them. Even Kamaru, the famous musician, wrote a song about him.'

'Ah, I remember the song playing on the radio when I was little,' I remarked.

'So Herina spotted the men coming down the dusty road to the compound where we lived in Igajo, and she knew they were in trouble. She knew Muniu used to find beautiful women and girls for the white people. They called them plucking chickens. She alerted Wanjira to apply soil to her face.'

'Soil? Why?' I asked.

'That's what women and girls did to disguise their beauty when they had no access to ash. They both smeared their faces with soil but it was too late. Muru Wa Itina had already seen Wanjira.'

'What happened to Wanjira?'

'He asked if she wanted sugar. She refused the sugar and said that she was married. Muniu dragged her off the stool and said she must be respectful to *bwana*. Muru Wa Itina asked again if she wanted sugar. Feeling afraid, she accepted and went with the men for the sugar.'

'What happened to Wanjira Mum?' I enquired impatiently.

'Muru Wa Itina was a very bad man. They took her to the forest and they slept with her. She was found the following day on the side of the road naked, nearby was her father's body. The village elders moved their bodies. Someone had alerted him, and he had gone to find his daughter. Muniu and the other men had tied him to a tree and made him watch his daughter being defiled.'

Maitu's stories shocked me. They were horrifying and distressing. I felt a chill go through my entire body.

'So Muru Wa Itina was arrested for murder?' I

asked. Maitu laughed sarcastically.

'Arrested by who? They were above the law. No one cared about us being beaten or killed. They were bandits. One time Herina and I were walking to Dagoretti market when we saw Muru Wa Itina on the other side of the road. Herina wanted to hide because everyone was frightened of him. He spotted a woman wearing traditional Gikuyu clothes who had *hangi* decorating her ears. He hated the way Gikuyu women looked in their traditional attire, so he walked over to the woman and, using his whip, he slashed both her ears off. I have never seen so much blood. He patrolled the whole place carrying a pistol and a whip. He was untouchable. His Land Rover was always covered in blood from knocking people down.'

When I begun my quest, my mission had been to discover what lay beneath my father's dysfunctionality. I was expecting to understand why Baba was the monster that he was, but never did I expect to hear anything of this magnitude. I found myself in a place far worse than I would ever have imagined. Why was there no curriculum about this? Why did the history books in my school in Thogoto not seek to explain why the people of Thogoto seemed so traumatized and helpless? They walked around like people in a zombie apocalypse. When I think of Riara Ridge and Thogoto, those two places looked like the aftermath of something I was never able to describe. I now understood why. These places whispered their secrets so silently that I felt there was something dark in the waters but I couldn't figure out what. Riara Ridge was the playground of the hedonistic white settlers who lived the high life at the utter expense of the Gikuyu. It was where all the food used to grow before they slashed it all down like locusts, leaving not a single crumb for my people. The more I thought about it, the more I realised that so many of these unanswered questions had lingered in my mind even as a child. The irreconcilable differences between the pristine calmness of Riara Ridge versus the chaos and sheer poverty in Thogoto. The people of Thogoto were all crammed within a square mile or so. What made them all want to live so close together? The villagers of Thogoto that I saw at the Church of the Torch sang sombre songs, as if life had lost all meaning, but the people in Riara Ridge were distinctly cheerful and sang jubilantly.

My history classes taught me about European noblemen and explorers like David Livingstone, but where were the lessons of *my* people? Who were the noblemen of *my* tribe? There must have been noblemen and women, like Wangu Wa Makeri. Whispers of her prowess still live in legend, but not in the curriculum, as the famous chief who was renowned for her nobility in the land of Gikuyu and Mumbi. It was not Adam and Eve who were the first people on earth, in our land it was Gikuyu and Mumbi. They gave birth to their nine daughters who formed the nine clans of the Gikuyu. That was not the core syllabus of descendants of these Gikuyu forebears, instead we covered Napoleon and other noblemen with moustaches and tights. These were just stories of white people. People I barely saw or came into contact with. They had no relevance in my mind and they were just stories, like Cucu Herina and Maitu told us during *kunyihia huai*. These men in tights were to me like the giants that always featured in our oral stories. Or the man who so desired a wife and family but no woman in the village wanted to marry him. He consulted the witchdoctor, who granted his wish. 'You shall be blessed with beautiful daughters,' the witchdoctor had told the sad lonely man. His knee began to swell, the swelling getting bigger and bigger and one day it burst, and inside his knee were the most beautiful daughters. Three beautiful daughters. I did not know the relevance of that story but I was happy for the man because he had a family of his own. He finally found a place of self-belonging and did not need to marry anyone. Those white men in tights and ruffled shirts from my history books looked alien. I did not know the relevance of their war, it was all imaginary in my mind.

I had more questions than answers. Why did I not learn about the disruption and trauma caused by the white man's activities in Thogoto? Don't the children of Thogoto have the right to know the truth, they being the inheritors of their parents' trauma? Surely they were the deserving bearers of truth. They needed healing but instead, the people of Thogoto were left walking around aimlessly like zombies with no knowledge of what had happened to their mothers and fathers. I had been to visit Cucu Herina in her home countless times and never did I realise that the reason they were all overcrowded was that they were the remnants of the concentration camps. The reason the corner she lived in was called *kiamburi, mburi*, meaning goats, was because it was where all their animals were kept after their being confiscated by the District Officer to be granted as rewards to the chiefs. The laundry of images in my head altered depending on my conversations with Maitu. The woman who was offered sugar and gang-raped in the forest with her father watching; what would that have done to the villagers of Thogoto? Each one could have been randomly selected and marched to the forest and ordered to dig their own graves, making sure they would fit in it. What about the babies of the mothers who were shot with their babies still strapped on their backs, left to suffocate slowly under the red soil in which they were buried alive, their blood tainting the soil? I needed the answers.

Baba

Baba was born at the most unfortunate of times, during
the mass starvation referred to as the cassava famine
amongst the Gikuyu, because cassava was all that was
available. Europe was ravaged by the Second World
War, with all food denied to the Gikuyu to help the
British with their food rations. Baba was found as a baby
suckling furiously on his dead mother. Frail and
weakened by hunger, she had been out in the forest
collecting firewood when she collapsed and died. Her
baby son was still in the sling when he was found
by passers-by, suckling on the cold dead body of his
mother. His mother was a young woman called
Wairimu, who was married to a man called Sang'i.
Sang'i spent all his time sat on a stool outside their hut,
plagued by elephantitis. People rarely went to the hospital in those days; even if they did, I doubt there was a
cure. Any medical ailments were treated by medicine
men or witch doctors if it was thought to have been

caused by the wrath of the spirits. Wairimu was one of three siblings, with an older sister called Nyambura and a brother, Wainaina, of whom no one knew his whereabouts.

After Wairimu's death, her children became destitute, condemned to scavenging in bins and sewers. All contact with their father, presumed dead, was lost. Therefore, Baba did not have the fortune of knowing his parents. In those days people rarely took photographs. Baba's survival was nothing short of miraculous. On numerous occasions his aunt Nyambura tried to rescue them but she was destitute and near death herself. It was then that she decided to drown Baba and his older sister Gacambi. Life was so hard that she considered it kinder to drown them in Undiri, the revered swamps. It was the way most people went when life got too difficult. Undiri is an old lake that turned into swamp. It was as though this old lake had given up too, neglecting the Gikuyu. When she got to the lake, Baba and Tata Gacambi looked at her expectantly, hoping she had taken them there for a surprise. She could not go through with it and instead began to run, and ran and ran. It was only years later when the three reconnected that Cucu Nyambura explained how she had nearly drowned them. They swore never to abandon one another, which I learned was the reason we kept a bedroom for Cucu Nyambura.

To save herself, Cucu Nyambura went off to live

with a man she had met called Riweri, and with that she was out of their lives. My father and his sister were left to fend for themselves and spent their days in the streets of Nairobi, joining the thousands of roaming juveniles. At this time Nairobi was swamped with destitute children, their numbers estimated at around 20,000. With nowhere else to go, many lived in squalid ramshackle dwellings with no sanitation and open sewers, bringing about the birth of the slums and shanty towns in Nairobi. It was in these dirty, smelly and poverty-ridden streets that Baba spent his days.

For a while he had lived with a distant relative in Thogoto. She treated him harshly, making his life absolute misery. She gave him no food and scolded him all the time. He would wake up early before she was up and sneak out to join the other children walking to Nairobi, where he spent his days begging for food and money. Before nightfall he would walk for miles back home to sleep in his relative's hut. One day when he returned, she was angrier than usual about something and she started scolding him as soon as he walked in through the door. She then took a red-hot charcoal and squeezed it hard on his shoulder, leaving him screaming in pain with severe burns on his shoulder. He fled in pain and tears and at five years old his options were very few. He sought refuge in the dumpsite at Kikuyu town, escaping death once again when he fell asleep in a bin when the municipal workers set them alight. It was this inhumanity and desolation that shaped Baba's life.

* * * *

Cucu Nyambura learned of Baba's incident with the municipal bins and that's when she decided to take him to live with a relative in Ruthimitu, a small town in Kiambu district where he was a chief. When Cucu Nyambura arrived at the chief's home with Baba, dirty and unkempt, Chief Mwangi and his wife barely listened to what Cucu Nyambura had to say. They stared at Baba in the most unfriendly manner and when Cucu Nyambura stopped talking, the woman outlined what was expected of Baba. He was prohibited from entering the main house where the chief, his wife and children lived. His dwellings were to be in the rat-infested outdoor building that was always smoky because it also served as an external kitchen. Baba was to sleep on the floor near the fire by himself on the sack they provided him. He was to wake up at four every morning and head to the cowshed, where he would start milking the cows. Once the cows were milked, he was to go to the farm to cut long grass to feed the cows. Once all the morning chores were done, he to was walk at least 2 kilometres to Kahuhira, the school that he was to be enrolled in. After school, he was to walk home, feed and milk the cows, and it would be long after dark that he would be sleeping. He was to eat sweet potatoes or potatoes which he would cook himself by burying them in embers overnight.

Baba's routine started the very next day. He could barely open his eyes when one of the workmen banged on the door, waking him up. They walked to the back of the main house where the cows were resting. The workman carried a paraffin lantern as it was still dark. He got two cows into a pen, tied the rope on their neck to secure them and closed the gate, penning them in. The workman had brought with him a bucket of warm water with a cloth, with which he was to clean the cows' udders. He then sat on a stool and called Baba closer for his lesson. The man greased the teats and holding a teat in each hand, began to massage them downwards, spraying milk into the cold shiny steel pail. He carried on until the pail was half full and then invited Baba to take up the rest. Baba sat on the stool, scared of the cow. It was big and it towered over him. After he had washed his hands and greased them, the farm worker gave the nod to get started. The man was cold and unfriendly and left Baba to get on with it. At his first attempt to milk he touched the teat too softly, irritating the cow, who kicked the pail, spilling the milk on the floor. The workman walked over to him, slapping him hard on his back, shouting at him for spilling the milk. Whimpering away, he carried on milking one teat at a time until he got the hang of it. When all twenty cows were milked, he and the workman, each carrying a machete, marched down the path to start cutting the grass. Once the cows were fed, he followed the workman back to the outdoor building where he had slept. He sat close to the fire, feeling the warmth whilst watching the workman eat his porridge hungrily. There was none for Baba.

The only thing Baba liked about his new life was the uniform. Navy shorts, a white shirt and navy blue jumper. It was the first time he had ever worn new clothes. For a brief moment he was happy. But by the time Baba got to school he was already tired and miserable. He hated school from the first day. His teachers beat him for everything: for not doing his work, for being late to school, for talking in class, for breathing; when they were bored, anything. He hated being confined in the classroom all day. He had no food to eat during lunch and ate whatever else he came across to and from school, fruit fallen from trees or food from bins. His life was significantly worse than when he lived in the dumpsite, if that was possible. At least there he had freedom to sleep and wake up when he wanted. In the dumpsite he did not receive constant beatings from his uncle, auntie, the workman and teachers. At the dumpsite he did not need to milk the cows or cut grass. Although he now had a roof over his head, he longed for the dumpsite in Kikuyu. A year went by and his life became one of a slave, just beatings, work and hunger. It was then that he decided to run away and return to his old life in Kikuyu dumpsite.

The expulsion of the Gikuyu from their lands had the expected consequences of the detribalising a tribe. The destruction of family homes dissolved tribal structures, leading to a breakdown in families, values, law and order. Vagrancy became the biggest headache for the colonial government as a result of homelessness and unemployment amongst the Gikuyu. It became a constant struggle and a thorn in the side of the Governor Sir Evelyn Baring. Vagrancy and Juvenile laws were introduced, mimicking those in Britain, but the government did not have the time or resources to deal with the problem. The numbers of street children and vagrants quadrupled in the months leading up to the declaration of the State of Emergency. The street children nicknamed Chokora became a law unto themselves. They filled the streets of Nairobi begging for food and money, ruining the smart streets of the city. Many children walked in groups and found innovative ways of extorting money and food from passers-by. They would carry bags of excrement and threaten the smart Nairobi workers with being plastered with faeces if they did not yield food or money. Many boys fell into petty crime such pickpocketing whilst many girls became child prostitutes.

The plethora of vagrant children was a growing challenge, the government resorted to collecting all the children in lorries and dumping them far away in the countryside. The children thought this was a wonderful break from their monotonous lives and besides, being carried in cars was the equivalent of being taken to a funfair. They gathered excitedly, waiting for the municipal lorries to take them. It was one such group of dumped children that Baba joined when he ran away from Chief Mwangi's residence. It was a long journey, thirty miles by foot back to Kikuyu, the place of his mother's birth. In those days there was little public transport. There were a few municipal buses, but no one had money for the fare, so most people walked everywhere. It took him the best part of eight hours, but he was finally reunited with his familiar environment in Kikuyu.

Cucu Herina's Compassion

They say it takes a brave person to walk away and that's what Cucu Herina did. She, old man Muraguri and Maitu listened to Baba's story. She was a woman of strong resolve, had great wisdom and immense compassion. What Baba had done to Maitu was an unforgivable crime that deserved punishment of the highest order, but life had dealt Baba the cruellest of punishments. The pathetic figure sat before her, whimpering in his ragged clothes and begging for forgiveness, deserved a chance he had never had. Every waking hour of his life, Baba had had to fight for his existence. He was the headless chicken that ran frantically without sight, parameters or direction. He was determined, with blind ambition but without the cognitive brain capable of making rational decisions, he was still able to function in some capacity. Finally, Cucu Herina spoke.

'You cannot atone for what you have done to my

daughter, but life has given you so much punishment that I don't wish to inflict anymore.' In any case, she had no options. She and the others were prisoners and despite their grievances, the only justice available was for white people. There was not much else she could do. She turned to old man Muraguri. 'Could you let this young man live with you to escape the dumpsite?' Old man Muraguri thought for a while. He had lost his entire family and was all alone. Baba too had lost his family. His face cleared and his answer was deliberate and definite. 'I will look after the young man.' It was past the curfew hour so they deemed it best to sneak back home before it grew too late. Over the coming months, Baba kept his distance from Maitu. It was as if he finally accepted that she would never love him. He avoided her gaze on the train, making sure they never shared a carriage. Baba worked harder than ever, focusing all his efforts on providing for him and old man Muraguri. One day, on his way home, he saw a rusty bicycle for sale. It was the first thing that Baba ever purchased.

If there was anything Maitu craved, it was to learn how to ride a bicycle. All her life she had watched the way people sat on bicycles pedalling, feeling the breeze in their faces. She marvelled at how they sat back whilst the bicycle wheeled them to their destination. She longed to be the one sat on the seat, pedalling away, feeling the freedom of being taken to her destination.

One day, when she was just about to alight the train, she spotted Baba getting on his bicycle and cycling off. She was captivated. He had acquired the one thing she desired most. It was then that her interest in Baba and his bicycle grew.

'Can I ride your bicycle?' she asked one day when their eyes met on the train.

'Sure, you can ride my bicycle.' Baba could not conceal his delight at possessing something of interest to Maitu. 'I will meet you at the station this evening if you like.' Maitu had never ridden a bicycle before and Baba became her dutiful teacher. Every day, after work, he waited for Maitu to alight the train and they spent their evenings riding the bicycle. It was undeniable that the two had finally fallen in love.

Cucu Herina was a tall, thin, gaunt woman, hunched forward as if suffering from constant stomach pain—which I now realise was heartache. She had very smooth skin, with a dark complexion and kind eyes that sometimes looked very distant. Her weather-beaten face had that look of struggle and hardship when she was serious but was completely transformed when happy. Her harsh life had not taken away her ability to leave friends and family in heaps of laughter. She was a gifted storyteller and a master of mimicry. She would imitate the soldiers, both their accents and the way they walked, in the most hilarious manner. She was the first comedian I ever knew and remains my favourite to this day. Sure, people like Dave Chapelle, Chris Rock, George Carlin and Bill Burr have all made me laugh, but never the big belly, rib-tickling laugh that Cucu Herina induced. She had such wit and a brilliant sense of humour. She learned to use this humour to get herself out of tricky situations, and I am slowly learning to use my pain on stage because making people laugh is the only medicine for my soul. She was loving and radiated warmth and kindness to anyone who came across her path. This is where fate met destiny for Baba and Maitu.

End of an Era

The station master bowed at the District Officer, who had just driven his Land Rover to the station entrance. He walked past without so much as a nod, straight to the platform, the villagers stepping aside to make way. The station master followed him, a look of concern on his face, wondering what the problem was. When the officer got to the bottom of the platform, he climbed down, pacing up and down as if looking for something, then lay across the tracks. The villagers watched in confusion as he held out a copy of the *East African Standard* and resting his head on the metal rails, began to read. The train tracks commanded little respect from the locals, who used them in numerous ways. The old idle villagers used the tracks as seats, whilst others spread out their meagre laundry on the hot metal. Even the stray dogs seem to be making a mockery of this knackered train line. They had never seen a *mzungu* use the tracks this way. The curious villagers began laughing, some mocking him, saying he had gone mad. 'Maybe he is trying to kill himself,' someone suggested. An old man wearing the traditional attire with a soiled trench coat gave this offering: 'The ghosts of all the women he had shot in the forest have come to get him.'

The tracks began to rattle as the distant whistle of the approaching train added to the unfolding drama. Muru Wa Itina turned to look at the villagers, a menacing grin on his face. The villagers watched in horror as the officer began yelling, 'I will never be ruled by monkeys.' His grin turned to a grimace as the tracks shook violently and the metal rims of the train crushed the end of an era.

The Present

When my mother decided to surprise Baba at his new workplace, she had no idea how much trouble she was about to cause him. She got up that morning, beaming with a smile. Nothing was going to ruin the joy in this sixteen-year-old. She hummed a tune as she went through her morning rituals. Reaching for the stick, she broke off a small section and began chewing, spitting the bitter saliva until she created bristles at the end of it. When the bristles were all soft, she began brushing her teeth, the minty taste of the eucalyptus stick freshening her breath. She then reached for the small *sufuria*—pan and scooped water from the black painted oil drum, leaning forward to wash her face. When her face was dry, she blew lungfuls of air into the metal cylinder pointed towards the embers to reawaken the fire. After eating her warm porridge, she headed for the train station.

When the train failed to arrive, my mother headed

to the bus stop and now sat staring out of the window of the old bus struggling up the hill, meandering round the scenic Gikuyu countryside. She was glad not to be going to work that morning. It had been a difficult few weeks since the orders had come from the chief asking everyone to attend the Barraza in Dagoretti market square. The chief had announced that the all the huts in the camps were to be demolished and everyone was required to destroy their homes. They would be granted a week in which to do so and anyone whose house was still standing by the end of the week would be reckoned with. 'Where will we go?' someone had dared ask, to which the chief replied, 'Anywhere but here.' By the following day, the guards were going round the village arresting those who hadn't attended the Barraza. They were taken to the chief's compound where they were lashed for their disobedience. Baba had been unable to attend because his new boss had refused to give him time off. It was the first time that Baba had ever worked for anyone.

'The chief's men are looking for you,' my mother had told him the day before.

'I don't care about the chief's men. All I care about is you,' he had replied, handing her a bag.

'What is it?' she asked curiously.

'Go ahead, have a look. It's yours,' Baba coaxed her. She reached inside the bag, pulling out the most beautifully knitted beige cardigan with pink roses embroidered on it.

'It's mine?' Maitu asked excitedly.

'It's a gift for you.' Maitu could not contain herself as she unfolded the cardigan, holding it close to her chest, stroking it.

'Put it on,' he said impatiently. It fitted her perfectly. She had never worn anything new before. All her clothes were hand-me-downs from her older sisters, which were usually oversized rags. Before Baba could stop her, she ran to her hut, calling 'Herina' excitedly to have a look at the gift. He had not seen Cucu Herina for nearly three months, since the incident. He was full of shame and couldn't bear to look at her. If only he could turn back time and undo what he had done, but he was determined to prove himself worthy of my mother's love. By the time Maitu came out of the hut with Cucu Herina, Baba was gone and she hadn't had the chance to thank him. Later that night, when Cucu Herina handed my mother 25 cents for the morning's train fare, she made up her mind that she would go to Baba's workplace to thank him personally for the gift.

One afternoon, an argument had erupted between hawkers on the train and Baba went to help. Distracted, he did not see the train inspectors coming and was caught with goods but without a hawker's licence, and with no money to bribe the officer, his whole stock had been confiscated. Distraught, and too proud to beg anymore, he was left with no other alternative but to go round the Indian quarters looking for employment in order to replenish his stock. He got a job in a factory that manufactured knitwear.

Now, as Maitu sat in the old bus filled with fumes ejected from an old exhaust, as it approached the bus station on the south side of Nairobi, she couldn't wait to see Baba's face at the surprise visit. She got off the bus, straightening her dress as she caught a reflection of herself in the window of a taxi. She used the sleeve of her cardigan to cover her nose against the overwhelming stench from the public toilets as she walked past the station entrance. She stopped for a moment, feeling something move inside her. It was a definite movement.

'We don't have vacancies for women,' declared the smartly dressed Indian man as my mother approached the factory entrance.

'I am here to see Njogu,' she replied. His face scrunched up as if angry as he instructed my mother to wait. Minutes later my dumbfounded father walked out alongside his boss. There was something wrong. He looked nervous and frightened. My mother had never seen that look on his face.

'Go wait for me at the bus station café.' Confused, she walked back to the bus station. Had she looked back, she would have seen the Indian factory owner drag Baba back into the factory. He led him to a pillar to which the foreman was instructed to tie him. Baba knew what was coming. If he cooperated it should be short and quick. He wrapped his arms around the pillar and the foreman tied his wrists together as the Indian boss walked back with his whip in his hand.

'What is the punishment for stealing?' he asked Baba.

'10 lashes,' he replied as the leather landed on his back, cutting through his flesh and causing him to shout.

'You stole the cardigan to impress your girlfriend; this is the price.' the Indian yelled at the eleventh lash. 'When will you thieving Africans ever learn? You must leave my premises now and never show your face here again.'

That day, Baba wept. He had never stolen anything in his life before, but he could not bear to see my mother wearing old rags which were let out at the sides to accommodate her growing bump. It was hours later when Baba finally composed himself to go and meet my mother at the bus station café. She had ordered tea and samosa, expecting that Baba would pay after he got his wages. He had been dismissed from his job without a penny. Thinking quickly, he asked her to go and wait at the bus stop whilst he paid the bill. When she was out of sight, he walked over to the waiter and pleaded with him to let him pay the following day. He would return to settle that bill, one day.

Epilogue

Like a shipwrecked couple in a rubber dinghy floating without a compass in the sea, having battled elements from all inconceivable angles, my parents clung to life without the know-how. In life, we can only play with the cards we are dealt, to the best of our ability. Baba did not a have chance but he did the best he could, with the hand he was dealt. Ask yourself, what kind of a human being do you become if no one ever held your hand and said, 'This is how you cross the road?' What kind of a human being do you become if no one ever offered you a hot meal and said, 'Soothe your rumbling tummy?' What kind of a human do you become if no one ever gave you a hug and said, 'Everything is going to be alright?' That human being was Baba. Finally, I got it. It was as if the coincidence of events was always meant to lure me into reaching an understanding of who Baba was. I was lured to his grave, as if Baba knew it would enhance my understanding.

In death, Baba spoke to me through Maitu. All those hours we spent on the telephone, helping Maitu to off-load her baggage whilst shedding light on the defective gene that contaminated our family. Through this process, I gained respect for my parents, with their resilience that enabled them to move on and give us the life we had in Riara Ridge, no matter how short and disturbing. Through Maitu, Baba communicated the reasons for his dysfunctionality, in the process binding the three of us together. My prayer that one day Maitu and Baba would be reunited was answered but not in the way I expected. The story kept Maitu, Baba and me together as a unit for all the time I carried out the research and wrote this book. Just like when Baba read our itinerary to a smiling Maitu the day we went shopping for my boarding school kit list.

Maitu was able to relay the story without bitterness, as if she had come to a place of forgiveness of Baba and the colonisers who caused our people so much heartache. Without forgiveness the wheels of time would grind to a halt. Baba would never have been able to explain all this to me; he did whatever he could with the life he was given. Finally, I found a place in my heart to forgive him. If Baba were alive today, I would walk over to him and I would give him the biggest hug anyone could ever give anyone, and I would say, 'Baba, everything will be okay.'

Bibliography

Alam, Shamsul S.M, *Rethinking Mau Mau in Colonial Kenya,* Palgrave MacMillan, 2007, New York

Anderson, David, *Histories of the Hanged: Britain's Dirty War In Kenya And End Of An Empire*, Orion 2005, London

Cagnolo, Fr, C, *The Akikuyu Their Traditions And Folklore,* Mission Printing School 1933 Nyeri

Clayton, Anthony, *Counter Insurgency In Kenya 1952-60*, Transafrica Publishers Ltd 1976, Nairobi

Crook Martin, *The Mau Mau Genocide, A Neo-Lemkinian Analysis*, Journal of Human Rights in the Commonwealth • Volume 1, Issue 1 (Spring 2013) • pp.18–37

Elkins, Caroline, *Imperial Reckoning: The Untold story of Britain's Gulags in Kenya*, Henry Holt & company, New York

Kags, Al *Living Memories, Kenya's Untold Stories*, No Boundaries Ltd, 2009 Nairobi

Kenyatta, Jomo, *Facing Mt Kenya, Vintage Books*, 1965 New York

Likimani, Muthon, *Passbook Number F.47927*, MacMillan Publishers 1985, London

Ng'weno, Hilary, *The Day Kenyatta Died*, Longman 1978, Nairobi

Routledge Scoresby and Routledge Katherine, *With A Prehistoric People, The Akikuyu of British East Africa*, Edward Arnold 1910 London

Wamweya Joram, Freedom Fighter, East Africa Publishing House, 1971, Nairobi